HOW TO BUY AND MANAGE INCOME PROPERTY

HOW TO BUY AND MANAGE
INCOME PROPERTY

Philip G. Wik

Prentice–Hall, Inc.
Englewood Cliffs, New Jersey 07632

Library of Congress Cataloging-in-Publication Data

Wik, Philip.
    How to buy and manage income property.

    Bibliography: p.
    Includes index.
    1. Real estate investment. 2. Real estate
management. 3. Rental housing. 4. Commercial
buildings. I. Title.
HD1382.5.W55 1986   332.63′24   86-17083
ISBN 0-13-403049-4

Editorial/production supervision and
  interior design: Tracey L. Orbine
Cover design: Marianne Frasco
Manufacturing buyer: Carol Bystrom

The publisher offers discounts on this book when ordered in bulk quantities.
For more information, write:

    Special Sales/College Marketing
    Prentice-Hall, Inc.
    College Technical and Reference Division
    Englewood Cliffs, NJ 07632

Printed in the United States of America
10 9 8 7 6 5 4 3 2

ISBN   0-13-403049-4   025

Prentice-Hall International (UK) Limited, *London*
Prentice-Hall of Australia Pty. Limited, *Sydney*
Prentice-Hall Canada Inc., *Toronto*
Prentice-Hall Hispanoamericana, S.A., *Mexico*
Prentice-Hall of India Private Limited, *New Delhi*
Prentice-Hall of Japan, Inc., *Tokyo*
Prentice-Hall of Southeast Asia Pte. Ltd., *Singapore*
Editora Prentice-Hall do Brasil, Ltda., *Rio de Janeiro*

To my parents, Harold and Lucinda Wik, with love.

Make no little plans; they have no magic to stir men's blood, and probably themselves will not be realized. Make big plans, aim high, and hope, and work, remembering that a noble, logical diagram once recorded will never die, but long after we are gone will be a living thing, asserting itself with growing intensity.

Daniel Burnham

"Would you tell me, please, which way I ought to go from here?"
"That depends a good deal on where you want to get to," said the Cat.
"I don't much care where—," said Alice.
"Then it doesn't much matter which way you go," said the Cat.

Lewis Carroll

CONTENTS

Preface   xi
Introduction: The Rules of the Game   1
Part I   How to Buy Income Property

1   *How to Buy   25*
2   *How to Finance   67*
3   *Who to Involve   93*
4   *What to Buy   107*

Part II   How to Manage Income Property

5   *Accounting   126*
6   *Insurance   138*
7   *Taxes   153*
8   *Tenant Management   169*

Conclusion: Risks and Rewards   207
Glossary   215
Appendixes:

A.   *Amortization Chart   223*
B.   *Settlement Costs   225*
C.   *Tools and Supplies   268*
D.   *Federal Taxes   270*
E.   *Property Management Contract   271*
F.   *Tenant Management   280*

Selected Bibliography   287
Index   291

PREFACE

Real estate is a well-traveled road to wealth. The fortunes of Harry Helmsley and Donald Trump of New York and Arthur Rubloff and A. N. Pritzker of Chicago are all tied to real estate. Real estate is unique among investments in its concentration of wealth-building elements. These include cash flow, equity buildup through amortization and improvements, shelter from taxes, and appreciation. Harnessing these factors can put you on the road to wealth.

PURPOSE

How to Buy and Manage Income Property is a practical guide to buying and managing income property. This book addresses two questions: How do you buy profitable income property? and how do you manage income property profitably? We'll answer the first question by looking at ways to find and finance income property. We'll answer the second by looking at aspects of property management, including accounting, insurance, taxes, and tenant relations.

AUDIENCE

Buyers and Owners of Income Property

I have written this book mainly for buyers and owners of income property. Income property generally means apartments, ranging from a duplex to syndications involving hundreds of units. But it can also mean commercial property, such as warehouses, stores, and offices. The single-family house can be another form of income property. Thus, throughout this book, I'll mention practices concerning the single-family house, such as homeowner's insurance.

The Small Income Property Investor

Some investors want an empire of houses, condominiums, apartments, and offices. But most are content with staking out a smaller beachhead. This book was primarily written for those people—the small income investor. I'll define the small property investor as anyone who controls less than a half-million dollars in income real estate or less than a dozen units. Although you may lack the resources of the empire builders, you share many of their problems.

The First-time Investor

This book was written for the first-time investor. You may be considering buying a duplex, as the carrying costs for a single-family home are too high. You may be a professional looking for ways to shelter your income from taxes. You may be looking for a second career, hobby, or source of income. This book was written for you.

The Professional

This book was also written for those involved in the transaction between buyer and seller. They include brokers, inspectors, appraisers, insurance agents, contractors, and bankers. This book tries to bridge specialties. For example, a lawyer will find little legal information in this book that is new. But he may not know so much about appraising or financing. Conversely, an expert in appraising may learn a few things about the law he didn't know. Awareness of areas outside of your specialty will make you a better professional.

Both Sexes

Since there is no singular personal pronoun in English that refers to both sexes, the word *he* has traditionally been used when the sex of the antecedent is unknown. Although I've adopted this custom throughout this book, the reader shouldn't conclude that I'm impugning the professionalism of women in real estate. "There is lots to be said for the economic and political equality of the sexes," C. S. Lewis wrote. "But the claim for grammatical equality of genders is an unmitigated nuisance." I wrote this book for girls and for boys, for men and for women.

CONTENTS

This book has two parts. The first part gets into the mechanics of evaluating, financing, and acquiring income real estate. The second part offers tips on managing income property finances and tenants.

We start by reviewing the rules of the game, those tasks you must accomplish and the attitudes you must have before you invest in income real estate. The successful investor may wish to skip that section. But if you're new to the game, I suggest you read the introduction with care.

The book concludes with a review of the risks and rewards of real estate, a glossary, appendixes, a selected bibliography, and an index.

This book is comprehensive, as it embraces bodies of knowledge that are the domain of professions such as banking and law. But I can tell you only so much with 100,000 words. Given the complexity of real estate, it isn't the last word. No real estate book could possibly be definitive, although all should avoid distortion. To make up for these constraints, I urge you to consult other authoritative sources. Some of these are in the bibliography. This book, sound professional advice, and hard work can be your formula for avoiding financial catastrophe and for achieving financial security.

Real estate writing lies on a spectrum, with clustering at the extremes. Folksy rags-to-riches tales are at one end. These writers dwell in proud detail on their exploits at a specific time and place. Like war memoirs, they're fun to read and inspiring. But they tend toward rapid obsolescence. At the other end, you've got tomes that delight in footnotes to footnotes, leaden prose, and a false air of objectivity. I don't want this book to be so theoretical that you have trouble making a connection between what you read and what you should do. Nor do I want it to be so idiosyncratic that you think you're reading my autobiography. I'm aiming for the broad middle. I wrote this book because I couldn't find credible information about topics that interested me when I was buying my first income property. Although I'm an income property owner, it isn't just my story. If you've bought or want to buy income property, it's your story as well.

ASSUMPTIONS

Many real estate books assume that the reader is in the 50 percent tax bracket, has ample time to investigate, rehab, and manage, has the credentials of a lawyer, accountant, contractor, broker, and banker, has access to single-digit financing, and lives in a part of the country that has constantly appreciating real estate values. The reader with average means has little in common with these Alice-in-Wonderland assumptions. This book arrives at some of the conclusions of those other books and describes many of the same techniques. But it doesn't assume knowledge or wealth out of the ordinary. For the sake of realism, I'll assume a 30 percent bracket, double-digit interest rates, and marginal appreciation. These conservative assumptions are necessary to correct the sometimes dubious advice presented in other books and seminars.

This book endorses no get-rich-quick schemes. You could say it's a get-rich-slow scheme, as I stress a systematic incrementation of net worth over a succession of 5-year periods. My recommendations are conservative, sometimes astringently so. If your goals and personality are inclined to speculation, you should take that path. However, the caveats in this book will give you something to ponder. Real estate creates a magic that can multiply your wealth beyond your dreams. It can also bankrupt you, a fact that the easy-money, no-money-down, road-show boys often fail to admit. But you want the truth. This book will try to establish the truth by addressing such deals with two questions: Is it possible? Is it wise?

The answer to the first question is often yes. The answer to the second question is often no. Most authors of real estate books write from the premise that you should buy income property. But I don't think income property is for everyone. I'll present the arguments and let you make up your mind. If I can discourage you from buying real estate if you lack the resources, I'll have achieved one of my goals.

The rules that govern real estate vary from state to state and even from county to county. Moreover, these rules are constantly evolving. I've tried to avoid details that could be misleading or rapidly obsolete. Building codes, tax laws, and brokerage regulations will change. But certain principles are applicable everywhere. I'll review these concepts at the end of each chapter. To make generalizations meaningful, I use specifics, such as Chicago's building codes. Readers elsewhere may read such sections with impatience. But they will appear more relevant if you read them as you would read a case study. In a case, the student studies a plethora of facts, from which he is expected to draw conclusions and render judgments. Likewise, when you review Illinois rental laws, you'll derive principles that will give you a better understanding of your laws. As you gain experience within your locality, you will adapt, modify, or discard these specifics when necessary. I wrote this book from the perspective of the middle 1980s and the industrial Midwest. Perhaps I would have written a different book if I had been living in the Sun Belt during the 1970s. However, I think the conclusions I derive from this perspective are valid for all parts of this country through at least the end of this decade.

Finally, this book isn't a substitute for professional advice. Read this book for broad guidance. Rely on your broker, lawyer, and accountant for tactical instruction. A recurring theme in my book is to seek professional help. That I'm not a broker, lawyer, or an accountant is both a weakness and a strength. It's a weakness because I've had to go to them for help. It's a strength because I can write about them "without fear or favor." The author and publisher aren't engaged in providing accounting, legal, or other professional services. For such advice, consult your own attorney, accountant, or other qualified professional. The reader buys this book with the understanding that the author and publisher disclaim any liability that may result as a consequence of this work.

ACKNOWLEDGMENTS

Grateful acknowledgment is made to the following for permission to reprint copyrighted material:

Vincent William Zucchero, *Rental Homes: The Tax Shelter That Works and Grows for You,* © 1983, p. 22. Reprinted by permission of Prentice-Hall, Inc., Englewood Cliffs, New Jersey.

Code Inspections and the Housing Court: A Study of the Impact of Pre-Trial Inspections in Non-Payment Proceedings When Tenants Claim Needed Repairs, Office of Program and Management Analysis, Department of Housing Preservation and Development, New York, 1982, pp. 134–35.

I wish to thank the Legal Assistance Foundation of Chicago and the Chicago Council of Lawyers for legal advice, as found in their noncopyrighted *Tenant–Landlord Handbook.* This book was edited by Gordon Waldron and Robert Ungerleider. The second edition was published in 1982, made possible by a grant by the Chicago Bar Foundation.

I also wish to thank Stetson Management Company, West Dundee, Illinois, for permission to use their property management contract in this book.

Finally, I must thank Prentice-Hall. My relationship with this publishing house has now lasted through two books and over five years. The staff has always been pleasant and professional. I want to specifically thank the following people at Prentice-Hall who helped me develop this book:

Jeff Krames, Acquisitions Editor
Tim Moore, Marketing Manager
Tracey Orbine, Production Editor

Their work and thought made this book possible.

Philip G. Wik

HOW TO BUY AND MANAGE
INCOME PROPERTY

INTRODUCTION:

THE RULES OF THE GAME

This chapter doesn't directly address the topic of this book. But it does lay the foundation. The sophisticated investor may wish to "fast forward" to Chapter 1. But if you fit one or both of the following types of people, I urge you to read this section:

1. You're a novice in investing. You've just graduated or you've just immigrated. Perhaps you've experienced a major life change—a new job, a divorce, the death of your spouse. Whatever your situation, you feel you face an uncertain economic future.
2. You're a loser in investing. You're making money, but you're not keeping it. You also feel you face an uncertain economic future.

You probably recognize real estate can mean financial security. But a precondition to buying real estate is to be financially secure. Thus, your ability to buy income property must be the culmination of wise decisions made over many years. These decisions assure you'll have enough funds to get the property, manage it, and still support your life-style. Your mastery of the principles of free enterprise will shape your future. These, then, are the rules of the game of capitalism.

INVESTMENT TASKS

All great religions have their Ten Commandments, their Five Pillars, or the like. Capitalism isn't a religion, but it is a moral imperative, for it promotes individual freedom of choice and the greater good better than any existing ideology. Here is your Eightfold Path to Prosperity:

1. Take stock of yourself.
2. Plan.

3. Nurture your career.
4. Eliminate personal debt.
5. Determine your annual net worth.
6. Save.
7. Diversify your investments.
8. Buy income property.

Many have walked this path. Some, like myself, started out with nothing in the material sense. Your pilgrimage may end in a Manhattan penthouse, a North Shore mansion, a Main Line estate. But, in the scheme of things, the trappings of wealth are peripheral. What counts is the joy you'll see in those close to you. By providing for them, you can shield them from some of the problems of life. If you buy income property, you'll also get satisfaction from knowing that your efforts bring shelter and employment to people with families and goals, that without your spirit of enterprise their housing would be less adequate, their prospects less certain.

Step 1: Take Stock of Yourself

"Know thyself," the ancient Greeks said. Before starting your investment program, do some soul searching. Honest answers will help you from falling into the trap of mindlessly striving out of compulsion rather than for positive reasons. Before you reach for the brass ring, make sure the ring really exists.

Ask: What do I value? What is important to my family? What do I want? What do I want to be? You're not getting any younger. The clock is ticking. You must focus your goals. The time to act is now.

At a more pragmatic level, you must answer these questions:

1. Do I have the time, desire, and expertise to manage my financial affairs? Perhaps one of your goals is to let others manage.
2. Am I looking for a tax shelter? Those with limited income may have little use for the tax benefits of some investments.
3. Is my income likely to remain steady? People in volatile businesses should be wary of making long-term financial commitments.
4. Do I move frequently? People who move a lot may be unhappy with the lack of mobility that comes from owning real estate.
5. Do I want to assume personal liability for all risks? One goal may be to assume only limited liability.

To the question "What do I want?" many people respond: "To be happy." Is that a legitimate goal? In my view, happiness shouldn't be your goal, but the residual of working toward that goal. President Ronald Reagan's secretary of education agrees. "Happiness is like a cat," William Bennett said.

"If you try to coax or call it, it will avoid you. It will never come. But if you pay no attention to it and go about your business, you'll find it rubbing against your legs and jumping into your lap. So forget pursuing happiness. Pin your hopes on work, on family, on learning, on knowing, on loving." By striving to benefit yourself, you benefit others. The essence of capitalism is that self-interest inevitably rebounds to the collective good. Your stocks provide employment, your property provides shelter.

But if happiness isn't a legitimate goal, is wealth? The little-engine-that-could spirit may be a mirage. Hard work may yield riches as well as broken marriages, loneliness, and physical collapse, as the lives of Howard Hughes and John Paul Getty would attest. Money won't solve your problems. It will only pay the bills. But those who have fought their way out of the projects or the barrios know that it's absurd to question the legitimacy of the pursuit of wealth. For poverty is the enemy of the human spirit. Wealth is more than an idle dream. It's a practical possibility, particularly for those who shun the image of wealth—the fancy cars, the pretty clothes, the social swirl. That's less important than the freedom it offers. If you have money, you have options. Riches become a side effect of personal achievement, a grade bestowed by capitalism for excellence, the payoff for winning the great game. A century ago, the Reverend Russell Herman Conwell went about this nation delivering a popular speech. He praised not only the virtues of hard work, but its rewards as well. "To secure wealth is an honorable ambition," he said "and is one great test of a person's usefulness to others. I say, get rich, get rich!"

Step 2: Plan

Unwilling or unable to plan for the future, most people let others plan their future. This refusal to decide is in itself a decision. Passivity in the face of a troubled economy threatens your security.

Both countries and corporations give planning high priority. It provides the basis for rational management. Planning checks impulsive actions and provides a map for future growth. The following plan by a real-estate developer is an example:

STATEMENT OF PURCHASING POLICY

A. Large properties only.
  1. Office buildings have a minimum net rental area of 80,000 square feet.
  2. Shopping centers in excess of 80,000 square feet of net rentable space or prime leasebacks.
  3. Industrial leasebacks, such as warehouses and research laboratories, to AAA-1 tenants.
  4. Apartment buildings have a minimum of 100 rental units.
  5. Vacant land to accommodate any of the preceding structures.

B. New or relatively new properties only.
   1. To ensure an attractive property for loan purposes at the outset and for refinancing purposes after acquisition. This policy recognizes that many lenders, especially insurance companies, avoid making loans on older properties.
   2. To ensure that amortization exceeds depreciation (actual wear and tear) so that the investor's equity is constantly increasing.
   3. To provide a desirable property for sale after depreciation is no longer attractive in its tax consequences to produce tax-sheltered income. (This should not rule out properties that have been or may be completely restored through the installation of new mechanical, electrical, or air-conditioning equipment.)
C. Large equities, never thin. The payment of sufficient equity capital above a conservative first deed of trust (mortgage) to ensure servicing of nonfluctuating debt service even in periods of economic recession.
D. Limited to Washington, D.C. and surrounding area. With approximately 50 percent of the employees in the metropolitan area employed by the federal and district governments and the other 50 percent occupied in providing goods for these personnel, the chances of a prolonged economic recession in the metropolitan area in Washington appear remote. We believe that Washington provides an atmosphere of economic stability enjoyed by extremely few metropolitan areas.
E. No speculative-type business properties. We do not buy any real property whose major source of income comes from operating speculative-type business ventures, such as hotels, motels, swimming pools, golf links or country clubs, amusement parks, bowling alleys, or stadiums; no single-purpose buildings, such as funeral homes, garages, or automobile retail locations.

For a much smaller operation, the next statement has sufficed:

STATEMENT OF PURCHASING POLICY

A. The purpose of income property purchases is to generate a reliable second source of income.
B. My salaried job will take precedence in commitment over this enterprise.
C. The property must generate enough income to at least initially service the mortgage.
D. The first consideration in buying the property will be a strong positive cash flow based on net income/asking price. Secondary considerations include location, rent increase potential, maintainability, manageability, selling potential, appreciation potential, and tax-shelter capability.
E. Each year, I will ascertain the value of the property, amount of rent increases, and feasibility of future acquisitions.
F. The property must be professionally appraised before making a bid and professionally inspected before making the purchase.
G. Tenants will pay for all recurring costs, except for taxes, insurance, and utilities that are not individually metered.
H. The property will be turned over to professional management after the turnaround phase.

Most people think of a budget as a one-year plan for managing money. You set up an income-outgo (expense) ledger with a year's worth of monthly totals and you revise your plan at the end of the year. But budget planning should look ahead in blocks of 5 years. Many investments take at least that long to germinate. Some people have trouble anticipating what they'll be doing next week, much less 5 years from now. To others, such planning comes easily. With practice, everyone should be able to methodically plan where he is going and what he'll be doing 5 years hence. Investment records, tax receipts, insurance policies, pension plans, and mortgage amortization schedules are examples of information on which to base these projections. Nothing is written in stone. You can deal with uncertainty by reviewing and modifying your plans. The best time to update is on the first of the year, the traditional day for making resolutions. Unlike the somewhat frivolous New Year's custom of making vows for the future, you should approach this task more analytically and critically. In the last year, pinpoint the causes of your failures and successes, especially in regards to making money.

The act of articulating specific goals unleashes the subconscious. You'll start to structure your life so that you'll accomplish those goals. You should write the plan in terms of decreasing abstraction, from a general objective to a timetable of concrete actions. Depending on your age, family situation, assets, life-style, and tax bracket, you will need to establish which of the following goals is preferred:

1. Immediate income, such as bonds that pay interest twice a year.
2. A long-term investment with potential for appreciation, such as some types of stock.
3. Tax benefits, such as you would get from tax shelters.

(The beauty of real estate is that it's possible to buy property so that all goals are met—income, appreciation, and tax avoidance.) As you review your plan each year, you will adapt it to new conditions. But you won't deviate from it. Razzle-dazzle hype and insider tips can sway you. A plan sets up criteria against which to weigh such thinking.

Here's an example of a personal financial 5-year plan:

FINANCIAL FIVE-YEAR PLAN

Updated: January 1, $19 \times \times$
Years: 19×0–19×5

    I. Objective: To achieve financial security.
   II. Goals:
       A. To increment my net worth by a minimum $\$ \times$,000 yearly.
       B. To put discretionary capital in investment vehicles that will overcome my tax liability and the inflation rate.
       C. To diversify sources of income (salary, interest, dividends, and rent) and sources of investment (money market, certificates of deposit, stocks, and real estate).

III. Aims:
  A. To assure myself continuing income.
    1. By not shortchanging my career.
    2. By keeping myself healthy and motivated.
  B. To maintain a perfect credit record:
    1. By meeting all financial obligations without error.
      a. Loans must be paid on schedule.
      b. Credit-card bills must be paid when due, not on installment.
    2. By not borrowing more than 25 percent of my net income, exclusive of investment property mortgages.
  C. To maintain a low-risk investment program:
    1. By consistently saving $×00 a month in a bank money market fund.
    2. By reinvesting all interest and dividends.
IV. Tasks:
  A. To determine my net worth, update my resume, prepare my budget, and evaluate my 5-year plans every year on January 1.
  B. To let blue-chip professionals handle my tax, accounting, insurance, and legal needs.
 V. Timetable of Major Purchases:

Objective	Amount Needed	Purchase Date	Amount to Save Each Year
Car down payment	$1,000	1/1/××	$500
New refrigerator	$ 600	6/1/××	$300

You should also draft 5-year plans for other areas of your life that could use strategic planning. These include educational, vocational, social, physical, spiritual, or entrepreneurial areas. You're a totality of interests and values, not just a money machine. Finally, integrate all plans into a comprehensive long-term master plan. This plan could be as short as 10 years or as long as a lifetime. It will give you a bird's-eye view of where you're heading and at what velocity. For example:

TEN-YEAR MASTER PLAN

Updated: January 1, 19×0
Years: 19×0–19×0

Year	My Age	Expected Net Worth	Comments
19×0	24	$ 5,000	Finished MBA
19×1	25	$ 8,000	Down payment on condo
19×2	26	$15,000	Paid off educational loans
etc.			

Step 3: Nurture Your Career

Your job provides the seed capital for investing. You must cultivate on-the-job competency. This will assure a continuing flow of money. Job security is the foundation to financial achievement. If you aren't a civil servant, tenured teacher, member of a strong union, or sure about the staying power of your job, you must protect yourself against layoffs. Don't depend on unemployment or welfare. These programs are inadequate and debilitating. To protect yourself, be prepared to put in long hours, save as much as you can, and job hop when necessary. Ideally, your job should pay well, require little travel, and offer long-term growth and security. Such jobs are often found in the service sector, such as banking and insurance. Avoid industries that are subject to swings of fortune, such as the automotive and construction industries. Consumer behavior in a recession is to retrench. They postpone luxuries and major purchases, such as a car and home. The long-term trend is toward service and information-oriented work and away from blue-collar, smokestack work.

You cannot always choose for whom you'll work and where you'll work. But our system lets you move from firm to firm and industry to industry as you like. In mobility lies opportunity. America is the land of the second chance. I don't minimize the difficulty of finding satisfactory work. It's hard. If you have children, impress on them that nothing good—including a career—comes without work, knowledge, courage, and sacrifice. If you're young, now is the time to start planning for the future. Let's say you're a high school dropout working at a gas station changing oil and tires. If you view yourself as a failure, you could be sandbagged in that dead-end job. But if you see yourself as a management trainee on the first rung of one of the most important industries in the world—the petroleum industry—and if you make an aggressive effort to learn all you can about that industry, you'll rise. Your future will be as bright as any college graduate. In fact, many college graduates are floundering in their careers. Why? They fail to see that upward mobility is the product of relentless self-assessment, self-improvement, and self-promotion. Education doesn't end with a sheepskin. Attitude is the key. There is no failure, save from within.

If you were born between 1944 and 1964, you face unique competition. As a member of the postwar baby boom, demographics has forced you to compete more intensely for good schools, careers, and houses than any generation before you. Jobs that might have been open a generation ago are no longer available. Baby boomers born just before you will block your rise up the corporate ladder. Those born just after you are snapping at your heels. Under these conditions, two strategies suggest themselves. The first involves trying to break out of your peer group into a higher age cohort where there's less competition by ruthless job hopping. The second strategy is less risky and possibly more fruitful. It involves being content with a well-paying, middle-level niche that allows you time to develop lucrative sideline activities, such as real-estate investing. Your dual income—a good salary plus rentals—could give you the life-style of those who live more precariously at the corporate apex.

Eventually, you could be making more money from real estate than from your job. But, until then, your salaried job has priority in commitment over your investments.

Step 4: Eliminate Personal Debt

Borrowing to invest can accelerate wealth building. If the return on investment is such, it makes sense to borrow. But accumulating debt to gratify emotional or egotistic impulses is irrational. It will ruin hope of long-term gain.

Loans and credit-card debts (excluding mortgages) shouldn't exceed 25 percent of your take-home pay. How do you get out of debt? Pay off all high-interest credit-card bills as soon as possible. Cut up your credit cards. Their interest rates are too high, the temptation to spend is great, and the temptation to delay payment is also great. Pay cash for consumer durables, such as furniture, appliances, and clothes. After paying off the car loan, keep it for at least five more years. It makes no sense to go into debt every few years just to have a new car. Avoid using unsecured lines of credit. Avoid bill consolidation loans. The use of such a loan is an attempt to treat the symptom, not the problem. The problem is the accumulation of debt by overspending. If you simply lower the payments by extending the term, it may help temporarily. But if your spending habits continue, your problems will multiply.

Step 5: Determine Your Annual Net Worth

You should work up a personal balance sheet at the start of every year to let you know if you're moving ahead. Although your obligations may be heavy at one point, if your net worth is solid and at least 10 percent ahead of the previous year, you're doing well. If your net worth starts to stagnate or decline, you must reassess your investment strategy and spending habits.

Net worth is simply total assets minus total liabilities. Assets are things of value owned. Liabilities are creditor's claims. Your net worth is the excess of the value of your assets over your liabilities or your liabilities over your assets. The balance sheet of a business is a statement of assets, liabilities, and net worth on a given date. It may be drawn up in the form illustrated next, which is an expression of the following equation: assets − liabilities = net worth.

THE X COMPANY

Balance Sheet: January 1, 19× ×

Assets:

Cash	$ 5,000
Accounts receivable	8,000
Merchandise	12,000
Total	25,000

Liabilities:

Accounts payable	7,000

Net worth: 18,000

The assets of a business are equal to the claims of the creditors plus the owner's equity. This relationship is expressed by the following restatement of the foregoing equation: assets = liabilities + net worth.

There's a tendency to exaggerate the value of your nonliquid assets, such as your house, appliances, and furnishings. Make an effort to be as precise as possible. A broker will give you a range in which he thinks your real property will sell. Your banker will suggest a fair market value for your car. An appraiser will give you the market value of your furnishings, stamps, coins, and jewelry. In theory, the value of an unexpired lease that you hold is an asset. But since this is virtually impossible to convert to liquidity, I ignore it. The principal due on all loans, including mortgages, must be included as liabilities.

Use the following chart to determine your annual net worth:

STATEMENT OF NET WORTH

Personal Balance Sheet for 19× ×
Prepared: January 1, 19× ×

Assets:

Cash on hand	$ _____ . __
Cash in checking account	_____ . __
Cash in savings account	_____ . __
Cash in money market	_____ . __
Certificates of deposit	_____ . __
Cash surrender value of life insurance	_____ . __
Current value of home	_____ . __
Current value of other real estate	_____ . __
Current value of annuities	_____ . __
Current equity in pensions	_____ . __

Market value of securities
    Stocks   ——— . —
    Bonds   ——— . —
    Mutual funds   ——— . —
Uncashed checks   ——— . —
Accounts receivable   ——— . —
Market value of durable possessions
    Cars   ——— . —
    Household furnishings   ——— . —
    Household appliances   ——— . —
    Recreation and hobby equipment   ——— . —
    Tools and office equipment   ——— . —
Other assets   ——— . —
Liabilities:
    Current bills outstanding   ——— . —
    Balance due on installment debt   ——— . —
    Balance due on mortgages   ——— . —
    Balance due on personal loans   ——— . —
    Amount due on taxes   ——— . —
    Loans on life insurance   ——— . —
    Credit-card debts   ——— . —
    Security deposits   ——— . —
    Other liabilities   ——— . —
Total assets   ——— . —
Total liabilities   ——— . —
Net worth   ——— . —
Last year's net worth   ——— . —
Net worth increase/(decrease) over last year   ——— . —
Net worth percent increase/(decrease) over last year   ——— . —

Step 6: Save

Saving is the capacity to forgo consumption. Investing is using savings to create producer goods. To invest, you must save. Even when you invest the savings of others, you must first show you can handle money responsibly by saving. The iron law of financial success is to retain a surplus of your earnings. To accumulate capital, you must live beneath your means. The time will come when you can buy furs and boats. But, until you've built a working investment program, you should adopt a spartan life-style. This will take discipline, but there's no other way. Hard work and planning isn't enough. You must also save. By saving more than you spend, you start the process of converting income to capital. From this dynamic springs all the great corporations and fortunes. If you make ten dollars and spend nine, you're on the way. "Money can beget money, and its offspring can beget more, and so on," Benjamin Franklin wrote. "He that kills a breeding sow destroys all her offspring to the thousandth generation.'' Save! Our society revolves around easy credit and easy living, so it will be hard. But still you must save until it hurts. Save, though you suffer hunger and cold! Save, though the heavens fall! For by so doing, you'll forge the foundations upon which your future will be built.

Commit yourself to a specific figure or percentage of your monthly take-home pay. Stick to that amount throughout the year. Some firms will deduct some of your pay to buy savings bonds or company stock. You may not like savings bonds or the firm's stock purchase plan. But don't despise these forced-savings programs. It's easy to rationalize not making the 10 percent or $100-a-month deduction.

You may decide to move this money into one-year certificates of deposit every month. For example, if you bought a $1,000 CD every month, at the end of the year you'll have $12,000 in CDs at an interest rate higher than the money market's. Your money will still be reasonably liquid, as $1,000 each month will come to maturity.

Reduce your checking account deposit to the minimum. Transfer your money from your savings account to a bank money market fund. What is a money market? When large corporations, banks, and the federal government need short-term cash, they borrow money from a group of institutions and individuals who have large amounts of money to lend for up to 6 months. Because the borrowers want large sums for a short time and because they put up no security other than their good name, they have to pay high interest. Thus, it's usually a good investment for lenders. A money market fund operates on the principle of pooling. It gets relatively small amounts of money from a large number of individuals and small businesses, pools that money, and lends it out in the money market. The interest earned is then passed along to the fund's investors as dividends. For savers, a money market that pays high yields, offers check-writing privileges, and is insured by the FDIC is a good deal.

Before investing, you should save at least 6 month's income. Even with ''no money down'' deals, your lawyer and insurer will still bill you. Unexpected vacancies could cost you hundreds of dollars, deferred maintenance thousands. Without this cushion, such investments as real estate don't make sense because they'll put your capital at risk. A classic mistake by real-estate investors is to underestimate costs and overestimate rentals. They often look at just the mortgage payment and property taxes, forgetting such costly but necessary expenses as management, furnishings, repairs, utilities, replacements, and insurance. In real-estate parlance, the investor has an alligator—negative cash flow—a rental property in which the expenses could gobble the property's owner. The usual result, foreclosure.

Let's get down to brass tacks. How much money do you need to get started? To prevent negative cash, I recommend that at least initially you follow these three rules:

1. Save 6 months of income.
2. Keep an additional reserve of $1,000 per unit in a liquid account.
3. Put 20 percent down on your purchase.

On a duplex costing $75,000, 20 percent down is $15,000. If you have a gross income of $30,000, your savings should be another $15,000. In addition, you should have $2,000 for incidental unit expenses. Your total cash reserve should be $32,000. For many families, that will seem forbidding. But, within the context of your 5-year plan, $32,000 is within your reach. If you save systematically, you'll be able to meet that target. You may get by with as little as $20,000. Much will depend on your skills as a negotiator, the local economy, availability of special financing, and interest rates. As your properties appreciate and as you gain experience in refinancing, you'll be able to operate with a more slender cash backup. But, for the first-time investor, if your cash liquidity for the preceding example falls much below $20,000, you may face financial problems.

Step 7: Diversify Your Investments

All investments must be characterized by prudence, research, discipline, and diversification, and be judged on the basis of safety, liquidity, and yield—in that order.

If all investments involved the same degree of risk and gave you about the same opportunity for reward, it would make little difference how or where you invested your money. But, of course, different investments have sharply different risk/reward relationships. In general, no-risk or low-risk investments offer a small but guaranteed return, such as money deposited in an insured savings account. Moving up the risk ladder, various types of bonds pay an interest rate that reflects in large measure the level of risk that they are thought to involve. Similarly, the degree of risk (*beta*) is one factor affecting the volatility of common-stock values. You've a limitless range of alternatives. It's axiomatic that what may be the best investment for you may not be the best—or even suitable—for someone else. Most people aren't in the financial position to make any high-risk investments, no matter how high the possible rewards. But others may want to consider the opportunities to substantially increase their return by placing some portion of their capital in investments that involve larger but affordable risks.

No hard rules govern who should consider speculative investments and who shouldn't. But there are some useful, time-proven guidelines. These guidelines are best depicted in the form of an investment pyramid. Everyone, regardless of his financial status, should give first priority to foundation investments—adequate insurance, savings earmarked for specific purposes, and sufficient liquid funds for family emergencies. Such investments should involve a minimum of risk and should constitute the largest part of your overall portfolio. For those who have adequate foundation investments, the second tier on the pyramid might best be termed growth investments. Included in this category are such investments as good grade common stocks or investment real estate, which can appreciate and produce a reasonably predictable income. These investments involve somewhat greater risks. Common stocks can go down as well as up. Real estate is subject to a variety of both physical and economic hazards and is often illiquid. However, they generally offer a greater reward potential than lesser risk investments.

At this point, the answer to the question "Should I speculate?" becomes clear. Until you have sufficient foundation investments to meet your family's needs and sufficient growth assets to accomplish your long-term financial goals, you must avoid speculative forays. Never speculate with money you cannot afford to lose. I won't dogmatically say that you should never trade hog belly futures. But you should have a clear appreciation of the risks of such speculative activities before you do so.

I get angry when I hear people promote their shortcut systems to wealth, which usually involve a measure of speculation and fraudulence. Despite valiant efforts by consumer watchdogs, suckers continue to pour their savings down these ratholes, often in the name of evading taxes. It seems they would rather hand their money to a swindler than the government. Those who lose so much money are our social elite—doctors, lawyers, entertainers, academicians, and businessmen. Perhaps because they're so smart in their careers, they despise first principles in investing. The British say that you can be "too clever by half." You can be so much in love with your plans and deals that you lose sight of the fundamentals: "Look before you leap." "Trust must be earned." "There's no free lunch."

You can call these aphorisms "bromides" or "cliches." But what are cliches but distilled common sense—which apparently isn't so common. They're like warning lights that flash on our brainpan when the flimflam man comes calling. The Buddhists speak of karma, the idea that acts operating in previous states determine successive states of existence. This concept suggests that acts have consequences, that if you break the rules, you will be broken by the rules. The Taoists speak of that essence of all nature—the Tao, or Way, through which man could find immortality. This concept suggests that norms exist independently of wish or will, and that if you stray from the path limned by these norms, you'll do so to your peril. These so-called platitudes are subliminal reminders of how we should act, for they encode the "wisdom of generations."

Here are ten guidelines to help you avoid getting "stung" by a bad investment:

1. Don't let yourself get rushed into anything. Never sign anything hastily. Few deals cannot wait until tomorrow.
2. Always know with whom you're doing business.

3. Beware of steals. You cannot get something for nothing.
4. Don't listen to high-pressure sales talk.
5. Beware of promises of spectacular profits.
6. Be sure you understand the risks.
7. Don't buy on tips and rumors.
8. Get all the facts.
9. Tell the broker to put the information in writing and mail it to you.
10. If you don't understand what is going on, consult a person who does.

These rules of conduct have "stood the test of time." Every year, millions of dollars are swindled from people who fail to keep these principles in mind. All these rules can be reduced to one: Buyer beware!

Don't let anyone manage your investments, unless they understand precisely what you want and you understand precisely what they are doing. These rules should prevent account churning or unauthorized transactions from clobbering your foundation investments. Inside information, esoteric financial jargon, and flattery are tools of the pin-striped crook. Old-line, blue-chip brokerage houses do employ and encourage such people. Actually, the broker who swindles gets a disproportionate amount of the blame. Greed, vanity, ignorance, laziness, sentimentality, impatience, and dishonesty are the investor's seven deadly sins. If you find you've been cheated, ask yourself which one of those traits or group of traits best describes you.

Don't "invest" in coins, gems, arts, antiques, or "collectibles." Storage and appraisal costs are high, liquidity is poor, and appreciation is by no means assured. These goods have the additional disadvantage of not generating income, interest, or dividends.

I don't deny that people have made money—sometimes fortunes—buying these things. And tangibles can be a good inflation hedge. Advisors, such as Harry Browne and Howard Ruff, have built a following promoting "hard money." In my view, such a strategy puts the cart before the horse. You shouldn't put your money into these goods until you've established your foundation and growth investments. If you do buy gold, gems, and the like, recognize what you're doing for what it is: speculating. Hope of gain comes out of your expectation that you'll find someone else who'll take it off your hands at a higher price than you bought it for.

Apart from their speculative quality, most of these goods have little intrinsic value. You cannot eat gold or wear stamps. Also, the small investor is competing with people and organizations with great resources and sophistication. Market manipulation, boiler-room scams, and mail fraud can wipe out the life savings of those who are dazzled by claims of high appreciation, time-payment plans, insurance policies, special financing, money-back guarantees, four-color brochures, and posh addresses.

The tangible itself may be a fake. That Maple Leaf could be brass. That diamond could be zirconium. That Chippendale could be made in Japan. Tangibles can suffer great reversals in value, especially if the economy undergoes disinflation. What happened to the one-karat investment-quality diamond is instructive. In 1980, such a diamond was selling for about $60,000. Here was an investment that had not gone down in value for over 40 years, had appreciated an average of 25 to 35 percent every year since 1970 and consistently outperformed gold, silver, and the stock market, and had outpaced inflation. In 1982, that same diamond was worth only $18,000, with a previous 12-month decline in value of 52 percent.

My final problem with a hard-money strategy is that it's pushed by people who have a dim view of our future. Ruff's book, for example, is called *How to Prosper During the Coming Bad Years.* I don't think the coming years will be bad. His analysis is largely predicated on the decline of the U.S. dollar and runaway inflation. We'll continue to have bouts of recession and inflation. But I don't see the kind of social dislocation that justifies a life-style based on bartar and hoarding.

If you want to invest in stocks, consider staying with an industry related to your line of work. You'll have a better grasp of the value the stocks are supposed to mirror. For example, engineers could put some of their money into the computer firms that have sprouted in California's Silicon Valley. Don't "plunge" or "play the market." Wall Street isn't a playground or a casino. You should plan at least 3 months of study, observation, and "paper trading" before you write a check to your broker.

A dog-eared but much-ignored Wall Street axiom advises investors to "cut your losses but let your profits run." Once you buy a stock, set a floor and sell it at that floor if the stock drops below it. If you buy stock at 100, you may set a floor at 80. If it falls to 79, sell, no matter what. Don't expect it to rebound. It might, but you must discipline yourself to assume it won't for the good of your entire portfolio. This ratchet device will protect you from the ruinous gambler's fallacy, the psychological need to justify previous efforts by redoubling your wager to win back your losses and make a profit. This principle applies to all areas of investing, such as commodities and real estate (after the turnaround phase).

You don't have to buy a block of houses to take advantage of the investment opportunities available in residential real estate. You can put your money into the stock of firms that build houses and apartments. You can also buy into mortgages that finance them. One way to invest individually in groups of mortgages with a high degree of liquidity and safety is by buying Ginnie Maes. These securities are backed by a pool of Federal Housing Administration (FHA) and Veterans' Administration (VA) mortgages originated and sold by professional lenders. The Government National Mortgage Association, a federal agency, issues them. They are backed by the full faith and credit of the United States. Although the initial price of a Ginnie Mae security is $25,000, Wall Street has been carving up the investments into smaller denominations through unit trusts or mutual-fund-type portfolios.

A cut below Ginnie Maes are participation certificates offered by the Federal Home Mortgage Corporation, or Freddie Mac, and the mortgage-backed securities offered by the Federal National Mortgage Association, or Fannie Mae. Collateralized mortgage obligations (CMOs), issued by Freddie Mac, are the sale of debt rather than assets. They are tiered instruments. Thus, the investor can buy short-, intermediate-, or long-term maturities. A CMO works much like a zero-coupon bond. It grows in value until the shorter-term classes are paid off. Then it begins paying off to long-term investors.

In some states, second trust deeds are another possible investment. A second trust deed differs from a second mortgage mainly in the foreclosure procedure, which is quicker, simpler, and cheaper. Often an investor makes a second trust loan to a homeowner who wants to spend some of the appreciation in his house without selling it or to a house buyer who cannot get a big enough loan. In either case, the loan is typically handled by a mortgage broker. He pairs an investor with the buyer or owner in need of extra cash. The loan's term is usually less than 6 years.

Step 8: Buy Income Property

I'll tell you how to do this in the remaining chapters. Steps 1 through 7 can be done at roughly the same time. Step 8 should be done only after you've done the previous steps.

INVESTMENT FORCES

Inflation, interest, and taxes shape your investment decisions. You must understand these forces to cope with their consequences.

Inflation

In the context of the 1980s, you may view this section with impatience. After all, inflation has subsided. However, the crises of the past have a way of recurring. The better part of wisdom is to refrain from making long-term suppositions about the economy.

Will a good job lead to financial independence? After 40 years on the job, your pension and Social Security will meet your minimal requirements. They won't be enough to assure "the good life." To retire comfortably and maintain a life-style similar to your current standard of living, 50 percent of your present income is needed, 60 percent if you want to travel. This doesn't factor in inflation. Inflation will boost costs and dilute the value of your savings and pension. Inflation results when the amount of money and credit increases in relation to available goods and services, forcing up prices. If a government prints money out of proportion to the economic production of the country, the value of the paper money declines. The paper money begins to mean nothing because it represents no tangible assets. As inflation gets out of control, banks will collapse, the machinery of government will break down, and cities will face chaos. Germany in the 1930s, China in the 1940s, and Hungary in the 1950s are examples.

How should you respond? The best strategy is to transfer a portion of your savings into hard goods, preferably goods with utility, such as real estate. Real estate is the best inflation hedge, because it represents a basic necessity. Yet it can be paid off over time in money of decreasing relative value. The more property you control, the better protected you are against inflation. You may be tempted to spend if you think prices will rise. But it's absurd to forgo a systematic program of savings. Everyone should have money for emergencies. Also, it's not always possible to convert hard assets into legal tender. Save during times of inflation. Spend during times of recession, when the economy is undergoing a general price decline.

Interest Rates

Interest is a key factor in property affordability. High rates are largely the financial market's expression of anticipated inflation and deficits. It's both a barometer of the inflation suffered to date and a prod on future inflationary surges. High rates are due to fears by lenders of being caught again with long-term loans at low rates in a new period of high inflation caused by federal borrowing to support record deficits. The government's demand for credit collides with private demand with such force that real rates are driven up. The government always stands first at the credit window. Interest rates are the pivotal variable in the dynamics of the economic system. It tells you what you should be doing. When interest rates go up, the stock market goes down. They always move in opposite directions. The most dependable signal of a turn in the economy is the relationship of short-term interest rates to long-term rates. Ordinarily, long-term interest is higher than short-term. When the short-term rates are higher than the long-term, it means that a recession is about 6 months away. When the short-term drops below the long-term, a recovery is no more than 6 months away. Long-term rates, by virtue of their being out of reach of government policy makers, are the reliable inflationary gauge. Every time short-term rates have moved above long-term rates, trouble followed, as it did in 1968–1970 and 1973–1974. The most disastrous case of short rates fetching more than long rates was in 1929. This signal was flying fully 18 months before the Crash.

For borrowers, rising interest rates mean paying back loans with cheaper dollars. Watch for signals of an interest rate peak. Rising unemployment and lower factory orders for machine tools are two good indicators. The 30-day Eurodollar rate is another leading indicator on interest rates, as it's sensitive to massive borrowings from around the world. But be alert for election-year pump priming and post-election credit tightening. If it looks like rates will fall, put your money into long-term debt instruments, such as 4-year Treasury notes and CDs.

Money markets and the forces that govern them are cyclical. The booming development periods of 1970–1973 and 1976–1980 were followed by tight money, high interest rates, and limited investment. These cycles hit all areas equally, providing periods of boom and dormancy. They do, however, tend to hit various investment strategies in different ways. In general, low interest rates and limited capital tend to support rehabilitation and recycling. Recessionary periods also create demand backlogs. Housing starts drop. Office vacancy rates decline. On the other hand, easy credit and low interest rates can signify major overbuilding, as many projects vie for the same markets.

What happens to the market value of real estate when interest rates fall? Its value rises as more prospective buyers can qualify to buy it. Thus, the increased price of the property could eat up any savings you get by waiting for a fall in interest rates. Developers often exploit this interest rate psychology by offering financing with lower-than-market interest rates and a higher selling price.

Taxes

Tax considerations enter into every stage of real-estate investment decision making. Potential tax liability or savings influence the cash flow from the investment, thus determining the price the investor could pay and still earn the desired rate of return.

For owners of real estate, the tax blessings include the following:

1. Income real estate gives you substantial deductions for interest, property taxes, repairs, operations, and maintenance. These deductions result in a tax savings. And, because of the way the federal tax rates are set up, the higher your taxable income, the greater your tax savings.
2. Rehabilitation of old and historic buildings provides special tax credits for those willing to spend money for rehabilitation.
3. Each year that the building is in existence, it wears out. To encourage investors to buy real estate, tax laws permit the investor to deduct that amount of depreciation from his income. The mortgage doesn't affect the depreciation allowance. The depreciation is based on the total cost rather than your equity.

4. On the sale of a real-estate investment, the investor may be taxed at a lower capital gains rate.

5. The investor can exchange real property for other property, allowing him to increase his equity without tax cost.

The following table is a summary of tax treatment for different kinds of holdings:

Type of Holding	Depreciation Allowance	Treatment of Gain	Treatment of Loss	Repairs, Maintenance	Interest
Personal residence	No	Capital gain	Not deductible	Not deductible	Deductible
For sale to customer	No	Ordinary income	Ordinary loss	Deductible	Deductible
Trade or business	Yes	Capital gain	Deductible	Deductible	Deductible
Investment	Yes	Capital gain	Deductible	Deductible	Limited

INVESTMENT ATTITUDES

Real-estate investors share several traits. These include the willingness to learn, energy, realism, and independence. These traits can be learned. They are no less important than capital and expertise to achieve your financial goals.

Knowledge

The investor must be open to new information. He must know the local market. He doesn't have to be a financial wizard. A basic knowledge of math and the ability to learn from mistakes is sufficient. Many strikingly successful real-estate tycoons came from backgrounds of limited formal education. Conversely, people of great education and intellect have sometimes done poorly in practical finance. It seems that dogged tenacity is more important than education, at least in the long run.

News articles, magazines, other books, and courses at the local community college can fill gaps of knowledge in such key areas as accounting and business law. If you want to get into corporate real-estate development, a JD, CPA, MBA, or even a Ph.D. may be necessary. If you plan to take that track, make sure your goals are sharply focused. Some people get good grades, but their long-term goals are a never-never land of wishful thinking.

I would discourage you from attending those real-estate seminars often advertised in newspapers and over cable. The cost is expensive, the atmosphere is emotional, the recommendations are questionable, the pace is frantic, and the expectations that are raised are unrealistic. The speakers may know what they're talking about. But the techniques they push may not work in your area. Many brokers would be happy to spend an hour with you talking about some of their ideas for free.

Energy

Arabs say that health is the digit one, love is zero, glory is zero, success zero. Put the one beside the others and you are rich. But without health, everything is nothing. Health is energy. Energy is work. And work is capital. Tycoons often have boundless energy, a "driven" quality that possibly derives from a combination of genetics, greed, and filial piety. Real estate is a long-term proposition. The rewards often mature only after a long incubation.

Meanwhile, you must be willing to work long hours even if it doesn't appear that you will make a lot of money. At least at first, you must agree to having your leisure time interrupted. Landlording is a business conducted during odd hours. If you aren't willing to accept this, you will find it a burden. Income properties inevitably have a succession of problems—people problems as well as material and financial problems. If you're a brooder, paranoid, suspicious, and furtive, you won't survive. You can neither be impulsive nor compulsive. If you have the kind of personality that feels you must always remain in control, you'll find that your reward isn't wealth but anxiety, humiliation, disorientation, frustration, and a loss of creativity. If you're sick, you won't enjoy the fruits of your labor. You'll just want to get well.

For these reasons, you should take stock of your habits. These considerations aren't moralistic, but pragmatic. What's the cash value in how you live? Lack of exercise, drugs, a tense personality, bad driving habits, hedonism, underinsurance, and divorce can retard or wipe out your efforts to build a fortune. Human nature being what it is, perfection isn't a reasonable expectation. But the apprentice capitalist must see that the barriers to accumulation aren't just financial and educational, but also physical, psychological, motivational, and moral.

The rules for success won't work unless you do. Discipline, delayed gratification, and sweat are the engines of wealth. To enjoy a better future, you must forgo the pleasures of the present. This runs contrary to our society's pleasure ethic, but there's no alternative. Although your eyes are on distant shores, you cannot lose sight of the here and now. It's easy to dream of some magical rose garden over the horizon, while ignoring the roses that are blooming outside your window. Despite your temporary poverty, life can still be vital and joyous.

Realism

Investment real estate is a business. There's no room for self-deception in business. Can you agree with these statements?

1. The customer is always king and business exists only to serve the needs and wants of the customer.
2. The simple truth, well presented, is the most effective form of advertising.

High ethics is good business. This doesn't presuppose a Pollyanna view of human nature. It simply means that you shouldn't let contractors who cheat and tenants who connive corrupt your standards.

W. Somerset Maugham wrote, "The common idea that success spoils people by making them vain, egotistic, and self-complacent is erroneous. On the contrary, it makes them, for the most part, humble, tolerant, and kind. Failure makes people bitter and cruel." But the realist will learn from failure and redouble his efforts. The attitude expressed in the statement "I'm a failure" and the attitude expressed in the statement "I've failed" are worlds apart. Failure subtracts nothing, whereas successes are cumulative. Brooding about what you missed in life will only attract more failure. It it's a bad deal, the realist will bail out with a minimum of pain and loss, rather than languish in an unhappy job, relationship, or investment.

Self-reliance

In corporations, personal success is defined as being part of a team. The group ego supersedes the individual ego. "The nail that sticks out," the Japanese say, "must be pounded down." The real-estate investor is more independent. He is a contrarian, distrustful of creed and crowd. In the face of dissent from his attorney, accountant, and friends, the investor decides and acts. Few real-estate deals are unambiguously desirable. He will, therefore, have to weigh his own reservations against his instincts and knowledge. He is unwilling to take statements, figures, or people at face value. Statements must be tested against reality, figures must balance and add up, and people must prove their trust.

Self-reliance also means believing that ultimately he—not his parents, his friends, his firm, his school, his church, the army, the state—is responsible for himself. "We do not choose to be born. We do not choose our historical epoch, or the country of our birth, or the immediate circumstances of our upbringing. We do not, most of us, choose to die; nor do we choose the time or conditions of our death. But within all this realm of choicelessness, we do choose how we shall live," Joseph Epstein writes. "We decide. We choose. And as we decide and choose, so are our lives formed. In the end, forming our destiny is what ambition is all about." The investor will aggressively seek information that contradicts his inclination. But he will always keep his sense of independence.

Psychologist Alfred Adler believed that the great motivating force behind all achievement is insecurity. In fact, most people of attainment lost a parent early in life through divorce or death. Such a loss possibly breeds a sense of insecurity that drives him to pile up wealth as a buffer against further blows. The prevalence of parental absence in the histories of tycoons was confirmed in a Small Business Administration (SBA) study of 110 company founders: "The picture that comes through the interviews is one of a lonely child, grubby fists in tear-filled eyes, accepting the loss and facing a dangerous future." From such beginnings, it's not hard to see how such people were forced to develop independent judgment and self-reliance. Having no one else to guide them, they looked within themselves for guidance.

Wealth means the farewell to dunners, lien servers, and repossessors. It's the shortest, speediest route to self-esteem and security. But what you start to learn once you've reached your financial goals is that there is no security, save what you've got between your ears and in your heart. Let's not confuse net worth with self-worth. Security ultimately comes from who you are, not what you have.

To succeed as an investor, you must form a winning team. It might consist of your lawyer, accountant, brokers, and contractors. The most important member of your team is your family. It's both the goal toward which your efforts are focused and the mainspring behind those efforts. Even if you don't buy income property, you should get your family involved in your finances. They should know what you make, how you made it, and where it's going. Money is the last taboo, a subject not to be whispered among the well-bred. But none of us is born with a money sense. From you, your children will learn how to work, save, invest, negotiate, and consume. There's nothing a banker or broker does that cannot be learned by any 10-year-old. It's a mistake to shelter your kids from money considerations. An early grasp of practical finance will give them an edge in our increasingly competitive world.

Whatever your financial goals, you'll need the support of your spouse and children. If you're getting a lukewarm response from them, perhaps you should reconsider your intentions. You must decide that your success must nurture your family. To succeed at anything, you must support your family and have the support of your family. Any view that neglects the family is a jaded view. You cannot succeed—no matter what you accomplish—if you lose your family. "For what shall it profit a man, if he should gain the whole world, and lose his own soul?" The greatest success is the success that nourishes your family.

SUMMARY

Here are some of the main points from this introduction.

1. Make the 5-year plan the unit of personal financial planning.
2. Increment your net worth by a set amount each year.
3. Save at least 6 months of gross income before investing.
4. Monitor economic forces that shape your investment decisions.
5. Evaluate your abilities and personality.

1

HOW TO BUY

OVERVIEW

In a nutshell, the process of successfully buying income property follows this sequence:

1. Establish neighborhood, income, and property selection criteria.
2. Review a volume or file of multiple listings. Select properties that meet your criteria.
3. Visit the properties by yourself. Case the neighborhood. Eyeball the grounds and exterior.
4. Make a tentative selection of properties. Visit properties again with a broker and seller. You may also wish to bring along an appraiser and inspector. Establish the extent of delayed maintenance and true market value.
5. Bid—percent below market on the property, if still interested. Fill out offer form but don't sign it. Have your attorney insert protective clauses. Negotiate closing terms.
6. Submit bid and earnest money. The earnest money must not exceed that amount that a small-claims court can adjudicate.
7. If rejected and if still interested, increment bid by—percent but no greater then appraiser's market estimate.
8. If seller accepts your bid, contact funding sources, beginning with the seller.
9. Receive loan guarantee with an interest rate not to exceed—percent.
10. Enforce compliance by seller of all agreements, such as making repairs and showing income and expense records.

11. Sign loan acceptance form, if loan terms are acceptable and contract terms have been met.
12. Close.

Assess for yourself what figures to use in the blanks. These values will depend on market conditions and the amount of risk you're willing to assume. These 12 steps are a broad-brush overview of a complex, idiosyncratic process. The text that follows will explain these steps more fully.

ANALYZING PROSPECTS

How do you evaluate a prospective property? Consider three factors:

1. The neighborhood in which it resides.
2. The income it generates.
3. The structure itself.

That should be the order of your investigation. Don't visit the property until you know the area and the building's cash flow. It's easy to fall into the trap of buying a building because you like its appearance rather than for its profitability. Don't overanalyze a prospect. Your projections probably won't be accurate anyway. You must nevertheless base your decision on something more than intuition. You need facts. This chapter will tell you how to get and weigh those facts.

Neighborhood Analysis

Every broker offers the same old chestnut: "The three most important factors in buying real estate are location, location, location." What's wrong with this truism? First, a property can be well located and still generate negative cash and a sales loss. Second, location is one factor among many that you must consider, not the least of which includes return on investment. Third, all real estate is well located. It's just a matter of timing. The ghost towns of the Old West were built for a purpose. Babylon wasn't erected without reason. Today's slum is tomorrow's Gold Coast. In the life of a building, the value of a location is as variable as the economy. Many old European cities have gone through great changes, including market collapses, physical destruction, and racial transitions. Yet individual neighborhoods within them have survived over the centuries. They have either been continuously maintained or have gone through cycles of decline and renovation. Fortunes have been made by those who have anticipated these changes and have acted accordingly. Location isn't the only consideration, or even the main consideration, but it is a consideration. Sizing up the community is as important as evaluating the property itself.

What is a good location? Consider the following four points:

1. Vitality.   Critical for commercial buildings, economic vitality is also important for residential structures. Tenants may like to live on a quiet side street. However, a vacant unit near a bus or train stop, banks, or stores will command premium rents and will be easier to rent.

Jobs create housing. Jobs also determine the type of housing in an area. Be wary of investing in one-business towns. A review of the local press and a drive down Main Street will tell you where the local economy is heading. Check with the town's planning department to see if it is planning any initiatives to enhance the area's economic vitality. These initiatives could include low-interest loans, building rehab assistance, systematic code inspection, capital improvements (curb, gutter, and sidewalk reconstruction), selected rezoning and property purchase, and business technical assistance. Check if the city plans to implement rehab mechanisms, such as the following:

1. Tax increment financing. Tax revenues from a downtown district are frozen while increases in revenues are put into improvements. The districts sometimes last for 20 years, can give officials special condemnation powers over downtown property owners, and often involve extensive street renovation.
2. Special-service districts. These districts tax downtown property owners for special improvements, such as sewer lines, decorative streetlamps, and parking ramps.
3. Outright government ownership of property and partnership in development via industrial revenue bonds.

The U.S. Census Bureau provides local planners with analyses of where the town's population is heading. If you have a speculative frame of mind, you can use such data to follow John Jacob Astor's dictum: "Buy on the periphery and wait."

2. Accessibility.   Some buildings have visibility and are surrounded by vitality. But, because of traffic flow and congestion, they make poor investments. How hard is it to get to the building? An apartment with a garage is better than a brownstone with on-street parking. A corner-lot store with ample parking is better than a storefront on a hill or on a one-way street hiding behind a row of parking meters. The demise of some urban malls demonstrates the importance of accessibility. City planners touted urban malls as the answer to the afflictions of aging downtowns. Under the banner of urban renewal, streets were blocked, paved with cobblestones, and planted with trees and flowers. Full pedestrian malls, where you close the streets and reroute traffic, start to look like graveyards. The "store for sale" signs start appearing. As consumers drove to the shopping malls, stores in the urban malls died.

3. Quantity.   What is the competition? Some locations may be over-built. Rents will reflect this market saturation. As a city grows, congestion often rises in such public facilities as highways, parks, court systems, museums, and schools. Such crowding usually makes these facilities less desirable, thereby restraining the city's growth. Anything that restricts the city's growth will protect your rents. These include zoning restrictions, mountains, and parks.

4. Quality.   Look for a neighborhood that has stabilized or is coming into favor. Many of these neighborhoods are close to urban areas or next to pockets that are making a comeback. However, choosing a structure in an up-and-coming area will probably mean that renovations are needed. An architect or structural engineer usually can tell you if the building is worth preserving. Make sure the neighborhood isn't deteriorating. If the value of your neighbor's property decreases, the value of your property will go down. Diversify your real estate into varied areas so that a single neighborhood's decline won't tarnish your entire estate. Look for a property in a section of the city that has good schools, easy access to a major business district, and recreational and cultural amenities. Ask: Are there any objectionable smells or noises? What public transportation is available? Are streets well lighted, well patrolled, well maintained? What is the outlook for special assessments?

What is a bad location? These signs mark an undesirable neighborhood:

1. Overcrowding of buildings with people.
2. Overcrowding of land with buildings.
3. Poorly planned land use.
4. Lack of public facilities and services.
5. Lack of adequate shopping facilities.
6. Gang activity.
7. Lack of convenient transportation.
8. More than one structure out of every five in a state of severe deterioration.
9. Evidence of disinvestment. Disinvestment is a complex process involving property owners and bankers who decide that the return on a particular building or area is no longer worth investing more money. This leads to a reduction in services, the physical deterioration of the building, and often to its abandonment and eventual seizure by the city for tax delinquency. Arson is often a quicker solution.
10. Rent control. Congress once authorized rent control in all defense-rental areas. Because rent is the largest item in most people's budget, high rent and threats of eviction contribute to labor discontent. Rent control tended to reduce labor turnover and thus contributed to worker productivity. Even in peacetime, the law often fixes maximum rentals. But rent control

is good for no one—property owner or tenant. It discriminates against tenants who are willing and able to pay market rates. Rent control inhibits new private construction. It creates a disincentive to maintain the property, as the margin of profitability narrows and is eventually overcome by rising costs. Controlled rents in New York City are currently 40 to 60 percent below market. That percentage is the discount a seller must make to induce a buyer to acquire a unit with a rent-controlled tenant as part of the package. Largely because of rent control, New York City apartment real estate is a house of horrors. In the same building, you can have two adjacent apartments that are identical in all respects except for a 500 percent difference in rent. Rent control is often found in cities with a tenant majority and liberal politics.

Income Analysis

The section will help you to analyze the value of the property from the standpoint of cash flow. View all data from the listings with skepticism. It may be wise to add 10 percent to all expense values and deduct 10 percent from all income values. However, at this stage, absolute precision isn't necessary. You are looking for patterns and exceptions to patterns.

WORKSHEET

A. Investor Goals and Resources:
    1. Goal: To invest in residential/commercial real estate in the _____ area.
    2. To earn __ percent per year on an after-tax basis over an expected period of __ years, 19 __ to 19 __ .
    3. Personal Data:
        a. Tax bracket: __ percent
        b. Tax status: _____
        c. Share in equity: __ percent
        d. Share in sale: __ percent
        e. Share in profits: __ percent
        f. Net worth: $ _____
        g. Liquid worth: $ _____
B. Ratios:

As you flip through the listings, you should use ratios to deduce the property's income value. The net income/asking price is the best indicator of value, assuming that the income figure is accurate and that the delayed maintenance isn't too bad. The assessed value/asking price is another accurate ratio, but it's sometimes difficult to get fair assessments of many properties on short notice. The property tax/asking price and insurance cost/asking price can point to an unexpected value. Taxes are generally a function of market value (what it would sell for). Insurance is generally a function of replacement value (what it would cost to rebuild). High insurance and low taxes suggest massive depreciation. Low insurance and a high asking price suggest the property is either underinsured or overpriced. As you consider dozens of kindred properties, you will see the values emerge from these relationships. But these ratios are less important than the preceding, because of the capricious and complicated relationship between property values and taxes and insurance.

1. $\dfrac{\text{Net income}}{\text{Asking price}} =$

2. $\dfrac{\text{Assessed value}}{\text{Asking price}} =$

3. $\dfrac{\text{Property tax}}{\text{Asking price}} =$

4. $\dfrac{\text{Insurance}}{\text{Asking price}} =$

Save time in calculating these ratios by rounding. For example, for a net income of $6,214 for a $86,900 property, simply divide 6 by 9. As the result starts to exceed 1.0, you should slow down and consider other elements in the prospective purchase. In the preceding case, the net income should exceed $9,000. After looking at hundreds of listings, this process of rounding becomes so routine you won't need a calculator.

We've scanned all the listings and have made some tentative selections. Now we must determine the property's bottom-line benefits.

To find out the property's profitability, we must forecast the expected cash flows. These come from net rental collections and the sale of the investment. The after-tax cash flow represents the amount of cash the property is expected to generate after all obligations have been met.

C. Cash Flow
    1. Calculation of After-Tax Cash Flow:

Multiplied by	Rent
Equals	Number of units
Less	Potential gross income (PGI)
Plus	Vacancy and bad-debt allowance
Equals	Miscellaneous income
Less	Effective gross income (EGI)
Equals	Operating expenses
Less	Net operating income (NOI)
Equals	Debt service
Less	Before-tax cash flow (BTCF)
Equals	Taxes
	After-tax cash flow (ATCF)

2. Calculation of Taxes from Operation:
   Plus   Before-tax cash flow
   Plus   (BTCF)
   Less   Principal payment portion of debt service
   Less   Replacement reserves
   Equals   Depreciation reserves
   Multiplied by   Amortized financing costs
   Equals   Taxable income (TI)
                       Investor's marginal tax rate (tax bracket)
                       Taxes
3. Annual Cash Flow From Operation:

Years:	1	2	3	5	10
PGI					
EGI					
NOI					
BTCF					
ATCF					
TI					

Over time, the following will generally happen:

1. Rents will increase more than expenses.
2. Depreciation will shelter less income.
3. The proportion of principal to interest will increase.
4. The value of the property will appreciate.

In combination, these factors will reduce your tax shelter but increase your cash-on-cash return.

D. Capital Growth
   1. Down payment $ _____
   2. Principal payoff
      a. Annual loan payment   _____
      b. Less first-year interest   _____
      c. First-year principal payoff   _____
      d. Percent of down payment   _____
   3. Cash flow
      a. Annual gross income   _____
      b. Less expenses
         (1) Fixed   _____
         (2) Variable   _____

The purpose of capital growth analysis is to determine the return on what you've invested. That is, as a percentage of your down payment, what is the equity buildup, cash flow, and tax benefit in owning the property?

    c. Net operating profit   ———

    d. Less annual loan payment   ———

    e. Net cash flow   ———

    f. Percent of down payment   ———

  4. Tax calculation

    a. Net operating profit (3c)   ———

    b. Less loan interest   ———

    c. Less depreciation   ———

    d. Tax write-off   ———

    e. Times tax bracket   ———

    f. First-year tax reduction   ———

    g. Percent of down payment   ———

  5. Recapitulation

    a. First-year equity payoff (2c) ———

    b. First-year cash flow (3e)   ———

    c. First-year tax reduction (4f) ———

    d. First-year property appreciation ———

    Total amount   ———

    Amount as a percent of down payment ———

E. The Operating Statement

The operating statement is a sheet of paper that many real estate investors use as a guide to buying. They often put blind faith in these figures. Operating expenses include such items as property taxes, repairs and maintenance, property insurance, management fees, collection losses, and utilities. It's the cost of all goods and services used in the process of getting rental income. Expenses may be classified as follows:

1. Maintenance expenses are costs incurred for such items as management, wages, utilities, decorating, repairs, and similar operating expenses.

2. Fixed expenses are costs that vary little from year to year. These include taxes and insurance.

3. Reserves for replacements are allowances set up to replace equipment that has a short life expectancy. Reserves should be set up for heating systems, roof replacements, air conditioners, ranges, refrigerators, carpeting, and other items that will wear out during the economic life of the building.

Four types of expenses aren't operating expenses:

1. Financing costs. Principal and interest payments may be looked on as personal expenses of the owner, showing that he doesn't own the property free and clear. Property is appraised as though unencumbered.

2. Income tax payments. Since personal income taxes depend on a person's income and family situation, it's not possible to compute a tax that's representative for a property. Thus, income taxes aren't treated as expenses for appraisal purposes.

3. Depreciation charges on buildings or other improvements. An annual depreciation charge is an accounting method of recovering the wear of the structure. It rarely reflects the building's true erosion of value, because of the rising cost of construction and the demand for real estate.

4. Capital improvements. Sometimes an owner overstates his operating expenses by including the costs of recarpeting, buying new refrigerators, and the like as operating expenses. These items should be written off according to IRS rules. Although replacement reserves may have been set aside for these items, the payments themselves aren't treated as operating expenses. They are taken from the replacement reserve monies.

Operating expenses consume up to 70 percent of gross rentals in an apartment building, depending on the geographic area. All expenses should be verified by actual bills. Ask the seller or broker for a warranted rent schedule. This should tell you if the unit is furnished or unfurnished, the number of baths, and the number of bedrooms. You'll also insist that the seller supply a warranty that no rent concessions have been made to any tenants. In analyzing a potential purchase, buyers tend to underestimate operating expenses. Fudging of current or future income can cost an investor tens of thousands of dollars. It's easy to overlook the omission of figures for trash removal, pest control, snow removal, and other occasional services.

The most common distortions are claims of high-paying tenants. Some high-paying tenants may be affiliated with the seller. Sellers may operate the building themselves to avoid a management fee. If you cannot take care of the building personally, this fee must be added to the operating expenses. If the previous owner overstated the net income from a building, a new owner can seek a court judgment against him for damages, and maybe punitive damages for fraud. If the fraud is flagrant, the buyer may cancel the purchase and get his money back.

F. The Capitalization Rate

Income-producing property is usually bought as an investment. The purchaser wants the property for the return it will yield on the capital he uses to buy it. The value of an income-producing property is measured by the net income it can be expected to earn during its remaining useful life. Net operating income is effective gross income less operating expenses. The rate of return the investor receives is the capitalization rate, which can be expressed as a relationship between the net income a property produces and its value. Mathematically,

$$\frac{\text{Net income}}{\text{Value}} = \text{capitalization rate} \quad \text{or} \quad \frac{I}{V} = R$$

This formula is useful for appraising because of its two corrollaries:

$$\text{Capitalization rate} \times \text{value} = \text{net income}, \quad R \times V = I$$

$$\frac{\text{Net income}}{\text{Capitalization rate}} = \text{value}, \quad \frac{I}{R} = V$$

If the effective net income of a property and the capitalization rate are known, you can find the property's value.

Comparable properties have comparable caps. If a property the appraiser thought was comparable has a cap rate a half-percentage point or more in either direction from those of other comparable properties, the appraiser should discard that example. Even a slight difference in the cap rate will have a serious effect on the estimate of the property's value. For example, if a property was assigned a cap rate of 9 percent and its net income is $18,000, its value would be $18,000/0.09 = $200,000. If the cap rate was 8 percent, the value would be $18,000/0.08 = $225,000. One percentage point difference in the cap rate would make a 12.5 percent difference in the value estimate. By discarding extremes, the appraiser should have a narrow range of cap rates from which the property's cap rate can be averaged. Capitalization works best for large properties, such as shopping centers.

Here are several techniques to arrive at the price to pay for the property:

1. All cash method.

$$\frac{\text{Net operating income}}{\text{Cap rate}} =$$

This is the amount you should pay for the property if you were to pay all cash and were satisfied with a cash flow equal to the cap rate from your investment.

2. Financing method.

$$\frac{\text{Before-tax cash flow}}{\text{Cap rate}} =$$

This is the amount you can afford to invest in cash to get a return on investment equal to the cap rate. To arrive at the BCTF, each year the payment on mortgage debt, referred to as debt service, is deducted from the net operating income.

3. Cash-on-cash method.

$$\frac{\text{Before-tax cash flow}}{\text{Total equity}} =$$

To calculate the cash-on-cash rate of return, the investor divides the expected first year before-tax cash flow by the amount of cash he plans to invest in the project. If the percent rate of return meets his required rate of return, he might conclude that he invest. The problem with the cash-on-cash criterion is that it takes into account only the first year's cash flow. It ignores the tax benefits or costs from the investment. It also ignores the expected cash flow from the sale of the investment at the end of the holding period.

4. Gross income multiplier method.

$$\frac{\text{Sale price}}{\text{Gross income}} =$$

The gross income multiplier is obtained by dividing the price of the property by the gross annual rentals. Because they are subject to essentially the same market influences, rental prices and sale prices tend to move in the same direction and in the same proportion. If rental prices go up or down, sale prices will usually follow suit and to the same degree. Generally, annual gross income multipliers are used in appraising industrial and commercial properties, while monthly gross income multipliers are used for residential properties. The gross income multiplier is a quick way to check the validity of a property value. It's a rough measure that varies over time and by location. The multiplier might, however, provide you with a good first estimate of the investment's feasibility. (For readers acquainted with the stock market, the gross income multiplier is similar to the price/earnings ratio used in stock analysis.)

5. Payback method.

$$\frac{\text{Down payment}}{\text{Equity payoff + cash flow + tax reduction + appreciation}} =$$

The payback period of an investment is the number of years in which its initial outlay can be recovered by profits. If the payback is less than the time requirement the investor sets, the proposal is accepted. This method doesn't measure return on investment or profitability. It shows only how long it will take to recoup the cost. With real estate, the first year's payback should include all costs involved in getting the property and turning it around. The larger the down payment, the longer it will take for the investor to recover his initial expenses.

6. Return on investment method.

$$\frac{\text{Equity payoff} + \text{cash flow} + \text{tax reduction} + \text{appreciation}}{\text{Down payment}} \times 100 =$$

The return on investment method tries to establish the percentage of the return to the initial investment. It's the benefit the investor gets over his original investment. If there is a loss, the return on the investment is less and below the original investment. If a capital item costs $20,000 and earns an average of $5,000 per year over the asset's 10-year life, the return on investment would be $5,000/$20,000 = 25 percent. The average rate of return is the ratio of the average annual profits after taxes to the total outlay of funds.

7. Discounted cash flow method.   This method involves placing a present value on future cash flows, both cash inflows and cash outflows. The discounted cash flow method takes into account the time value of money; for example, a dollar of earnings today is worth more than a dollar next year. To use the DCF method, a table giving values of factors is needed. These tables are arranged by interest rates and number of years. As the name implies, discounted cash flow models estimate the value or rate of return for an investment by discounting the expected cash flow. The best measure of the expected cash flow is the after-tax estimate. For the small investor, the discounted cash flow method presents an unnecessary dimension of sophistication.

Property Analysis

You've pinpointed the neighborhood in which you want to invest. You've tentatively selected several buildings that seem to fit your cash flow requirements. Now you must determine the condition of the property. Basically, you will be looking for three things:

1. The quality of the original construction. The structure may be water and smoke damaged, but you may be able to turn it around if the structure is fundamentally sound. On the other hand, a superficially attractive building with fundamental structural flaws arising from land shifts, termites, and the like is a bad deal at any price. Like a good doctor, you will have to learn to see the skeleton beneath the skin.
2. How well or poorly it has been maintained. The age of the building isn't a good indicator of maintainability. If something looks like its broken, it usually is. The broker may tell you that the basement has no lights because the light bulb burned out. The odds are that you will probably have to rewire the basement and replace the service panels.
3. The peculiarities unique to the building's history. Every structure has unique components and a unique history. In viewing a property, your

attitude should be a balance between skepticism and tolerance. While you should be skeptical when the broker paints his word pictures, you should also be tolerant of the mess you see. Distinguish between cosmetic problems such as an uncut lawn and substantial problems such as a leaking roof.

A general guide for weighing these three factors follows:

1. Documentation.

Dimensions.   The exact dimensions of a property are shown on the assessor's map. If the dimensions are in acres, remember that an acre is about 200 by 200 feet. In rural developments, lot lines often extend to the center of the road. In the city, the lot line may extend just to the inside of the sidewalk.

Legal Owner.   The ownership of real estate is a matter of public record. You're entitled to this information. It can help you evaluate the property and negotiate with its owner. These records are in the county registry of deeds or the assessor's office at city hall. You don't want to deal with anyone except the legal owner of the building. No one else can make a binding commitment, unless the owner gives that person written permission to do so. If the legal owner isn't the same as the person with whom you're negotiating and the owner hasn't given your contact written authority, get in touch with the owner directly. His name and address are also included on the master list.

Unpaid Taxes.   The seller should pay any unpaid taxes. Back taxes are usually indicated in the master list of assessed properties. The year of delinquency is often shown, but not the actual amount. If the taxes are current, there won't be an entry. Your attorney or title company can easily find out the delinquent amount.

Liens or Claims.   You need to know about liens or claims by people who have done work on the property but who haven't been paid. As with back taxes, if the seller doesn't pay these liens, the buyer has to do so. Recorded liens can be checked at the county courthouse.

Existing Mortgage.   Using the name of the owner and the coded date of purchase, consult the property owner's index. One of the code numbers will be the document number of the deed that gave the property to the present owner. Read that document closely and inspect the documents recorded just before or just after it. Also, consult the name index for the later mortgage. Mortgages are always recorded.

Seller's Original Cost.   The amount of tax stamps on the deed is supposed to be based on the price of the property. Some people place excess stamps on the deed. If they sell the property, they have an apparent basis for claiming they paid more for the property than they did.

Pending Foreclosure.   If the seller is seriously behind in his mortgage payments, the lender will probably have recorded a document that says so. If a notice of foreclosure was filed, the seller is likely to be eager to sell. He probably doesn't have much time to come up with his delinquent payments.

Other Properties.   If the owner's name appears frequently in the index, you're dealing with a real-estate veteran.

Sophisticated Sellers.   If the owner's name appears on second or third trust deeds or on wraparound loans and complicated leases, the seller will know a lot about creative financing.

Assessed Value.   The county assessor must estimate how much the property is worth to compute the property tax. The estimate is usually at least a year old. It's usually lower than the market rate.

Here are items to bring with you when you visit a property:

Flashlight

Level

Tape measure

Notebook and pen

Flash camera

Water bucket, to test water flow and purity

2. Foundations.   Check the foundation for deterioration that may let moisture enter the basement. More importantly, check for uneven settlement. This will distort the house's frame and even pull it apart. It may rack window and door frames out of square, loosen interior finish and siding, and create cracks in the plaster. Minor settling can be corrected by releveling beams or floor joists. That isn't sufficient reason to reject the structure. Many failures and general uneven settlement, however, would indicate a new foundation is needed or that the house isn't suitable for rehabilitation. The foundation supports the entire house. Its failure can have profound effects. Many old houses have stone or brick foundations. Some may be supported on masonry and even wooden piers. Check the masonry foundation for cracks and crumbling mortar. This common defect can usually be repaired. Most foundation walls or poured concrete have minor hairline cracks. These have little effect on the structure. But open cracks indicate a failure that may get worse. Whether a crack is active or dormant can be determined only by observation over several months.

Defects are most obvious in the basement. Check walls for inward bulges, cracks or crumbling mortar, and high-water marks. Check the floor for signs of leaks, seepage, or dampness. Look for a sump pump, suggesting frequent flooding. Check the basement piping for heavy corrosion. Hot-water pipes should be copper. They should also be insulated if they're long. Cold-water pipes should be copper or plastic. Damp or leaky basement walls may require a major repair, especially if the basement is used. Causes of dampness are clogged drains, broken downspouts, cracks in walls, lack of slope away from the house foundation, or a high water table. The most common source of dampness is surface water, such as from downspouts discharging directly at the wall or condensate from an air conditioner that is improperly draining. These problems can be resolved easily. A high water table is a more serious problem. There's little possibility of getting a dry basement if the water table is high.

3. Chimneys. The most obvious chimney defects are cracks in the masonry. Such cracks are usually the result of a foundation settling or attaching antennas or other items that strain the chimney. They are a particular hazard if the flue doesn't have a fireproof lining. The chimney should be supported on its own footing, not by the house's framework.

4. Siding and trim. Problems with siding and trim stem from moisture. One contributor to this problem is the lack of a roof overhang, allowing rain to run down the wall. Moisture may also enter from the inside, because of the lack of a vapor barrier. Decorative trim is sometimes excessive and presents decay and maintenance problems, particularly where water may be trapped. Good shingle siding appears as a perfect mosaic. Worn shingles have a ragged appearance. Close examination will show individual shingles to be broken, warped, and upturned. You will have to replace these shingles.

5. Windows. Windows usually present one of the more difficult problems of old frame houses. If they are loose fitting and not weather-stripped, they will be a major source of uncomfortable drafts and high heat loss. Check the tightness of fit and examine the sash and sill for decay. If the sills are freshly painted and the rest of the house isn't, the paint may cover rot. Casement windows should be checked for warp at top and bottom. In cold climates, windows should be doubled glazed or have storm windows, both to reduce heat loss and to avoid condensation. If windows aren't a standard size, storm windows may be expensive. Check if screens are rusted, torn, or missing.

6. Doors. Exterior doors should fit well without sticking. They should be weather-stripped to avoid air infiltration. This is a cheap item to add. Warping usually causes difficulties in latching a door. The lower part of exterior doors and storm doors are particularly susceptible to decay and should be checked. Also, check the condition of the threshold. It may be worn, weathered, or decayed.

7. Roof. If the roof leaks, it should be clear from damage inside the house. A look in the attic may reveal water stains on the rafters. These indicate small leaks that will eventually cause damage. Damage inside the house isn't always attributable to the roof. It could be caused by faulty flashing or from condensation. Study the building from the outside. Line up the top ridge of the roof to make sure it's straight. A sagging roof or bulging walls means the frame is weak. Rebuilding will be costly. Check the roof for broken shingles, tar paper bubbles, and broken patches. Check metal sheathing around the chimney and ventilators. It should be watertight and made from rust-proof material. Look for leaks and breaks in gutters.

Asphalt shingles are the most common roof covering. They are made of a wide range of weights and thicknesses. The most obvious deterioration of asphalt shingles is loss of surface granules. The shingles may also become quite brittle. A good asphalt shingle should last for about 20 years.

Built-up roofing on flat or low-sloped roofs should be examined by going onto the roof and looking for bare spots in the surface and for breaks and separations in the felt. Bubbles, blisters, or soft spots also indicate the roof needs major repairs. The life of a built-up roof varies from 15 to 30 years, depending on the number of layers of felt and the quality of application.

Flashing should be evident where the roof intersects walls, chimneys, or vents and where two roofs intersect to form a valley.

8. Floors. Look for buckled or sagging boards. If the floor is generally smooth and without too much separation between boards, refinishing it may put it in good condition. Some type of new flooring will have to be added if the boards are too thin to sand.

Floors with resilient tile should be examined for loose tiles, cracks between tiles, broken corners, and chipped edges. Replacing any tile in a room may mean replacing the flooring of the entire area because tiles change color with age and the new tile won't match the old.

9. Walls and ceilings. The interior wall covering in an old house is usually plaster. Plaster almost always has some hairline cracks. Minor cracks and holes can be patched. A new wall covering should be applied if large cracks or holes are evident. The same rule applies to ceilings.

If walls have been papered, check the thickness of the paper. If more than two layers of paper are present, they should be removed before applying new paper. All paper should be removed before painting. You may need to sand off the glue residue before you resurface.

10. Insulation. Look in the attic to see the amount of ceiling insulation. The ceiling represents the greatest source of heat loss on cold days and the greatest source of heat gain on hot days. At least 3 inches of insulation should be provided for homes in mild climates and 4 to 6 inches for those in cold climates. To find out if walls are insulated, some siding or interior covering must be removed. Insulation is also needed under floors or crawl spaces in houses in cold climates. The R factor is a rating given to insulation to denote its ability to resist heat flow. Depending on the climate, good ratings for ceilings are R-22 to R-38 and R-13 to R-19 for exterior walls.

11. Plumbing.   Old plumbing fixtures may be rust stained and require replacement. The plumbing drainage system consists of a sewer lateral, the underfloor drains, the drainage pipes above the floor, and vents. Pipes may be clogged, broken, or too small. Venting may be inadequate and below code requirements. In extreme cases, the vents may cause water in the traps to be siphoned out, allowing sewer gas to enter the house. Note any excessive suction when a toilet is flushed. Sewage disposal drainage may be inadequate. Run water for a few minutes to check drain lines between the house and the sewer main.

Water pressure is important. Check all faucets to make sure the flow is adequate. What causes low pressure? The service pipe may be too small or clogged with lime. The supply pressure may be inadequate. If the house has its own water system, check the gauge on the pressure tank. It should read a minimum of 20 and preferably 40 to 50 pounds. Anything less than that suggests the pump isn't working properly or the pressure setting is too low. Check shutoff valves at various points in the system to see if they've become frozen with age or disuse. Rust, white, or greenish crusting of pipes or joints may indicate leaks. Private well water should be tested.

12. Heating and cooling.   Because of rising energy costs, the cost of heating and cooling the property is a major consideration. Heating system advances and concepts of comfort outdate the heating systems in most old houses and apartments. Central heating with heat piped to all rooms is needed in all but the most tiny structures. The only way to really check the adequacy of the heating system is through use. Gravity warm-air systems are common in old structures. Temperature control and heat distribution won't be as efficient as with a forced-air system.

One-pipe steam heating systems are also common in older structures. They provide adequate heat but little control. Steam systems can be modernized by replacing standing radiators with baseboard heaters.

With a hot-water heating system, water may be heated for cooking, bathing, and other needs. However, with a hot-air furnace, the water heating coil seldom provides enough hot air. Furthermore, during summer months when the hot-air heating isn't needed, a separate system is needed to provide hot water. A gas water heater should have at least a 30-gallon capacity. An electric water heater should have a capacity of 50 gallons for an average structure of about 1,500 square feet.

Considerations of energy efficiency are also important for buyers of income property in states with warmer climates. To properly select an energy-efficient structure, you should look at its energy-efficiency features, such as insulation and equipment. And you should examine energy cost estimates from builders or dealers. Make sure the seller or real-estate agent provides you with a copy of energy bills for the past year. Most utilities will give you a copy of these bills, if you provide the company with written permission from the property's owner. If the structure has air conditioning, get the year's electric bills along with the gas or oil bills. You may need to adjust the figures for inflation. If the last winter or summer was cooler or warmer than usual, take that into account.

You can get an idea of the comparative cooling power of a structure's air conditioner by estimating its energy-efficiency ratio (EER). The higher the EER, the less it will cost to operate. The EER ratings of air conditioners vary from 6.0 to 9.0 or more. An air conditioner with an EER of 9.0 uses only two-thirds as much energy as one with an EER of 6.0. The Air Conditioning and Refrigeration Institute (ARI) publishes a directory with the EERs of nearly all air-conditioning models. Most air-conditioning contractors have a copy of this directory and can tell you the EER of a unit if you tell them the exact make and model number. The ARI will also answer mail or telephone inquiries about specific models. Write the Air Conditioning and Refrigeration Institute, 1815 North Fort Myer Drive, Arlington, VA 22209, (703) 524-8800.

13. Electrical.   So many electrical appliances have come into use in recent years that some old structures may not have adequate wiring to accommodate them. The service should be at least 100 amperes for the average three-bedroom house.

Examine the electrical wiring whenever possible. Some wiring is usually exposed in the attic or basement. Wiring should also be checked at several wall receptacles or fixtures. If any armored cable or conduit has rusted or if wiring has deteriorated, the wiring should be replaced. At least one electrical outlet on each wall of a room and two or more on long walls are desirable. Ceiling lights should have a wall switch. Rooms without a ceiling light should have a wall switch for at least one outlet. Check the fuse box. Sixteen to twenty circuits with circuit breakers are needed for an eight- to twelve-room house or a two-bedroom duplex.

14. Termites and other pests.   Termites cost the people of the United States many millions of dollars each year in repairs to structures and in control measures. There are two major kinds of termites—subterranean and nonsubterranean. The former occurs in every state except Alaska. It's particularly prevalent in the southern half of the country. The latter is restricted to the southern half of the country and the Pacific Coast states. Subterranean termites live in nests in the ground, close to a source of wood, and often build tunnels upward to attack the wood in structures above them. Nonsubterranean termites fly directly to the wood they attack, and live in colonies in cavities they make in the wood itself. They damage all kinds of wooden objects, including structural timbers, furniture, posts, poles, and piles of lumber.

The techniques of termite control are too extensive for adequate discussion in this book. To detect and control termites, call a pest control operator. Before you buy a structure in a termite-infested area, make sure it's inspected by a professional. When you walk through the structure yourself, consider using a screwdriver or knife to probe beneath the paint on a beam to ensure its solidity.

You should also look for intrusions by these other household pests:

Ants	Mice
Bats	Mites
Bedbugs	Mosquitoes
Carpet beetles	Powder-post beetles
Centipedes	Rats
Cloth moths	Scorpions
Cockroaches	Silverfish
Crickets	Spiders
Fleas	Ticks
House flies	Wasps

An unusual infestation by any of these creatures is reason not to buy the property.

15. Appearance.   Taste is largely a personal matter. But here are some basic guidelines. Simplicity and unity are major considerations. However, a structure possessing "charm" may be appraised somewhat higher than plainer ones. Buildings of historical or architectural significance are in a special category. For the appraising of these buildings, get professional advice.

Simplicity is one of the first principles. Observe the main lines of the structure. Some variety adds interest. But numerous roof lines at a variety of slopes present a busy, confused appearance. Strong horizontal lines are often desirable to give the structure the appearance of stability. It should appear as a unit, not as a cluster of unrelated components. In the case of a duplex, both sides of the structure should be identical, so as to maintain its value. To the extent possible, this should include all exterior trim and landscaping. (In this book, I've defined duplex to mean any two-unit rental property. But some brokers use the more narrow definition of two identical units, usually side-by-side.)

Windows and trim should be in keeping with the style of the structure. Windows should be of a limited number of sizes. Porches and garages should blend with the house rather than appear as attachments. Trim should appear to be integral to the design rather than stuck on as afterthoughts.

List the number of materials used as siding. There should never be more than three. A rule of esthetics is that what appears in nature is better than something made to look like it was natural. Thus, real bricks are better than plastic imitations, real plants are superior to plastic plants, cedar shingles are preferable to aluminum siding.

A combination of building styles can be grotesque or comical, as in the case of a Tudor revival that ends up as a Mediterranean.

A building out of proportion to its lot is also a minus. At the turn of the century, the Victorian Gothic may have been built on a 3-acre lot. As the press of urbanization eroded its boundaries, the house today may sit on a quarter-acre or less.

Interior colors should not deviate from earth tones, pastels, or white. Tenants react unfavorably to harsh primary color schemes.

Note the owner's exterior decor. In an expensive neighborhood, he may festoon his grounds with statues of lions and nymphs. In a poorer location, he may settle for plastic windmills, pink flamingos, and painted tractor tires, all of which conveys an unintentional sense of kitsch.

Look beyond the grime and tackiness for property that you can improve. The top of the heap has no place to go but down. Fresh paint, wallpaper, and landscaping can dramatically upgrade a basically good property.

Although there may be emotional considerations in buying any piece of property, pride of ownership isn't a main concern with an investment building. Neither the bank nor the buyer will allow anything for sentimental value. Your building is a business. This doesn't mean that you should skimp on maintenance. Address maintenance problems immediately. Otherwise, not only could rents drop, but you could endanger your equity and perhaps even the lives of your tenants.

Look for a building that is relatively new. It has been a common practice on new buildings for the owner to take some form of accelerated depreciation to obtain a greater tax shelter. As the amount of depreciation diminishes after about 10 years, the owner, who still wants a high shelter, may be forced to sell. This usually puts a large group of 8- to 10-year-old buildings on the market. The seller may be so eager to move to another property, you may be able to negotiate a below-market selling price. Unlike a new building, a 10-year-old structure has been tested by time. Problems of plumbing, wiring, roofing, and insulation have usually been worked out. The records of rents and expenses in the past decade will give you solid data on which to estimate profitability. There may also be an old mortgage that you can take over at a low interest rate. However, the older the building, the more money you will probably need for repairs and maintenance.

Unfurnished buildings are preferable to furnished buildings. Tenants don't move so often if they must pay a moving company to transport their things.

Here are physical grounds for rejecting a structure:

1. The foundation cannot be repaired.
2. The entire frame of the house is out of square.
3. The frame is rotted or termite infested.
4. The cost of buying and rehabbing the structure exceeds the fair market value of houses in the area. A rule of thumb for a presently owned structure is that the rehabilitation cost shouldn't exceed two-thirds of the cost of a comparable new structure.

The cost can be arrived at in two ways:

1. If the work is to be done on a fixed-price contract, the contractor's bid will give you a definite figure. Increase this figure by 10 percent for unforseen extras.
2. If you plan to do most of the work and are concerned with the economics of the project, first get bids on those items that will be done by others. Second, figure the cost of all materials for work you will do. Third, estimate your labor time and establish costs using a fair hourly rate. If you aren't experienced in building construction, increase your labor estimate by 50 percent because much time is lost in doing work a little at a time, and there is also a strong tendency to underestimate.

Property should be analyzed from two perspectives—quality (how good is it, what needs to be repaired, what is obsolete) and quantity (what is included with the structure). Listings in real-estate offices usually give a fair quantitative review of the property. They rarely address the qualitative side, except with generalities. The following worksheets will help you analyze the property from both perspectives.

QUALITATIVE ANALYSIS   Date: _____

Address: _____

Asking price: _____

Best use: _____

Investment features: _____
_____

Neighborhood factors: _____

General physical condition: _____

Age: __

Circle the appropriate option:

1. Type of structure
    a. Single-family house
    b. Apartment: number of units __
    c. Condominium
    d. Commercial

2. General appearance
   a. New
   b. Good
   c. Fair
   d. Bad
3. Condition of lot
   a. Good
   b. Fair
   c. Needs extensive landscaping and planting
4. Exterior (siding or paint)
   a. Good
   b. Fair
   c. Poor
5. Roof: Type of roofing material _____
   a. Good
   b. Fair
   c. Poor
6. Driveway: Condition _____
   a. Blacktop or concrete
   b. Gravel
   c. Dirt
   d. None
7. Foundations
   a. Good
   b. Poor
8. Exposed structural beams
   a. Good
   b. Indications of termites or decay
9. Basement or crawl space
   a. Dry and clean
   b. Damp or musty
10. Floors: Type _____
    a. Firm, solid, level
    b. Weak or sagging
11. Chimney condition
    a. Good
    b. Fair
    c. Poor
12. Insulation (R value)
    a. Roof or ceiling __
    b. Walls __
    c. Floors __
    d. None or impossible to evaluate
13. Interior walls: Type of materials _____
    a. Good
    b. Fair
    c. Poor

14. Wall and ceiling finishes: Types _____
    a. Good
    b. Fair
    c. Poor
15. Condition of windows
    a. Good
    b. Poor
16. Window screens and storm sashes
    a. Yes
    b. No
17. Electrical wiring
    Capacity of service entrance
    a. 30 amperes
    b. 100 amperes
    c. 200 amperes
    d. Other _____
    e. None
    Electrical outlets and fixtures
    a. Adequate
    b. Needs additions
    c. Needs complete rewiring
18. Water supply
    a. City
    b. Drilled well
    c. Shallow well
    d. Other _____
    e. None
19. Sewage system
    a. City
    b. Septic tank
    c. Cesspool
    d. None
20. Water pipes
    a. Copper
    b. Galvanized iron
    c. Other _____
21. Hot-water heater
    a. Type _____
    b. Age _____
    c. Condition _____
    d. None
22. Bathrooms
    a. Number __
    b. Condition of fixtures _____
23. Heating
    a. Type _____
    b. Age __
    c. Condition _____

24. Kitchen cabinets
    a. Adequate
    b. Additional units or remodeling needed
    c. None or not serviceable
25. Condition of garage/shed
    a. Usable
    b. Requires repairs
    c. None or not serviceable
Other comments:

As you walk through and around the building, take careful notes of flaws and problems. Look at the property from the perspective of a tenant and a future buyer. Take snapshots of everything that strikes your eye, including all sides of the exterior, every room of the interior, close-ups of less desirable features and delayed maintenance items. Your notes and photographs will help you negotiate a lower price.

QUANTITATIVE ANALYSIS   Date: _____

Address: _____
                _____
                _____
Asking price: _____
A. Single-family home/Townhouse/Condominium   Asking Price: $ _____
    1. Address: _____
               _____
               _____
    2. Number of bedrooms:
    3. Number of baths:
    4. Subdivision:
    5. Township:
    6. Age:
    7. Style:
    8. Financing:
    9. Owner:
   10. Phone number:
   11. Existing mortgage:
       a. Name:
       b. Rate:
       c. Balance:
   12. Garage spaces:
   13. Lot size:
   14. Zoning:
   15. Property tax:
   16. Schools (with busing, you may not know):
       a. Elementary:
       b. Junior high:

    c. Senior high:

    d. Parochial:

17. Fuel:

18. Dimensions:

	Lower Level	Upper Level
a. Living room:		
b. Dining room:		
c. Kitchen:		
d. Bedroom 1:		
e. Bedroom 2:		
f. Bedroom 3:		
g. Bedroom 4:		
h. Family room:		
i. Bathroom:		
j. Other:		

19. Items to be included (circle each applicable):

a. Basement	n. Dishwasher
b. Slab	o. Garbage disposal
c. Crawl space	p. Carpeting
d. Septic	q. Clothes washer
e. Sewer	r. Dryer
f. Central air conditioning	s. Porch
g. Unit air conditioning	t. Patio
h. Drapes	u. Pool
i. Blinds	v. Barbecue
j. Rods	w. Fence
k. Refrigerator	x. Shed
l. Microwave	y. Storm windows and screens
m. Oven	

20. Association dues:

21. Real estate agent:

22. Comments:

Note: As defined in this analysis, a single-family house, townhouse, and condominium represent a type of property that consists of a single income unit, in contrast to multiunit apartments and offices. As defined elsewhere in this book, a condominium is a form of ownership, rather than an accounting unit.

B. Apartment Building   Asking Price: $ _____

                                                    Unit Price: $ _____

    1. Address: _____

                    _____

                    _____

    2. Number of units:

    3. Township:

    4. Zoning:

    5. Age:

    6. Owner:

    7. Financing:

8. Existing mortgage:
   a. Name:
   b. Rate:
   c. Balance:
9. Fuel:
10. Lot size:
11. Parking:
12. Style:
13. Floors:
14. Basement:
15. Utilities:
16. Lease:
17. Items to be included (circle each applicable)
    a. Range
    b. Refrigerator
    c. Dishwasher
    d. Garbage disposal
    e. TV antenna
    f. Clothes washer (Leased?)
    g. Clothes dryer (Leased?)
    h. Compactor
    i. Security
    j. Elevator
    k. Drapes
    l. Shades
    m. Blinds
    n. Screens and storms
    o. Furniture (Leased?)
    p. Pool
    q. Patio
    r. Balcony
    s. Barbecue
    t. Tennis court
    u. Recreation room
    v. Furniture
    w. Other _____
18. Income:

Number of Units	Rent @	Total Rent
Efficiency		
1 Bedroom		
2 Bedroom		
3 Bedroom		

19. Expenses:
    a. Taxes:
    b. Insurance:
    c. Maintenance:
    d. Utilities:
    e. Management:
    f. Other: _____
20. Recapitulation:
    a. Gross income:
    b. Annual expenses:
    c. Net income:
21. Real-estate agent:
22. Comments:
C. Commercial/Office Building   Asking price: _____
   1. Address: _____
      _____
      _____

2. Town:
3. Location:
4. Business name:
5. Type of business:
6. Financing:
7. Owner:
8. Mortgage:
9. Construction:
10. Zoning:
11. Lot size:
12. Documentation:
13. Parking:
14. Improvements:
15. Living quarters:
16. Licenses:
17. Rooms:
18. Square footage:
19. Taxes:
20. Gross income: Type of lease: Amount of security:
21. Annual expenses:
22. Net income:
23. Miscellaneous (circle each applicable):

a. Central heat	n. Office equipment
b. Central air conditioning	o. Cash register
c. Separate heat	p. Booths
d. Separate air conditioning	q. Tables
e. Security	r. Walk-in freezer
f. Fixtures	s. Scale
g. Display room	t. Tools
h. Carpet	u. Machinery
i. Drapes	v. Exterior signs
j. Reception	w. Loading dock
k. Modernized	x. Conveyors
l. Furniture	y. Sprinklers
m. Appliances	z. Elevators

24. Real-estate agent:
25. Comments:

D. Land/Lots   Asking price: $ _____
  1. Address:
  2. Township:
  3. Zoning:
  4. Dimensions:
  5. Owner:
  6. Documentation:
  7. Use:
  8. Acres:
  9. Terrain:
  10. Soil: (Can it support construction?)

11. Taxes:
12. Financing;
13. Improvements/Miscellaneous (circle each applicable):

a. No improvements	k. Residence
b. Gas	l. Shed
c. Electricity	m. Barn
d. Water	n. Garage
e. Sewer	o. Fruit trees
f. Telephone	p. Pond/creek/lake/river
g. Cable	q. Fishing
h. Septic	r. Golf course
i. Well	s. Nursery
j. Sidewalks/curb/gutter	

14. Real-estate agent:
15. Comments:

WHEN TO BUY

Buy when times are hard. Buy when blood is running in the streets. Buy after a flood, blizzard, riot. During such times, insurance firms and banks have properties they don't want. Owners are also desperate, as they suffer the anxieties of having to feed a white elephant.

Winter and summer are real estate's dead seasons. Check the units in the spring or fall. At the start of winter or summer, bid on what is left. In the summer, sellers who don't have their houses sold by June start worrying if they'll be out in time for their children to change schools. In the northern states, November and December are panic times for sellers, especially if the house is vacant. Thoughts of heating bills and water problems loom large. Any buyer looks good at that time of the year. During the winter, sellers tend to price their properties more realistically because there are fewer buyers. Because there will be less demand for mortgage money during this time, affordable mortgages may be easier to get.

Try to find a motivated seller, someone who wants to sell for such compelling reasons as divorce, death, a job change, or old age. Brokers generally aren't too candid about the seller's motivations. And, as agent to the seller, the broker doesn't have to reveal these motivations if that is what the seller wants. However, you should get a sense of the seller's desperation by his reaction to your first offer. (In some states, in the eyes of the law, the broker represents the seller until a purchase agreement has been signed. At that time, the broker is also obligated to act as the buyer's agent. Even though the law is changing in this regard, I question whether the broker can truly serve two masters, since he has a financial interest in representing the seller's position.)

THE OFFER

Negotiating

There are three areas of commerce in which prices and terms are set by negotiation—antiques, used cars, and real estate. Fixed labels and prices have little meaning. Real estate is the most complex of these areas. Numerous factors come into play: financial, legal, and the individual circumstances of each property.

Face-to-face bargaining rarely works well in real estate. Pride of ownership gets involved. Personalities clash. But middle men with expertise in real-estate negotiations can keep the dickering unemotional. You may consider having your attorney negotiate for you, as the real-estate agent isn't a middle man but the seller's agent.

A skilled buyer tries to understand the seller's viewpoint. Find out what he is like. Talk to people who have done business with him. The more you know, the better you can bargain. You will try to strike a bargain that will be fair to both sides. All truly successful negotiations end with all parties convinced that they have gained. There is room for him to get a decent price and for you to get a lucrative deal.

The Contract of Sale

In contract negotiations, the seller and buyer agree on the terms of sale A document should embody the exact terms, so that each side understands precisely what he is to give and get. Neither party is compelled to rely on the honesty or memory of the other party. Common sense alone, therefore, would point to the need of putting the agreement in writing. As a matter of law, also, it's necessary that a contract for the purchase of real estate be in writing. Furthermore, the entire contract must be in writing. It cannot be partly in writing and partly verbal. In any litigation involving the contract, the court will reject oral testimony offered to supply omissions in the written document. Hence, great care should be exercised in preparing the contract. Every lawyer knows that virtually no oral representations made before the signing of a written contract are binding. Under the "parole (oral) evidence rule," they aren't even admissible into evidence should the case go to court. It's the law that once the parties reduce an agreement to writing, the document speaks for itself. Don't rely on verbal explanations from the seller or his broker as to what any terms in the contract mean.

To cross the Rubicon means to adopt some measure from which it's difficult to recede. The Rubicon was a small river separating ancient Italy from Gaul, the province allotted to Julius Caesar. When Caesar crossed this stream, he passed beyond the limits of his own province and became an invader of

Italy. When you've signed a contract of sale for real estate, you must assume that you will follow through. You have crossed the Rubicon, you have committed yourself to buying the property. Even if you festoon the contract with escape clauses, your ability to get back your earnest money could be a lengthy and costly process if the seller and broker choose to sue.

The actual sequence of events that occurs in making an offer, acknowledging acceptance, and agreeing to terms varies around the country. But, in many areas, you make a written offer to purchase. This is backed by some cash, referred to as "earnest money." Getting the seller's signature on your offer will constitute a binding agreement. It binds both parties to a price and assures the buyer's option to negotiate a binding contract before anyone else. The seller may not use your offer as leverage to get a better price from someone else. Your offer should always require that the seller accept or refuse it within a specific time period, usually one or two days.

If your offer is accepted, it becomes the receipt for the deposit that accompanied it. If buyer and seller fail to come to terms during the subsequent negotiations, this money may become an object of dispute. Your primary concern, therefore, is to protect your money and get a valid, binding commitment from the seller. The seller will try to get as big a deposit as he can with an agreement of sale favoring the seller all the way. If the buyer defaults, the seller can keep the deposit, even though it may be several thousands of dollars. (The broker may also get part of the defaulted escrow.) Thus, it's important for the buyer to keep his deposit as small as the seller will let him and to make the deposit in a way that will give him the best chance of getting it back if trouble should arise. As a rule, the buyer should make a deposit no higher than can be adjudicated in a small-claims court, usually under $3,000. If the seller wants a larger deposit, put the remainder in an escrow account with your lawyer. The earnest money must be in a noninterest-bearing account, unless both the buyer and seller agree to do otherwise. This agreement must be in writing. The buyer will receive the interest. For expensive acquisitions that involve a long closing period, this kind of an account is desirable.

It's general practice for brokers to wrap up a deal quickly without any "interference" from the seller or buyer's attorney. Accordingly, they often use simple on-page purchase and sale agreement forms. These agreements have dozens of names: a binder, offer and acceptance, agreement to buy and sell, or preliminary sales contract. Such forms are acceptable if your attorney inserts clauses to protect you and if he checks the small print. Never let a broker or the seller's lawyer get you to sign a contract that your own lawyer hasn't drafted or reviewed.

The agreement to purchase must cover price, earnest money, the kind of deed, dates for closing and occupancy, items to be left with the property when the seller moves, title exceptions, the survey of the building and lot, taxes, and insurance. A real-estate contract is generally held to be all-inclusive. Only in special circumstances will a court consider other evidence that isn't actually recorded in the contract. So, as you proceed from the binder to the negotiations over the terms of the final agreement, you must insist that everything of importance be written into the contract. Your attorney will make sure that no important consideration is overlooked and that the seller performs his obligations.

A contract is formed the moment acceptance is communicated back to you. Until that moment, you are free to revoke your offer. Once your offer is rejected by the seller, the offer is dead. He cannot revive it and accept it later. Most contracts that aren't completed fail because the buyer cannot find acceptable financing, or the seller is unable to deliver an acceptably marketable title. The smart seller will reserve the right to finance the purchase himself, according to the terms the buyer stated in the contract that he would need. Without this, the buyer could ruin the deal by not trying seriously to qualify for a loan. In most contracts, the financing clause favors the buyer. He usually states the precise terms and conditions he will need to be able to purchase. These terms include the total amount to be mortgaged, the interest rate to be charged, and the term over which the loan will be repaid. The seller will try to limit your time to search for a loan commitment. Try for at least 30 days. This will give you adequate time to compare mortgage loan offers.

You should submit an offer and deposit check to the broker only with the following precautions:

1. Your check should be made out to the broker, not to the seller.
2. The broker should hold the check in escrow until he gets an acceptance from the seller and your attorney has had the chance to draw up a purchase and sale agreement satisfactory to you.
3. On the back of the check, you should write the following: "To be used only as a deposit on an offer to purchase property at . . . (address)."

Many contracts provide that if the escrow is forfeited, the agent gets half of it. However, the broker has many incentives not to cheat you out of this money if the deal falls through. Not only has he a reputation to maintain, but he is tied to the area where he does business. The Chamber of Commerce, state or local consumer protection agencies, the state licensing board, and national broker associations can help you get your deposit back. If possible, retain the right to get your deposit yourself. State somewhere in the contract that all monies will be refunded out of escrow if the sale in not consummated within, for example, 30 days of the scheduled closing. If the escrow arrangement is being used, have the "subject to" clauses in the contract tied to the refund from escrow within a stipulated time period. In this way, you will be assured that you will get your deposit back if anything goes wrong.

Your lawyer should include the following contingency clauses in the contract:

1. Violation of ordinances.   The seller should maintain the property until closing. Itemize violations of building, electrical, and plumbing codes in the contract. Whether you can get the seller to pay for these repairs will depend on how serious they are and how candid he has been with you about them. Contracts often require the seller to deliver the title free of such violations. It may provide that he deposit cash to correct the violations.

2. Inspection.   Make a complete inspection of the structure, lot, and all subsystems. Check for land slippage, soil conditions, health of the grass and shrubbery, city encroachments or easements, and the building's shell, foundation, roof, frame, plumbing, wiring, heating, and cooling. Get a termite inspection and pest report. If the seller has used low utility or tax bills as a selling point, have him guarantee those figures for a year or so, or make up the difference. It's difficult to get warranties for an old house. But it's sometimes equally hard for a seller to unload an old house. You should at least insist on a warranty that makes your agreement to buy contingent upon a satisfactory inspection, with a clause like this:

> Subject to inspection by a licensed inspector, such inspection to meet the buyer's approval.

With your agent's help, you should verify that all utility bills are real and that the firms have been paid. This is especially true with water bills. They are usually billed to residents although the charges may have been incurred for a time during which you weren't in possession of the property.

You should walk the boundary of the property to see if any fences or structures overlap onto your neighbor's property or if any of the neighbor's improvements seem to encroach on yours. You may consider making a stake survey, to mark out the angles of your lot.

On the same day, just before closing, you should again inspect the property. This inspection will ensure that the premises are in the same condition as when you made the offer to buy. The time for the buyer to inspect and note defects for correction by the seller is during the contract negotiations and before the sales agreement. Note repair or replacement items in the contract. Most resale properties are sold in "as is" condition. It's up to the buyer to perform the inspection, not the seller. Verify that all utilities are working and that all items of personal property that were listed on the broker's listing sheet are still on the grounds. If you don't make a comprehensive inspection, it's unlikely that personal property that was improperly removed or structural damage can be compensated for after the closing. It's often an expensive and time-consuming matter to seek recovery from the seller. Accordingly, any questions about the condition of the property must be raised before closing. All deficiencies should be noted, and funds may be withheld at the settlement for repairs if the seller doesn't correct those problems. Upon receipt of bills indicating that repairs are complete, your attorney will release the balance of the funds to the seller.

3. Lawyer.   The sale should be subject to your attorney's approval. This catchall escape clause will let you back out of the deal without having to make elaborate explanations or meet conditions set by the other side.

4. Records.   Make sure your offer to buy is contingent on reviewing certified copies of the property's tax records, leases, and rent records. If they don't tally with the alleged total income from rents, the deal should be re-negotiated. A fraudulent representation of rents, income, and profits from the property is grounds for canceling the contract.

You should be able to tell how much income an apartment property brings in based on the number and size of the units, the property's location, and the condition of the property. For commercial and office property, this information is more difficult to estimate.

5. Financing.   The agreement should specifically state that the sale is subject to your obtaining whatever terms of proposed financing are specified. The contract becomes void if you cannot qualify for a loan at those terms. The seller may try to offer you those terms himself, rather than see the deal collapse. Always insist that a specific interest rate be given in your contract. Don't use phrases such as "at market rate" or "best available." The contract probably provides that, if you cannot get that mortgage commitment, you must notify the seller as specified or you will be stuck with the contract. The contract often provides that the seller, once notified, can get the mortgage for you or provide equivalent seller financing.

6. Taxes.   The seller must give the buyer a good title free and clear of any liens not mentioned in the contract. Unless the contract provides otherwise, the seller must give the buyer a title free of taxes, which were a lien at the time the contract was made. The contract usually specifies the taxes to which the property will be subject when the deed is made. The contract often provides for proration or apportionment of the current year's taxes. You should insert into the real-estate sales contract a provision requiring the seller to escrow, either with the broker, his lawyer, or yours, a sum that you feel is sufficient to cover the payment of any potential increase in taxes for this year.

7. Personal property.   Problems often arise over what personal property is to be included in the sale. The strict legal definition of this doesn't seem to stop sellers from removing anything they consider theirs. Have a general inclusion clause drafted that enumerates everything that you care about— refrigerators, stoves, carpeting, and so on. Also try for a guarantee that all appliances are in working order. Don't sabotage the sale over a birdbath. At the same time, remember that sellers have been known to rip out the plumbing, light fixtures, stained glass windows, and paneling. It's a good idea to take photographs of the property as it looks when the agreement is signed. Have the date certified and keep copies. This gives you conclusive evidence if there is a dispute later.

8. Time.   The phrase "time is of the essence" often appears on standard contract forms. Either party may insist on it. Courts interpret this phrase to limit extensions and penalize tardy performance. Make sure you abide by all intermediate deadlines. Otherwise, you could find the contract voided and the seller suing you for damages. With a structure that is undergoing construction or rehabilitation, expect the worst. Builders often fail to complete by the promised date. Provide for cash damages if there are delays.

The contract specifies the time and place of settlement. If you think you need more time, add a clause that provides for an extension for a reasonable cause.

9. Misrepresentation.   So many statements are made in the course of the sale of property that often untrue statements are made. An untrue statement is a misrepresentation. The law has started to recognize that nondisclosure is also misrepresentation. Even if the seller is not aware of a defect, the law may obligate the broker to reveal the defect. Misrepresentations won't affect the contract if they concern a trivial matter. An important misrepresentation doesn't necessarily make the contract void. The party who was deceived may still want to enforce the contract. A buyer may be able to get out of the contract if the seller has misrepresented the property with legal or structural defects.

10. Default.   If the seller refuses to perform, the buyer can pursue one of the following courses:

    a. He may rescind the contract and recover his deposit. This is the buyer's normal remedy where the property has decreased in value.

    b. He may sue to compel specific performance of the contract, such as compelling the seller to give him a deed on receiving payment of the purchase price. The buyer will use this remedy when he wants the property for a particular purpose or when he anticipates that it will appreciate in value. This remedy is more effective than a suit for damages, since damages are hard to prove and personal judgments are hard to collect.

    c. He may sue the seller for damages. This remedy is used when the buyer is content with a personal judgment against the seller for the amount of the profit he would have made had he acquired the property at its contracted price and resold it at its market value. Obviously, this remedy shouldn't be used where the property has declined in value.

The Deed

When the owner accepts your offer and complies with all the protective clauses that you have inserted, your attorney can draw up the deed. A deed describes the property in detail and formally conveys title of the property from the seller to you. The deed symbolizes the seller's relationship to the property and the title that he is passing to you. With a quitclaim deed, the seller doesn't establish his rights or interest in the property. He merely says that whatever he does have, he is passing it to you. You may need to deal with former owners who had no part in the contract for sale. A quitclaim deed conveys title with no warranties. The limited warranty deed is also known as a quitclaim deed with covenant. The grantor conveys whatever present interest he has in the property and promises that he has done nothing to impair the title during his ownership of the property. The grantor doesn't make any promises to the grantee concerning previous owners, who may make a claim to the property, alleging to have a better title. The best deed you can get is a general warranty deed with full covenant. A general warranty deed is a deed in which the seller agrees to protect and defend you against rightful claims to the deed as long as the basis of the claim originated before the title was transferred to your name. It guarantees that the seller will defend the title against anyone who may claim an interest.

Two steps must be taken before the deed can change hands at the closing. Execution occurs when the seller fills in the appropriate blank spaces in the deed and then signs it. Delivery takes place when he turns the deed over to you. This gives you ownership and possession of the property. When you get the deed, make certain that it's properly recorded in town or county records. Deeds require federal revenue stamps, for which the seller must pay. You will get the receipt of the recorded deed and the title insurance policy about 6 weeks after closing.

THE CLOSE

Settlement Procedures

In 1974, Congress passed the Real Estate Settlement Procedures Act (RESPA). Until then, there was little uniformity on the variety of costs associated with buying and selling homes. Under the provisions of this act, most purchases of private homes that involve third-party financing must conform to a sequence of interactions between lender and buyer designed to protect you from paying high fees for poor service. When you file an application for a loan, the lender must give you the government's "Special Information Booklet," plus a good faith estimate of the closing costs required at settlement. This estimate should be based on the size of your mortgage and the specific services the lender provides. They have 3 days to get this information to you (see Appendix B).

The lender can suggest or require the use of particular providers for services. But, unless he gives you a choice of at least two required providers for any given service, he must make a formal disclosure to you about the one he does recommend. He must give the full name, address, phone number, the fee that person charges for a particular service, and whether or not a business relationship exists between that provider and the lender. This restriction applies only to title services, legal work, or the use of a particular person to conduct the settlement. No kickbacks or unearned fees are allowed for referrals. One way of hiding unearned fees is by allowing the provider to maintain larger interest-free accounts at the bank. Ask if a recommended provider has an account at the bank. If you uncover an illegal arrangement, you can sue for three times the size of the fee charged.

One day before settlement, you should see the Uniform Settlement Statement. This government form is used to record the costs of the settlement under RESPA rules. It must be used, whether the actual closing is conducted by the lender, an escrow agent, title company representative, or anyone else. The actual finished statement must be delivered to you at or before the settlement meeting. Another important task on the day before settlement has to do with verifying the provisions of the contract. Many of the conditional issues written into the contract will be cleared up and certified on the final day by the mortgage, survey, and inspection statement. The more subjective aspects of the purchase will require a last-minute inspection of the property. The last stop before settlement is at the county clerk's office, or wherever the deeds and other documents get recorded. Your lawyer must make sure no liens have been registered against your property at the last minute. Sometimes this can be checked by telephone from the settlement meeting.

Mortgage Clauses

Conditions that seem minor when signing a mortgage loan contract can end up costing a lot of money during the life of the agreement. Some clauses to read before signing:

1. Transfer clause.   The lender will want a clause giving him the right to sell the mortgage to another lender. He may deny you the right to do the same thing, that is, sell the mortgage to another buyer by assumption.

2. Prepayment clause.   A prepayment clause lets you pay off the loan before it's due without being charged a fee for the privilege. Prepaying will save you money if interest rates drop and you refinance. FHA and VA loans allow prepayment without penalty. Different lenders have different rules. Some don't allow refinancing for the first 5 years, but then allow prepayment without penalty. Others charge a percentage of the balance, say 6 months income, as a prepayment penalty. Most prepayment penalties diminish over the life of the loan as the principal is reduced.

3. Add-on clause.   The add-on clause is often used in a contract to cover a series of installment purchases. It essentially makes earlier purchases security for later ones. If the buyer defaults on his payments, he may lose not only the new merchandise but also earlier items on which he had completed payment.

4. Acceleration clause.   The acceleration clause means that all payments are immediately due and are payable at the lender's discretion in the event of certain contingencies. Default is one of them. Transfer of title, even within your family, is another. Try to get this clause removed or limited to new buyers by agreeing that you will remain liable for the indebtedness.

5. Balloon clause.   The balloon clause stipulates a final payment that is substantially larger than the preceding installments.

6. Due on encumbrance clause.   The due on encumbrance clause makes the first mortgage due in full if the property is pledged as security for another loan, including second mortgages. This clause may not be legal in some places.

7. Other items.   In addition to the preceding clauses, make sure you understand the following before you sign the mortgage note:

1. The amount being financed.
2. Explanation for penalties and charges.
3. The amount of the finance charge.
4. The date on which the finance charge begins.
5. The annual percentage rate of the finance charge.
6. The number, amount, and due dates of payments.
7. An itemized list of charges not included in the finance charge.

The Closing

The closing is a solemn ritual attended by you, the seller, the listing and selling brokers, and a loan officer. In some areas, attorneys will be present. The seller should bring warranties on equipment and instructions on maintenance and operating. Your attorney should have searched the title and resolved property inspection problems. You'll sign the trust deed, mortgage note, and settlement sheets. The banker may require you to start an escrow account for taxes and insurance for the coming year. If that isn't required, you may have to send the lending bank a copy of paid property tax receipts for each installment and a copy of the property insurance coverage in an amount equal to the mortgage balance. The closing statement will contain all debits and credits. It will state exactly how much money is due from the buyer and exactly how much money is due to the seller.

In some areas, transactions are closed at the lender's office. Unless you've arranged to have an escrow closing, the time and place of the final settlement will depend on when the title and mortgage companies are ready with their documents. The papers may include the contract of sale, the deed, the seller's insurance policies, his receipted utility and tax bills, a property survey, the title abstract, a title insurance policy, a bill of sale for personal property, and documents certifying that the seller has cleared up code violations. The balance of the money that you're required to pay under the terms of the contract is roughly the difference between the purchase price and earnest money and the net mortgage proceeds. You should be prepared to have this amount available by cashier or certified check on the date of the closing. The exact amount will probably by known the day before closing. Your lawyer will call you with the figures at that time.

The lender has brought along the check for the mortgage loan. He will want your signature on the note and the mortgage. The note is your promise to repay. The mortgage is proof of his first lien on the property. If you assume the mortgage, you will need to sign an estoppel certificate that declares the exact status of the loan at present and a new note that releases the original borrower or includes both of you as liable. The appraisal, survey, and inspection reports will provide useful information about the status of your new property. They will also be needed if any errors or discrepancies arise. If the lender has permitted you to get your own hazard insurance, he will now want to see that proof in the form of a binder from the insurance firm.

Check all documents containing factual details for the accuracy of numbers. Make sure that there are no extra zeros on the mortgage note and that prorations have been done properly. Make sure the physical description of the property on the contract, survey, and title policy match. A number of bills representing ongoing expenses will have to be divided between you and the seller. Make sure this is done correctly. Your interest payment will be figured to cover the time until your first payment is due. Make sure you've filed the appropriate papers if you're expecting tax exemptions. If the seller's taxes and insurance have been escrowed, the seller will receive credit at settlement for an excess balance on the assumption. On new financing, the seller will get this refund from the lender at settlement. Taxes and homeowner's dues or condominium fees will be prorated on a daily basis. The seller, buyer, and brokers are supplied a copy of settlement sheets for their records.

The house keys are passed. You should test all keys and put them into an envelope for each key. You should have all locks changed, particularly in circumstances where there has been a multiple listing showing and it may be difficult to keep track of the keys.

Immediately after you take possession of the property, you should reinspect to make sure that there are no changes in the condition of the property as you recall it. This is especially true if there has been a substantial period of time between the closing and your possession.

HOW TO SELL INCOME PROPERTY

When to Sell

Select income property good for the long run. Selling is time-consuming and expensive. It will take at least a few years to earn an above-average return. The capital-gains tax can be devastating, especially in cases where the depreciation has been depleted.

Sometimes it makes sense to sell. You may want to focus your efforts on a particular type of property or in a particular location. You may get an offer that's too good to refuse. You may have emergency expenses. These are good reasons. But, if you want a premium price, the time to sell is when business conditions are favorable and the future is bright. The worst thing an owner interested in selling a prosperous enterprise can do is wait until the business starts turning down. Sell your apartment when occupancy is up to 100 percent, rents are at market level from way below, and the building is throwing off lots of cash.

How to Price

After conferring with the listing broker on market conditions, comparable sales and listings, and available financing, set the asking price. A rule of thumb: A price more than 5 percent over market value discourages offers. Buyers who can afford the property can get "more property" for their money elsewhere. Buyers who cannot afford the price simply won't look. A property priced right is half-sold. A fair market value is determined by comparing the property with similar properties that have recently sold and with similar properties on the market. This market-analysis approach is more accurate than the replacement cost or potential rental income methods. Call in a professional appraiser to determine its fair market value. Also, check the property's assessed value. Often a property is assessed at a certain fraction of its market value. The assessments may have been made years ago when the property was selling for less. FHA and VA appraisals tend to be lower than sales prices in a rising market.

Here are ways to attract offers:

1. Price your property within 5 percent of fair market value.
2. Help finance. Particularly for commercial properties, buyers need help with down payments or reducing monthly mortgage payments. It's to your advantage to appeal to the greatest number of buyers by accepting the greatest range of financing plans. However, make sure you understand the risks of "creative financing."
3. Consider picking up some of the closing costs or giving an allowance for repairs and redecoration.

Improvements

The motivations for improving a house or an apartment building are a need for more space, comfort, and convenience and a sense of pride. Consideration is seldom given to whether these improvements will increase the resale value of the property. Some improvements may not add as much to the property value as you paid for them. Buyers are generally unwilling to pay extra for finished basements, greenhouses, bars, tennis courts, and saunas—anything that's out of the functional mainstream. They are willing to pay for such items as heavy insulation, paved driveways, modern kitchens, and finished laundry rooms.

Stick to improvements that add top dollar value and strive to present a clean, neat structure. Create a general impression that the property has been well cared for.

Showing the Property

When someone asks to see the property, take his name and telephone number and ask him to give several times that would be convenient for him to see the property. Try never to refuse an appointment. Check with your tenants and arrive at a time satisfactory to all. When the prospect arrives, draw his attention to the property's good points. Don't exaggerate. Answer all questions honestly. Anticipate answers to these questions:

1. Why do you want to sell?
2. Are you willing to trade?
3. Will you finance?
4. Will you consider an installment sale?
5. What repairs need to be done?

Answer these questions cautiously. You don't want to commit yourself to an unfavorable deal. Nor do you want to close the door on a sale.

If the broker accompanies the prospect, it's best to leave. Let the broker handle objections and discuss terms, price, possession, and other factors. Keep chatting to a minimum. If you plan to be away, be sure to leave word on how the broker can reach you.

Offer, Acceptance, Disbursement

A buyer makes an offer by submitting a written, signed offer to buy. This will become the sales contract when ratified by the seller's signature. Once the seller and buyer sign the paper, they're bound by the contract conditions. The presentation of a contract starts when the selling broker registers the offer with his office and tells the listing broker of the offer. The listing broker then arranges a presentation appointment with the property seller. The presentation of the offer includes the following:

1. Date, name, and address of the buyer and seller and the legal description of the property.
2. Amount of earnest money deposit, usually held in a noninterest-bearing account by the listing broker.
3. Sales price.
4. Size of down payment and how remainder of purchase price is to be financed.
5. Proposed settlement and occupancy date.
6. Contingencies, such as review by attorney, structural inspection, and financing.
7. Other provisions include time limit during which the seller must accept the offer, a list of items that convey with the sale, stipulation that the title must be insured, and who is to pay the various settlement costs. A contract exists when all terms, including changes, are ratified by the initials of all principals and notice is given to all parties. When the contingencies are satisfied, the contract becomes firm. In some cases, the property may remain on the market with a 48/72 hour kickout clause, which allows time for reflection.

Time is of the essence, and a decision on an offer should be made at presentation. The seller has these options:

1. Accept the offer as written.
2. Make a counteroffer on unacceptable aspects. Counters are written in the margin of the contract or in addenda and are initialed by the seller. The buyer can withdraw, accept, or counter the counteroffer.

All offers registered prior to acceptance must be presented to the property's seller in order of registration. No action is necessary until all offers are heard. If more than one offer is accepted or countered, the seller must establish an order of precedence, such as primary, first backup, second backup.

Consult with your listing broker on all offers. Your first offer may reflect the price it should sell for. But a patient seller should be able to get within 10 percent of his asking if he is willing to wait. Multiple listing volumes often provide an analysis of how many days it took to sell a property. In general, a single-family home usually sells within 2 to 3 months of listing. A multi-family house usually takes 3 to 4 months. Commercial property and farms usually take 4 to 6 months. Lots often take more than a year to sell. This assumes that the property is desirable and properly priced. Owners may not be able to give away some properties because of their location and expenses. Other properties may be on the market for only a few days. These averages suggest the relative difficulty in selling commercial property in contrast to single-family homes.

The multiple listing service volume often provides other interesting statistics, such as the average price of properties of different types and in different areas, the average list to sale price difference for properties sold that week or quarter, and the percent of list to sale price for those time periods. Listings may also be broken down according to street and price. The MLS volume is a good tool for getting an idea of market prices and rents.

If your property doesn't sell, analyze the situation with your listing broker. Adjust for shortcomings and relist the property.

Your attorney or title company will disburse funds after all certified funds are in hand, the new lender has reviewed the papers, the title has been rechecked, and the deed recorded. Sellers usually get their funds with a certified or cashier's check at the closing. Some escrow agreements may call for payment a few days after closing.

If the buyers fail to make a full settlement, the earnest money may be forfeited and divided between the seller and the listing broker.

SUMMARY

Here are some main points from this chapter:

1. Have the property inspected before you buy.
2. Retain legal counsel before you sign anything.
3. Buy when times are hard.
4. Make sure you understand all mortgage clauses.
5. Put all verbal understandings in writing.

2

HOW TO FINANCE

FUNDAMENTALS OF INCOME PROPERTY FINANCING

Leverage

When buying income real estate, the general rule is to use as little of your own money as possible. Although leverage can be a handicap, it can also be a powerful asset. Leverage is the use of borrowed money to magnify gains and losses. You pledge the property as security for the debt. You can borrow up to 100 percent of the cost of the property. Having realized large profits via great leverage, the real-estate investor can shield most of his earnings from income taxes through allowances for depreciation and other expenses. From interest and depreciation alone, there is often a significant paper loss in excess of the positive cash flow. This can be used to shield other profits from taxes.

Leverage multiplies the economic benefits of your investment. For example, if the property appreciates at 10 percent each year, a $25,000 equity investment that buys $100,000 worth of property will enjoy a 10 percent increase on the entire $100,000. The property will increase by $10,000, a 40 percent return on the $25,000 investment. In this case, leverage has quadrupled the appreciation as a percentage of the equity investment.

Leverage also multiplies the tax benefits. Depreciating is the key to the real shelter, and it is based on your entire investment, not just your equity. Consequently, the greater the leverage, the greater the tax benefits in relation to the size of your investment. With leverage, fewer dollars of cash are buying more property that in turn produces more tax benefits.   An example of this is shown in the table on the following page.

But leverage is a double-edged sword. Just as it multiplies your benefits when you have a good deal, it will multiply your losses when you have a bad deal. For example, if the property cited earlier declines in value by 10 percent,

	$60,000 Purchase for 100% Cash	$60,000 Purchase for 80% Cash ($48,000 loan)
Gross income	$12,000	$12,000
Operating expenses	4,440	4,440
Interest	0	5,760
Depreciation	6,000	6,000
Total deductible expenses	10,440	16,200
Net taxable income (or loss)	1,560	(4,200)

you would lose money at the rate of 40 percent per year. A second problem with leverage is that you must be able to carry the debt service. If you don't have enough money from the property itself to pay for interest and expenses, the property will decline. The greater the leverage, the greater the debt service. If you have to keep putting your money into the property, eventually you will sell it—probably at a loss. A property is overfinanced if it doesn't produce enough income to cover the payments on the PITI and still have a positive cash flow. A property may also be overfinanced if the total debt against the real estate exceeds the value of the real estate. If the property is overfinanced on either of the criteria, you have problems.

Be sure that the gross income is high enough to cover all operating expenses and to repay the debt with something left over. Since the property may generate a fluctuating gross income over the years, the debt can only be serviced if a prudent amount was borrowed when you bought the property. Thus, no-money-down deals can be as unwise as all-cash buys. A 10 to 20 percent down payment with the balance financed at a favorable interest rate is often enough to assure both positive cash and reasonably high leverage.

Down Payment

The down payment varies. With some loans, it's 20 to 25 percent. With others, it's as low as 5 percent and, in some cases, nothing. At closing, however, you'll have other expenses—closing costs, prepaid taxes and insurance, points, and other costs totaling 5 to 10 percent of the sale price. To build up your down-payment account, cut the frills and save. Keep making purchase offers until the seller accepts one.

A cottage industry of books and seminars has evolved around no-money-down real property purchases. Before I cite some ways to buy a property with little or no cash, consider what attorney Vincent W. Zucchero has to say on this subject:

> First, the average seller is interested in a cold cash down payment. Period. He doesn't know you or your record. What if you are a fraud? Then the seller is stuck with a worthless promise to pay. Second, the person who doesn't want

cash in a lump sum but prefers a steady income stream must be found. If you are like me, your other activities already occupy the bulk of your time. And, since time costs money, this expense must be added to any no-money-down deal you do arrange. Third, your real estate contacts cannot come close to those of the renowned speakers in the no-money-down area. They have been in the business for years and have the experience in this field. Even they will tell you that the same person seldom closes this type repeatedly.[1]

The premise behind no-money-down books is that property values inevitably rise. Their idea is to buy the property with no money, wait for the property to appreciate, refinance, and use the money to either pay off the original debt or to invest in other highly leveraged properties. Thus, you build your pyramid. I don't deny that people have done well using creative financing and no-money-down purchases. In some parts of the country for short periods of time, this has happened. But, in my view, this strategy has no place with the average investor who lacks the resources and contacts of no-money-down experts. Investors with little equity and high negative cash flows are often forced to sell when faced with a balloon. Also, lenders are often reluctant to refinance a mortgage above its original amount. The go-go years of the 1970s are over. Deflation and depreciation are the new realities, even in the so-called recession-proof Sun Belt. In Houston's nine-month housing collapse of 1983–1984, the market value of the average house fell 15 percent. Buyers who put down only 5 or 10 percent found their properties worth less than their mortgage debt. In recent years, the value of farmland has dropped. Overbuilding and tax reform have eroded apartment and commercial property values. Local or regional economic problems have hurt real estate. Cities and towns with just one or two employers are especially vulnerable. Beware of the fallacy of appreciation. If your chief motive in buying property is for short-term appreciation, you're gambling. There are surely many easier and more enjoyable ways to gamble than to buy income real estate.

Seminarians speak fondly of OPM—other people's money. They urge you to get into the habit of using credit to extend your holdings so that you can use your cash reserves for other purposes. OPM can take the form of rent advances, multiple security deposits, credit cards, and lines of credit. A variation of OPM in no-money-down deals is using "paper" to the hilt. This means borrowing against the assumed value of leases, paid-down mortgages, car, boat, or land titles, or using promissory notes, including personal IOUs. If paper is accepted, it usually has a discounted market value, especially if its liquidity is in question. But need the obvious be stated? OPM remains other people's money until the debt is paid or the security returned. It's not yours to gamble. If the carrying cost exceeds the cash-in-the-pocket return, using OPM can be as debilitating to your estate as opium is to your body.

[1]Vincent W. Zucchero, *Rental Homes: The Tax Shelter That Works and Grows for You,* © 1983, p. 22. Reprinted by permission of Prentice-Hall, Inc., Englewood Cliffs, N.J.

The proponents of such deals suggest the following techniques. Your real-estate agent can recommend more.

1. Get a nothing-down-payment VA or low-down-payment FHA mortgage.
2. Borrow the down payment on your car or other personal property from a bank or finance company.
3. Equity squeeze by creating as your down payment a second mortgage on property you already own.
4. Borrow the down payment on your credit card or via an unsecured line of credit.
5. Buy on a land contract with little or no cash down.
6. Exchange your professional services for the down payment.
7. Give the seller a piece of the future profit in lieu of the down payment.
8. Use advance rents or security deposits as your down payment.
9. Prove to the seller that your labor will turn the property around and that if he sells to you for nothing down and holds 100 percent of the paper, he will benefit.
10. Make your offer with nothing down, giving the seller a note or mortgage secured by the property you're buying.
11. Exchange something you don't need or want for the down payment.
12. Give stock on interest in the property to the seller for the down payment. You could incorporate and give the seller some stock, with the single asset being the property.
13. Using promissory notes, including personal IOUs, second and third mortgages, balloon down payments, and payment deferral plans.
14. Some agents or sellers may suggest kiting, but it's illegal. (Sometimes, it's called a "silent second.") It works like this. A house has an asking price of $84,000, which is its true market value. However, the seller will accept $72,000 cash. You write two offers, one for $72,000 and the other for $80,000 to show the lender to get a 90 percent loan. It's better to buy the house for $72,000 with the seller to get the $72,000 cash in 6 months. You get the title, upgrade the property, and apply for a new $72,000 mortgage based on the $80,000 market value.[2]

Points

Because of usury laws, the lender is often forced to lend money at an interest rate below the market rate of interest. Under this situation, a lender must seek alternatives to the interest rate by making an appropriate charge

[2]For full coverage of no-money-down angles, I recommend Robert G. Allen's *Nothing Down* (New York: Simon & Schuster, 1980).

for the loan. This charge is called points. Points occur because of artificial restrictions placed on the market by government intervention. Without points, lenders would make fewer loans. Each point is 1 percent of a new loan. On a $50,000 loan, four points would equal $2,000. Either the buyer or seller can pay the points, depending on their agreement. With new VA mortgages, the buyer can only be charged one point and the seller must pay any other. Points paid on the financing of your own home is a tax-deductible expense as prepaid interest in the year you pay them. For investment property, points must be amortized over the length of the loan.

Loan Processing

The selling broker and lender usually handle the loan processing. Most contracts require the buyer to make a loan application within five working days after contract ratification. The lender's loan officer takes the buyer's application. He orders a property appraisal and verifies the buyer's employment, income, deposits, credit rating, and debts. After the officer has gathered all this information, he submits the package to the VA, FHA, or loan committee. Under some circumstances, the lender may specify requirements that must be met before the loan will be made, such as certain repairs. When the loan is approved, a commitment is issued to the buyer. After the loan approval, selling and listing brokers will coordinate a settlement date.

LOAN SOURCES

There are almost as many sources for mortgage money as there are types of mortgages. Shop for financing. Closing costs aren't the same at every lending institution, nor are interest rates the same. A 1 percent initiation fee or an extra 1 percent in interest can amount to a considerable amount of money. Each type of lender has its own regulations and preferences in terms of the size of the mortgage and degree of risk it's willing to take. Some of these lenders may only loan money for single-family homes or another specialized segment of the real-estate market. As a rule, it's more difficult to get funding for commercial and multifamily real estate than it is for a single-family home. Such properties often carry mortgages with stiffer terms and higher interest rates.

Savings and Loans

Savings and loan associations are the largest source of single-family residential financing. They are tied to the immediate local area, are generally run as smaller operations emphasizing personal contact, and will make a more knowledgeable appraisal of the property and neighborhood than most other lenders. Their mortgages tend to be made with longer terms and a high loan/ value ratio. They almost always require a note of personal liability. The loan will probably cost more in fees and points, be nonassumable, and carry a prepayment penalty.

Commercial Banks

Commercial banks generally extend further than the savings and loans. They will make a loan at a somewhat higher interest rate. Commercial banks want your other banking business and may therefore be more lenient on some features like prepayment. They prefer a shorter term. Commercial banks tend to be conservative and terms tend to be stringent. For example, nationally chartered commercial banks are barred from granting mortgages with a maturity greater than 30 years and an amount greater than 90 percent of the property's appraised value. Most commercial banks won't go beyond 25 years and 80 percent.

Insurance Companies

Insurance companies prefer to invest in large commercial development mortgages, often using a mortgage broker to arrange the deal. This orientation toward larger sums makes them less likely to haggle over a few hundred dollars. If they like your property, you may be able to save significantly on points, fees, and the interest rate. Competition for these loans is intense. An insurance company mortgage generally offers the combined advantages of low interest and long maturity. The drawback is that most insurance companies require a large down payment. Insurance company mortgages, when available, are obtained mainly through mortgage brokers, rather than directly through the insurance company itself.

Mortgage Companies

Mortgage companies are privately owned firms that specialize exclusively in granting mortgage loans. Terms usually are flexible, but the interest rate is often a bit higher than at other sources. It's best to avoid mortgage companies, unless you simply cannot find a mortgage anywhere else.

Mortgage bankers issue mortgages to borrowers. Then they process and sell the mortgages to large investors or into the secondary mortgage market. Mortgage bankers generally don't have large cash reserves, but usually originate the mortgage by borrowing the money for a short time from a commercial bank. Then they sell it in a package to a large institutional lender or to one of the national federal mortgage corporations. Much of their profits come from servicing these loans, for which they get a small part of the outstanding balance.

Pension Funds

Pension funds will usually invest in packages bought from a mortgage bank or arranged by a mortgage banker.

Real-estate Investment Trusts

Real-estate investment trusts (REITs) often lend money for unusual deals with short terms. They are a good source of construction financing. A REIT is similar in many ways to a mutual fund, except that its investments are in real estate. Basically, there are two different kinds of REITs: equity trusts and mortgage trusts. Equity trusts generally acquire and own improved real properties, such as commercial, industrial, or apartment buildings. Mortgage trusts invest their assets in mortgages on real property. Most trusts limit their mortgage investments to first mortgages made either to finance the ownership or the development and construction of houses and other structures. The primary source of income for equity trusts is rental income. The chief source of income for mortgage trusts is interest.

Credit Unions

Federally chartered credit unions can write 30-year conventional and government-insured mortgages.

Government Financing

Many buyers who could qualify fail to look into a loan secured by the Veterans Administration (VA) or the Federal Housing Administration (FHA). These loans are coveted because they're cheap and secure—for both the holder of the note and the borrower. To qualify for the VA loan, you don't have to be an eligible veteran yourself, but you should be able to cosign with someone who does qualify. VA loans can often be assumed. The FHA offers several different categories of loan assurance programs.

There are difficulties with government-insured loans. Because a lender will be charging a higher interest rate for conventional loans, he will want to be compensated for the difference in profit, usually by creating a number of one-time charges. After all the charges have been added, the total is nearly equal to the cost of a conventional loan. The law forbids the purchaser of the loan from paying points. The lender will have to get them from the seller, who may either try to back out of the deal or inflate his asking price.

Another common problem for FHA or VA borrowers involves the refusal by the government to appraise the house for its selling price. Since the government will back loans based on their appraisal, many deals fall through when the appraisal differs greatly from the agreed price. You should anticipate this problem by stipulating in the contract that the seller must either agree to the government's appraisal price or give you the option to withdraw with a full refund of all deposits. Finally, there may be a lot of red tape involved and a long wait while the loan is being processed and while the FHA determines if the structure meets the government's standards of construction, location, and livability.

If you are persistent, government-secured loans can be desirable. They offer longer terms, lower down payments, and many regulations that protect your rights in the transaction. An appraisal will determine these loans. It's conducted according to standards that assure the worth of the property. Standards are especially strict with new homes. Some lenders categorically refuse to lend on them.

For details on FHA-backed mortgages, consult the Federal Housing Administration, Department of Housing and Urban Development, 451 7th Street, S.W., Washington, D.C. 20410. For details on VA-backed mortgages, consult your local VA office or the Veterans Administration, Washington, D.C. 20420.

Private Financing

Individuals, often home sellers, and organizations, such as the seller's employer, lend money. This source is especially helpful with second mortgages. Sometimes, a wealthy friend or relative will make a loan. Your real estate broker may know someone who can help you. However, I don't recommend you go to these people for financing. First, nepotistic relationships could develop. They may want more of the action than you can afford to give. Second, you will anger them if you default. Instead of asking friends or relatives for a loan, consider forming a partnership in which friends and relatives participate in raising cash for the purchase price. At some future date, the house is sold or refinanced to pay off your partners, including a share of the profits. The partnership owns the house and each partner has equity participation.

Creative Financing

Creative finance means buying property with methods other than the usual down payment and new bank loan. Most creative methods involve having the seller finance your purchase. The key to selling a property during times when mortgage money is tight is to help the buyer find the necessary financing and to use some creative financing techniques if the buyer comes up short. Many sellers effectively become bankers. They offer buyers first or second mortgage notes, funded by deferring a portion of the price at rates several percentage points below those at bank windows. Depending on the seller's needs, these notes are either held as investments for regular monthly income or are sold for immediate cash to the Federal National Mortgage Association or local mortgage investors specializing in discounted seller paper.

We will review some creative financing techniques in the next section.

TYPES OF FINANCING

Conventional Mortgage

A conventional loan is an indebtedness or mortgage made between a lending institution and a borrower without a third-party participant, such as the VA or FHA. Most types of conventional loans are paid off in equal monthly payments of 15, 25, or 30 years. The interest rate stays the same for the life of the loan. Therefore, the monthly principal and interest payments also remain constant. A loan can be obtained for a down payment of as little as 5 percent. When the down payment is less than 20 percent, the borrower may need to get private mortgage insurance (PMI) to protect the lender. A conventional mortgage is usually the fastest and easiest to get. Virtually anybody in good financial standing is eligible. There is little red tape and no set maximum amount that can be borrowed. The waiting period is usually just a few days. Down payments, frequently regulated by law, are relatively larger, often 25 to 40 percent of the appraised value. Interest rates may be higher and extra points may be tacked onto the stated interest rate.

Adjustable Rate Mortgage/Adjustable Loan Mortgage

As its name implies, an adjustable rate mortgage (ARM) doesn't carry a fixed interest rate. The rate can vary over the full term of the loan. The changes are usually tied to changes in some index, such as the Federal Home Loan Board's national average mortgage rate for existing homes. At each adjustment period, the rate of an individual mortgage rises or falls depending on whether the index has gone up or down. The adjustable rate mortgage is popular because it offers a low initial interest rate. With more than 200 variations of the ARM on the market, choosing the right one can be hard unless the borrower understands the agreement. The key points to look for in an adjustable mortgage can vary, making thousands of different combinations possible. They are as follows:

1. Introductory rate. An initial teaser rate is sometimes offered to attract borrowers. It can quickly adjust upward, often with a substantial increase in the payment. The start-up interest rate may be a trap. In the second year of the loan, the interest rate sometimes exceeds the market rate. Presumably, borrowers understand this. However, if market rates rise faster than they expect, they can face payment shock and the loss of their property.

2. Interest rate.   An ARM should be at least two percentage points less expensive than a fixed-rate mortgage. Some lenders may offer you the choice of an ARM or a fixed-rate mortgage. Where you see interest rates going over the long term will decide which mortgage to pick.

3. Payment cap.   A payment cap places an upward limit on the amount of payments that can go up in any year or over the life of the loan. With payment-capped mortgages, the interest rate may change frequently, but the monthly payments remain fixed for a set period.

4. Interest cap.   An interest cap places an upper limit on how much the interest rate can be raised or lowered during each adjustment period and over the life of the loan. If there is a cap on the interest rate, always ask for a worst-case example. Have the bank calculate how high your monthly payments can go. If you're dealing with a national bank, ask the bank to use the Optional Disclosure Form from the comptroller's office. It gives you a realistic look at what happens to your monthly payments if interest rates were to rise 1, 5, or 10 percentage points. When the interest rate changes, any one of four things can happen to the mortgage loan. The monthly payment can rise or fall, the principal of the loan can go up or down (with the eventual change in the monthly payment), the term can be trimmed or lengthened, or nothing need happen.

5. Negative amortization.   With negative amortization, the borrower can end up owing more than was borrowed. Don't permit a situation where the outstanding principal could exceed the value of the property. With certain mortgages, negative amortization can easily build up. ARMs with negative amortization are loans that defer interest payments, adding them to the principal. The disclosure statement may have a phrase that reads, "The principal amount that I must repay will be larger than the amount I originally borrowed, but not by more than 125 percent of the original amount." This statement says that if you borrow $100,000, you may end up paying for $125,000 of principal—not interest.

A severe swing in interest rates could create negative amortization. Say you start out at 9 percent interest, paying $483 a month. If the interest rate rises to 13.5 percent at the start of the second year, you would normally owe $689 a month, but your payment cap holds you to only $519 a month, a $170 shortfall. The bank takes that unpaid $170 and adds it to your mortgage. Every time you make a monthly payment, you are actually adding $170 to the size of your loan. Your debt is getting larger rather than smaller. The rise in debt also costs extra interest. A negative amortization ARM may be an option if you plan to own the property for a short time, live in an area of rapidly escalating real-estate values, or will have a marked increase in income. However, the marketplace offers such a cafeteria of more desirable ARMs that there should be no need to accept this alternative.

6. Index.   The index is the interest-rate bench mark that triggers the changes, either a short-term measure such as 52-week Treasury bills or a longer-term measure like the Federal Home Loan Bank Board's cost-of-funds index. There are indexes based on 90-day Treasury securities, 6-month, 1-year, and 2-year securities, and other types of paper. These move up or down with a great deal of flexibility. Other ARMs are tied to the Cost of Funds Index, published nationally by the Federal Home Loan Bank Board. This index is one of the most stable. Historically, it has moved both less rapidly and less steeply than other indexes. The FHLB averages the relatively stable costs of institutions' checking and savings accounts against the more volatile cost of maintaining their short-term instruments. This index may lag behind current market conditions. Avoid accepting a mortgage with an index based on a lender's own cost of funds—the rates lenders pay for deposits and for other borrowed funds. It's possible for a bank to manipulate such an index. It's better to choose an index beyond an individual lender's control, such as the national average mortgage rate, the 3-year Treasury security rate, or the 6-month Treasury bill rate.

7. Margin.   Regardless of which index the lender chooses to use, he will add a margin to cover his operating expenses and profits. The index plus the margin establishes the new interest rate after adjustment. These margins range from 0.5 to 3 percent over the index. Most margins are below 1 percent.

8. Adjustment interval.   The ARMs can adjust as frequently as once a month or as infrequently as once every 5 years. Most have an adjustment period of 1 year, although 3- and 5-year ARMs are common. If interest rates are relatively low when you take out the mortgage, select a mortgage with an infrequent rate of adjustment. If rates are high and you expect them to drop, take a mortgage with a more frequent rate-adjustment period so that you can quickly get the benefit of a drop in rates. Make sure the loan agreement states exactly when rates will be adjusted and that they will decrease if the index drops. The adjustment period for the mortgage rate shouldn't exceed the maturity of the financial instruments on which the index is based. For example, if the lender is using 6-month Treasury bills, the adjustment period should be no longer than 6 months.

9. Graduated payments.   Some ARMs have payments that go up even without changes in the index. Graduated payments are popular among those who think they will be earning more than at present.

10. Prepayment.   A prepayment privilege allows the loan to be paid off before the end of the term. If you have a high-interest mortgage, you may decide to pay it off if you can get a better deal from another lender. Some ARMs impose penalties for prepayment; others forbid prepayment.

11. Points.   Points are charged at the start of the loan, in addition to processing fees. Sometimes, you can get low interest rates by paying a number of points. Always compare initial costs in terms of dollars required for up-front payment.

12. Assumability.   Assumability allows the loan to be taken over by a later buyer. It will be easier to sell your home later if your ARM is assumable. An increasing number of ARMs are assumable.

13. Convertibility.   A convertible ARM means that the lender will let you convert it to a fixed-rate mortgage at the end of a certain period, perhaps for a fee.

Contract Sales

When an investor wants to buy a property and financing is scarce or too costly, one solution is a contract of sale. The buyer makes mortgage payments directly to the seller, who retains title to the property until the mortgage is retired. The purchaser puts down a certain amount on the contract and agrees to monthly payments of both interest and principal. Seller-financing arrangements have long been used in commercial real-estate transactions. Since the arrangements are often complicated, a lawyer should advise you at every stage.

The seller of a property should be the first person you consider when thinking about financing. Not only is he an excellent prospect for carrying back a large second trust deed or mortgage loan, but he may also make an attractive deal on the first. One advantage of seller financing is that he won't charge you a loan fee. Also, he will resist foreclosing. So, if you want to readjust the mortgage payments, he will probably consider working something out with you. The needs and motives of the seller will dictate how favorable a mortgage you can negotiate from the seller. Some sellers are just trying to get out from under their mortgage payments. You can step in and save their credit rating.

Most contract sales involve a negotiated down payment and a short-term balloon loan provided by the seller. The loan is like the balloon made by conventional lenders, but may carry a lower interest rate and no points are charged at closing. Under the agreement, the seller holds title to the property until the terms of the contract are met. The contract will spell out the amount of down payment, length of contract, and the amount of payments to be made by the buyer. Although the monthly payments in a contract deal are based on a 25-

to 30-year amortization schedule, most contract deals call for a lump-sum balloon payment at a specified time.

Contract buyers, however, don't have the same legal rights as other mortgage borrowers. The biggest risk for a contract buyer is fast foreclosure triggered by late payments. The biggest risk for a contract seller is getting the property back on his hands because of foreclosure because of not paying the property tax, making payments, or tolerating code violations. While it takes at least a year to foreclose on a mortgage, a seller can foreclose on a contract buyer in as little as 60 days.

If the contract deal is tied to an existing mortgage, problems can arise for the buyer if the seller doesn't meet his loan obligations. The buyer's lawyer should make provisions in the contract that allow the buyer to make payments directly to the lender if the seller fails to pay his mortgage. The deed should be placed in escrow at a title insurance company to avoid estate problems if the seller dies before the contract is paid off.

Seller financing may be a reasonable investment for certain sellers. It makes most sense when it helps the seller get the full price he couldn't otherwise get. Contract sales have played a major role in keeping the resale market alive during times of high interest. However, contract sales can backfire. If the new owner fails to make a payment on the mortgage, the bank will file a foreclosure suit and name both the original owner and the new owner as defendants. If this happens, you will have difficulty getting another loan or a charge account because of the lawsuit filed against you by the bank holding the mortgage.

The Assumption

Many existing mortgages are at rates below those on new mortgages. If interest rates are 12 percent, but the owner of the property you are trying to buy has an 8 percent loan, you are better off assuming his loan. It used to be easy for a buyer to assume such a mortgage simply by paying the seller a sum equal to his equity and by taking over the payments. Lenders have tried to stop this practice by enforcing the due-on-sale clause. This clause calls for a full payment of the loan when the property is sold. As contract sales and assumptions climb, some lenders have begun to crack down, insisting on a higher interest rate on assumed mortgages or the full payment of the loan. They threaten foreclosure if borrowers don't cooperate, although few cases have gone that far. Sellers contend that if lenders made an 8 percent loan for 30 years the institutions should be willing to live with that rate, no matter who owns the house. Lenders, however, insist that contractual rights are not assignable. They will honor their agreement as long as that individual has the title. But they didn't price that product for 30 years for other parties, whose credit may be less desirable than the seller's.

Some banks allow a buyer to assume a mortgage containing a due-on-sale clause if the buyer pays a prevailing mortgage interest rate or possibly a rate slightly below it. While that may save some of the closing costs associated with taking out a new mortgage, it doesn't provide the benefits of an outright assumption. Few savings and loan or banks will write loan agreements that allow a new buyer to assume the existing property loan. However, many insurance company loans are assumable at the original rate.

Court decisions or state laws may prevent lenders from enforcing due-on-sale clauses. In those states, buyers may be able to enforce their right to assume a mortgage. Ask your attorney about this.

One way to avoid due-on-sale is to assume a home loan backed by the government. All FHA- and VA-insured loans are assumable. Most conventional mortgages that were taken out before the 1970s can also be assumed. But the problem with these loans is that the value of most of those homes has increased so much that the amount that can be assumed is a fraction of what needs to be financed. The loan is small in relation to the property's market value, both because the loan has been paid down by the owner and because the value of the property has risen due to inflation. This leaves a gap that your down payment won't fill. Therefore, you should try to assume the seller's mortgage but also ask him to accept a second mortgage or second trust deed secured by the property as part of the down payment.

Second Mortgages

The need for a second mortgage arises when there isn't enough cash to cover the difference between the purchase price and the mortgage loan amount. Sellers often become a source for second mortgages so that the deal won't fall apart for want of a relatively small amount of money. (However, second mortgages can be written for any amount, as long as it's covered by the value of the property.) The terms, including the interest rate, are based on the buyer/seller agreement. It's often a short-term loan. Sometimes only interest is paid until the term date, when the balance is due. A buyer then can pay off the loan or refinance. For example, suppose a house sells for $100,000. The buyer makes a $20,000 down payment and takes over the seller's mortgage, which has an unpaid balance of $40,000. The buyer still needs another $40,000. So the seller grants the buyer a loan for that amount. If this loan is secured by a deed of trust, it's called a second deed of trust. If the interest rate on the existing mortgage is low, the buyer's combined payments to the bank and to the seller may be lower than if he borrowed the entire $80,000 from a bank. Second mortgages are well suited for the buyer with a small amount of cash for a down payment, but with a monthly income high enough to handle both mortgages.

Many lenders, however, won't allow a second mortgage. In an effort to conceal the second mortgage from the primary lender, most seconds aren't recorded until after closing. Also, the seller holding the second mortgage can be financially grounded if the buyer doesn't make payments on the first mortgage. A foreclosure on the first loan would wipe out money owed by the buyer on the second mortgage, because it's a secondary obligation. Only after that loan is satisfied and the mortgage retired can a lien that has a position junior to the first move up the ladder and become a first mortgage. For this reason, a lender making a second mortgage will want a higher interest rate and will usually offer less money for a shorter period of time.

Balloons

Balloon payment loans call for relatively low payments each month over most of the loan's life and one or more large payments, usually at the end of the loan's term. The balance of the balloon is paid in full when the mortgage matures. The house is sold or refinanced when the balloon is due. Balloon payment clauses are often written into second mortgage loans to make it easier for the borrower to meet his monthly installment payment obligations. Since most seconds are written for fairly short terms, a borrower may not want to sign up for equal monthly payments. The lender agrees to let him make fairly nominal payments each month until the final one, when the entire outstanding balance is to be paid.

Balloons are often used in short-term improvement loans or by people who think they will sell their house in a few years. Although such mortgages can include guaranteed refinancing, some lenders have been unwilling to make such a guarantee.

A balloon loan is attractive because it offers below-market rates and often no closing points. However, if the balloon bursts at an inconvenient time, the buyer could fall into a financial hole. If rates are high when the balloon bursts, a buyer's alternatives include getting a conventional mortgage or renegotiating the balloon loan at a higher rate. If a conventional lender extends the balloon, he may charge additional closing points. The homeowner could face foreclosure if the lender doesn't extend the loan. In times of high mortgage rates, your only protection is to write an automatic extension of the balloon into the contract, perhaps stipulating terms that you would see in an ARM. The seller should also protect himself in such a deal. His lawyer should attach a rider that says, if mortgage rates drop, the buyer has to go out and get a conventional mortgage.

Refinancing/Equity Loan

You can enjoy your home's appreciation in value now by refinancing your first mortgage. Or you can sell your home and buy another without using all the money you earned from the first to pay for the second. The equity in your home is the difference between its current market value and what you still owe on your mortgage. Your home equity started with your original down payment and has grown over the years with your monthly mortgage payments. And your equity has increased even more with the appreciation of the market value of your home.

Taking equity out of your home by selling it works like this. Say your home appreciates in value and you sell it for $60,000. Your old mortgage balance is $40,000 and you pay it off, leaving you with $20,000 in cash. If you buy another home for $70,000 and get the traditional type of mortgage on that home, you will have to put down 20 percent of the purchase price, or $14,000. But that leaves you with $6,000 to spend as you like.

The other method of tapping home appreciation involves either getting a second mortgage on your home or refinancing the first mortgage. Some banks will let you borrow up to 75 percent of your home's current appraised market value, less the amount you still owe on your mortgage. The actual amount of the equity loan will depend on your personal financial situation. Dollars received from refinancing are tax free because they are debt. Many homeowners are using the money they get from refinancing to buy other residential real estate as an investment.

Cash-flush lenders who want to boost the loan balances of their longtime mortgage customers often offer special inducements. Even in the face of lender's cut-rate blandishments, refinancing isn't always the right move. Going from an old, fixed-rate, single-digit mortgage to a new adjustable one shouldn't be undertaken without thought. Refinancing simply isn't economical for a large number of owners who would like to get rid of above-market or risky mortgages. Equity in your house is a capital asset. Borrowing against it turns capital into debt. In addition, anyone with a home equity loan cannot sell the home until it's paid off. This could hold you up if you suddenly need to move and you don't have enough money to pay off the home equity loan. Interest rates on these loans are usually higher than on a first mortgage and the term is shorter. A home equity loan is basically a second mortgage. Federal law prohibits the use of this money for investment in securities or other financial assets, although you can invest in realty, precious metals, art, and the like.

To calculate how well you would fare in a refinancing, answer these questions:

1. Is the equity loan's interest rate when combined with the interest rate of the first mortgage more or less than the current market rate for a new first mortgage?
2. Will you have to pay prepayment penalties?
3. What are the closing/refinancing costs?

4. Do the lower monthly payments outweigh the cost of the total transaction?

Some states, such as Texas, may not allow first mortgage refinancing.

Purchase Money Mortgage/Takeback/Installment Sale

With a purchase money mortgage, the seller finances the unpaid balance of the purchase price at an interest rate and under terms negotiated directly with the buyer. The seller makes a mortgage loan directly to the buyer. The seller grants the loan for the purchase price of the property, less any down payment. The buyer gets title to the property and makes regular payments to the seller. The loan is secured by a mortgage that can be enforced in court if the buyer defaults, as with other types of mortgages. A purchase money mortgage is sometimes called a takeback or an installment sale. If the owner holds title to the property without a lien and doesn't need the cash from the sale all at once, he can write his own mortgage contract and charge the borrower interest. Purchase money mortgages often carry interest rates below those of banking institutions, partly because the seller doesn't have a bank's overhead costs and partly because the seller may be anxious to complete the sale. The biggest difference between the contract sale and the purchase money mortgage is that under a purchase money mortgage the buyer gets the deed and title to the property at closing.

For unsophisticated sellers, the biggest pitfalls lie in setting the interest rate too low and in collection risks. The purchase money mortgage contract must call for late-payment charges or interest penalties to keep the buyer honest. The buyer will need to protect himself, as well. The seller isn't subject to all the federal oversight, reporting regulations, and recommended practices that commercial lenders are. Your attorney should write a mortgage agreement and contract that gives you all the safeguards and remedies you would expect from any lender, especially with regard to foreclosure.

Wraparound Mortgages

A wraparound mortgage is a financing technique that involves the placing of a new mortgage on top of an old one. The new mortgage is larger than the old one and "wraps around it." The seller makes a money advance that "wraps" both the balance due on the old assumable mortgage plus a new loan at a below-market interest rate.

The borrower actually assumes two loans—the old favorable-interest loan and a new high-interest loan. The rate on the new loan may still be lower than what the buyer could get from a bank. For example, the down payment on the $100,000 home is $14,000. The "wrap" loan amount is $86,000. The remaining old balance is $58,000 at 7 percent. The new balance is $28,000 at market rate. The "wrap" interest rate on $86,000 is 11 percent. Monthly payments are $820. If the buyer had taken a new first mortgage at 13 percent, his monthly payments would be $952.

Buyers using this arrangement should protect themselves by obtaining the right to make payments on the underlying mortgage if sellers fail to do so and to subtract these from the balance owed. Sellers also need protection. If they incur any late charges and penalties because the buyer defaults, the seller needs the right to add these charges to the outstanding principal.

A bank holding an underlying mortgage may not look favorably on a wraparound since the bank's aim is to remove low-rate loans from its books. Some first-loan agreements contain an alienation clause that says the balance of the loan comes due upon the sale of the property. If you cannot talk the lender into waiving this clause, the deal cannot be made.

Options

An option to buy permits you to walk away from the transaction if, within the option period, you decide the property isn't for you. All you lose is your time and earnest money. By contrast, a contract agreement commits both buyer and seller. An option is a contract by which a property owner gives someone the right to buy his property at a fixed price within a specified time. If, within that time, the optionee gives the owner notice that he wants to exercise his option, the option ripens into a contract. If the optionee lets the specified time go by without taking any action, he has no further rights to the property, nor can he recover from the property owner the money paid for the option.

In practical terms, options work like this. You see a property that has a market value of $100,000 but is selling for $90,000. You option to buy it in 6 months for $85,000. In 3 months, you sell it for $110,000. You pay the original owner the $85,000 and you take a profit of $25,000, less the cost of the option and resale costs, say $10,000. Options are speculative. You must know the market and you must know what you are doing. Otherwise, you may end up with a hungry white elephant. Furthermore, it's often difficult to get property owners to give you an option, which effectively removes their property from the market.

Leasing

With a land lease, you buy the improvements and lease the land from the seller. The contract must contain a long-term property lease giving the new owner the option to buy the land.

Under a lease-purchase agreement, the purchase price is agreed upon but the closing date is delayed until the buyer gets financing. Meanwhile, the buyer occupies the house at a stipulated monthly cost, part of which may be applied to the purchase price. The buyer can improve the house and refinance. Based on his new equity, he may be able to pay off all the price.

Shared Appreciation Mortgage

The rising value of real estate has led to the shared-appreciation mortgage (SAM). The seller gives the buyer a loan at a reduced rate in exchange for a share of any increase in the selling price when the property is resold. If it isn't sold within a certain time period, say 5 years, the property may be reappraised and the owner may have to pay the lender one-third of any increased value.

Buyers face two pitfalls. First, the IRS hasn't ruled on whether the appreciation payment to the lender is deductible as an interest payment. Even if it is, there may be smaller overall tax savings for the borrower than if he had chosen a conventional mortgage. The question of improvements could also trouble a homeowner. He may be less inclined to improve the property if the added value has to be shared.

A variation on the SAM is the shared equity sale (SES). The seller will provide the down payment. The buyer will make the mortgage payments. At the end of an agreed term, say 5 years, the property will be sold and the profits will be equally shared. Of course, the main assumption behind the SAM and SES is that the property will appreciate. This may not happen.

Auctions

It's possible to acquire income properties at below market at auctions. The Department of Housing and Urban Development (HUD), private, and tax sale auctions are the most common. Let's look at these types of auctions.

HUD offers its selling list directly to the public, in contrast to city homesteading programs in which title is assigned to the city for future sale. The list includes photographs and estimated repair costs. Houses are classified as repaired, buyer rehabilitation required, and as is. Most properties fall into the buyer rehabilitation category. They usually have code violations. The buyer must correct these within 6 months as part of the sale requirement.

Bids are written. Thus, the bidder is seldom given a second chance to make an offer. Most properties are in run-down areas. Inspect the properties during the day, because the electricity is probably turned off.

Rehab property buyers must provide a $2,000 escrow deposit at time of closing. This is returned when the rehab work is done and all pending suits are dismissed. Owner-occupant bids are given priority over investor bids. Adjacent property owners take preference as long as their bids meet minimum stated sale prices.

HUD will pay all past water bills, taxes, and special assessments. Taxes and special assessments not yet due will be prorated to the date of closing. Closing is usually within 60 days. A 30-day extension is allowed with proof of a financial commitment or an additional deposit.

The properties carry no stated or implied warranties. Buyer rehab houses may be subject to court action for building code violations. Houses built before 1950 may have lead-based paint hazards that also need to be corrected. The estimated repair costs can be considerable. Despite these drawbacks, HUD properties can be bargains. There are no closing costs and, in most cases, no commissions. Properties are priced to sell. This means good buys for those able to handle repairs. Properties are advertised in newspapers. The bidder should visit a HUD-registered real-estate broker. He will explain the requirements and paperwork.

HUD also sells packages of properties under the following terms:

1. Properties listed are offered in separately numbered packages on an all cash, as is, no warranty, no FHA insurance basis.
2. The listed properties are offered as bulk packages only. Prospective purchasers of any listed bulk package must bid on all properties included in the numbered package.
3. Purchasers are to submit one total bid amount for each package they want to buy. HUD will consider only the highest acceptable offer for each package. The packages have no stated minimum price. HUD reserves the right to reject any or all bids or waive any informality or irregularity in any bid.
4. Offers are to be submitted in the form of a sealed bid with the envelope containing the words "Bulk Sale: Package #—." The bid cutoff date must be included on the envelope. The envelope should be marked "Sealed Bid: Do Not Open in Mailroom."
5. Sealed-bid offers must include the following:
   a. HUD Form No. 9551: Offer to Purchase and Broker's Tender.
   b. HUD Form No. 9544: Contract of Sale and Purchase (All Cash) Bulk Sale.
   c. Forefeiture of Earnest Money Deposit Form (HMP 5.1-5).
   d. An earnest money deposit of 10 percent on the bid price in certified funds or money order.
   e. Schedule A: List of Properties in Bulk Package.
6. HUD will pay an 8 percent sales commission to the broker, if any, who submits the accepted offer on behalf of the prospective purchasers upon closing of the transaction. However, offers may be submitted directly

without the services of a broker. In such cases, there will be no reduction in the sales price by virtue of saving the commission. No sales commission will be paid to an individual firm or broker submitting an offer on its own behalf.

7. Closing must be completed within 30 days on HUD's written acceptance of the sales offer. Failure to close the sale within that time will result in forfeiture of earnest money.

Private real-estate firms, such as Sheldon F. Good, 11 N. Wacker Drive, Chicago, also offer savings through auctions. Good has auctioned thousands of properties in 27 states. He suggests watching newspaper real-estate ads for advance information and coming to auctions with second, third, and fourth choices in case other bidders top you.

Developers and builders sometimes auction lots, condos, and houses to get rid of excess inventory and the carrying costs associated with maintaining unsold units. Although auctions can mean savings, they aren't the best way to sell homes and apartments. The traditional way of negotiated sales between buyer and seller has worked better. Some auctions have been successful, but the fallout rate among accepted bidders has been high.

Many counties auction outstanding taxes to investors. The investor's motive generally isn't to acquire property. He wants to be able to collect the interest due him from the original owner on the taxes. If the original owner doesn't redeem the tax certificate, which the successful bidder has acquired, the bidder can gain possession of the property. The period the owner has to redeem the certificate and the interest rates for those certificates vary according to state. The interest rate the state permits the bidder to charge the original owner is often higher than the actual interest rate, because of market pressures. If the property has liens, the mortgage holder will want some part in the foreclosure process. Thus, although it's possible to pick up a property for its outstanding taxes, it's rare this happens.

Most of these counties hold tax sale auctions once a year. They often prepare a booklet of properties that have outstanding taxes. Sometimes it will list thousands of properties. The county may publish this list in local newspapers. The list consists of the tax number of the parcel, the outstanding tax, and possibly the address. It's not unusual for professionals with large sums of money to attend these auctions. They may spend hundreds of thousands of dollars and snap up everything that has value. They can afford to make mistakes. The small investor cannot. Make sure you research all properties on which you are considering a bid. If you have any questions about the bidding procedure, call the county collector's office.

IRS tax auctions and auctions of foreclosed properties are usually advertised in the larger local newspapers. Call the IRS district office for further information.

Foreclosure

The source of any good real estate deal is a motivated owner. There isn't a more motivated owner than one in the process of foreclosure. Distressed real estate is creating attractive deals, because the owners or partners need cash in a hurry. These include developers who are overextended, families who fell behind their payments when their ARM interest went up or when their balloon loans came due, and people facing unemployment, tax troubles, or maintenance difficulties. Many of these properties are bought by professional investors for just the delinquent payment. Little or no money was paid for the equity. The investor was able to buy at substantially below the market value, deduct from his taxes the money paid for delinquent payments, assume the old loan at the old rate and terms, and use leverage to the maximum. The savings can be considerable—sometimes as much as 50 percent below market value. Some people have the misconception that foreclosures happen only in the slums. They happen all over.

To locate distressed properties, check legal notices in newspapers for foreclosures, bankruptcies, and tax delinquencies. Peruse the records at the municipal clerk's office. These records list those properties facing pending legal action. Contact real-estate agents, lawyers, accountants, and managers. They sometimes have clients who are eager to unload their property. Be alert for houses placed on the market for quick sale by contractors having trouble with unsold houses or recently divorced couples who are desperate to get rid of the house.

Buying foreclosed property can be a bargain. But often it only looks like a bargain. Sometimes the property's back taxes exceed its market value. Zoning restrictions may prevent renovation or conversion. The previous owner may have the right to reclaim the property after paying the back taxes and penalties. The result is an unclear title, making the property hard to resell. The foreclosed property may be more trouble than it's worth. Most foreclosed properties have been poorly maintained and vandalized. Previous owners may have even stripped the house of its wiring and plumbing. Inspect before you buy. Finally, some banks may not permit bids lower than the money they loaned out. For example, on a property with an original selling price of $100,000, the foreclosed owner financed 90 percent. The bank's minimum bid will probably be $90,000, even though the property has deteriorated so that it's market value is $70,000. If the owner previously owned the property free and clear and used the property as collateral on a defaulted loan, the bank's minimum bid will probably be its appraised market value of $70,000. These bids sometimes require high, noncontingent, nonrefundable escrows. Real-estate brokers will also snap up foreclosed properties that are truly desirable and resell them at fair market value. Brokers can do this because they are in constant contact with the banking and legal community. These negatives all militate against the small investor acquiring a "steal." It isn't impossible, but it's rare.

Renovation/Rehabilitation/Sweat Equity

On a scale both large and small, the idea is the same: Buy a property offered at below-market price because it has problems, fix those problems, and resell it at or above market.

Select basically sound properties that have been neglected due to the former owner's cash-flow problems. Don't be the first in to a run-down neighborhood. Its renovation potential may never be realized. Don't be the last in. You will pay dearly because there's no risk. Try to buy when about 30 percent of a neighborhood has been renovated, evidence that the trend has momentum. Beware of buying fire- or water-damaged buildings. Structural damage may be too great to justify renovation. With some spending on improvements and maintenance, you can boost tenant morale and attract a better grade of tenant. Sweat equity, then, means using your sweat to improve the property's equity. Much of the work revolves around important but inexpensive tasks, such as trash removal, painting, and landscaping.

Look for a property that can be changed to a better income-producing property. You should look for a property well below the going market. In the case of a rental property, rents should be about 40 percent below typical levels in the area. And the thing that keeps rents at $275 in a $500 neighborhood is the building's superficial ugliness. Replacing peeling paint with siding, linoleum with carpeting, and cracked walls with paneling are ways to increase your real-estate profits. Attractive units will rent faster and will bring in better rents than unattractive units. An attractive building will also sell better and will command a better price than a run-down building. Cosmetic renovators are likely to fare best in areas where new construction is limited. Lack of new buildings means there will be high demand for rental space and that your renovated building won't have to compete with the new properties. The most common mistake is to buy a building that is essentially renovated, but not perfect. Then you spend thousands achieving perfection and discover that the market rental value has hardly moved up at all. Related to the face-lift is property that lends itself to a complete conversion. Find a building zoned for a duplex but presently being used as a single-family. Add a bathroom and a kitchen and either rent or sell as a duplex. Converting commercial structures to apartments, cooperatives, and condominiums is another possibility. Investors have converted bowling alleys into single-family homes, trains into apartments, barns into condos, and factories into high-priced lofts. You're limited only by your budget and your imagination. Sometimes the property's potential is an attached lot. You can keep the lot for a few years and build on it, thus increasing your income properties. Or you can split it off and sell it at a profit.

The positive aspects of renovating an old building include a sense of accomplishment, an outlet for creativity, and the possibility that it will be a good investment. The reward of hard labor comes in the satisfaction of being able to work with your body as well as your mind and to see and enjoy the fruits of your labor. There's a revitalization of the spirit that allows you to tackle the next job with renewed vigor. It's good to work hard.

However, the experience of returning a house to its former glory can be frustrating and overwhelming to anyone who tries it. The worst aspects include not knowing what you are getting into, living amid the chaos of construction for long periods, and running out of money. Also, players of the turnaround game seldom place any value on their own labor and rarely ever adjust their profits downward by taking into account the number of hours they put into their holdings. Here are renovating rules of thumb:

1. Time: Plan to spend 2 hours for every square foot of living space you are working on.
2. Money: Budget an amount equal to 25 percent of the purchase price for renovation costs.

Study local zoning laws before you make major changes. Removing a pipe or a wall frequently requires a building permit. However, after you get the permit, your tax assessment will be raised, probably by as much as the value of the renovation. See if you can get an exemption for renovating. Sometimes the assessor will only exempt or partially exempt new additions, not renovations.

It costs a lot of money to hire even unskilled labor. The more work you do yourself, the more money you will have for other improvements. To find the best skilled workers, get names from the previous owner, neighbors, real-estate agent, insurance agent, or bank. Look into a middle route between contracting out for construction work and doing it yourself. Find an amateur homebuilder or retired handyman with low overhead costs willing to work on a time and materials basis.

Even if you don't have any skill with a hammer or saw, you can surely tear out and cart away materials that aren't needed. You can dig trenches for water lines, sewer pipes, or footings. Interior and exterior painting is something even the neighborhood kids might enjoy doing. Wallpapering, stripping, sanding, and tiling are all areas you can get involved in.

There are two areas you should probably avoid, not because they require any great skill or understanding, but because shoddy work could be dangerous: electrical wiring and plumbing. Changes connected with plumbing and wiring are among the most expensive areas of renovation, as anyone who has relocated a kitchen or added a bathroom would testify.

Don't be discouraged by broken beams, crumbling interior plaster, or even a leaking roof. As long as the exterior walls and the foundation are solid, shabby interiors are secondary. A good foundation and a square frame are generally good indicators that a structure is worth rehabilitating. However, repair and replacement requirements should still be weighed against the increased value of the property.

Many older houses possess desirable qualities of appearance that should be retained. To retain the character of the house, all additions, new windows, doors, and covering materials must be in keeping with its existing character. Take no shortcuts but do a lot of research through tax records, deeds, documents on file at city hall, and photographs at the historical society. Document the existing interior with black and white photographs. Consider retaining a professional on a consulting basis, and then proceed to rehab on a selected-phase basis.

Here are rehab ideas:

1. Make all basic energy-saving improvements, pariculary those that provide maximum home insulation—weather stripping, storm windows, and the like.
2. Install an additional half or full bath in homes with only one bathroom.
3. Modernize or improve the kitchen with particular emphasis on cabinet space, seating capacity, natural light, and built-in appliances, especially the stove and dishwasher.
4. Eliminate the maze of fuse boxes in the cellar and consolidate them into a modern circuit-breaker panel. Increase amperage.
5. Paint the cellar floor and whitewash the cellar walls.
6. Repaint any interior rooms that need painting. Remove old wallpaper.
7. Improve the plumbing system and piping to increase water pressure throughout the house or apartment.
8. Remove worn-out carpeting, either putting down new carpeting or sanding and waxing the hardwood floor.
9. Provide additional closet space.
10. Remove excess cords and exposed wires and replace them with permanent outlets.
11. Replace all broken screens, cracked window panes, faulty light fixtures, loose steps, and dripping faucets.
12. Repair broken sidewalks and driveways.
13. Landscape.
14. Replace defective gutters.
15. Replace broken or missing tiles. If the roof leaks, fix it.

Here are some working tips:

1. Avoid working on your knees and tiptoes. These positions are uncomfortable, time-consuming, and dangerous.
2. Avoid working on ladders and scaffolds. If necessary to do so, be sure that they are secure and stable.

3. Keep scrap and debris clear of the working area. Clean up after each day's work.

4. Schedule deliveries to correspond with the progress of the work.

5. Unload and stack or pile the materials as close as possible to the place of use.

6. Stack lumber in separate piles according to the sequence of use.

7. Lift materials into place by means of a front-end loader.

8. Call a scavenger service and have a roll-off delivered.

9. Children often play at construction sites. Keep the building fenced and locked.

10. Buy locally to avoid shipping charges and in quantity to avoid the higher cost of small deliveries.

11. Buy the cheaper material when it will do the job. Never compromise on lumber, wiring, plumbing, and mechanical items that are subject to wear.

12. Shop around to get the most for your money. Take advantage of warehouse sales and preseason promotions.

13. Buy stock materials in standard sizes.

14. Know what materials you need and where you can substitute should you find a bargain.

15. Limit the number of types of materials used.

SUMMARY

Here are some of the main points from this chapter:

1. Sources of loans include the seller, insurance firms, and government agencies.

2. Don't allow negative amortization.

3. Don't overfinance.

4. Understand the risks of creative financing.

5. Foreclosures and auctions are sources of below-market property buys.

3

WHO TO INVOLVE

The purpose of this chapter is to describe your relationship to the broker, appraiser, inspector, lawyer, and banker as you buy the property. We will also look at the contractor's role after you have acquired the property. Absent from this list of participants is the seller. The reason for this is that your contact with the seller during the buying process should always be through a third party—your attorney or a broker. After the sale, your contact with the seller should cease forever. In short, the one person you shouldn't involve in the real-estate transaction is the seller, except at the closing formalities. Instead, make these people work for you. Delegate duties. Demand results.

THE BROKER

In 1972, Congress ordered the Department of Housing and Urban Development, the Federal Trade Commission, the Federal Bureau of Investigation, and others to study the conduct of professions involved in real estate—brokers, bankers, escrow agents, and title company specialists. Investigation revealed a system of kickbacks and covert agreements that coerced buyers into buying services at noncompetitive prices. The study found great interdependence among agents, curbing the flow of information to consumers and resulting in excessive and uniform brokerage fees. The study also found that most sellers mistakenly believed commission rates weren't negotiable. Buyers were often urged to accept creative financing that they couldn't afford. The government responded to these activities with reforms designed to separate the various providers, force certain disclosures, and educate buyers about how to protect their interests. The Real Estate Settlement Procedures Act of 1974 has reduced the incidence of these abuses, but illegal practices persist. This section will outline the relationship of the broker to the buyer and seller.

If You Are a Buyer

Probably the biggest advantage in using a broker is that he knows what is available in which price range. This can save you time, money, and trouble. Another advantage is that he knows the financial market—what kinds and types of mortgages are available and whether the house you want can produce the financing you need. He will know where the nearest schools are, the location of main and secondary store centers, how far it is to the hospitals, and so on.

If a broker tells you that you must use a particular provider for any service, that broker has broken the law. He may recommend but not insist. His recommendations must be in good faith and must reflect his experience in the field. The main problem is that buyers who work with brokers think that the agent represents them or is a neutral intermediary. He represents the seller. Except in rare instances, it's the seller of a property who pays the agent's fee. The broker has been hired by the seller and has fiduciary responsibility to him. This special legal relationship is one of trust. It includes the obligation to be loyal, to obey the seller's general instructions, to inform and account to the seller, and not to be negligent. In the past, the only duties the broker had to buyers were to deal in good faith and not commit fraud. But, lately, consumer pressures have forced the courts to expand this responsibility. In most jurisdictions, the agent must also be "fair and equitable" to the buyer. You, the buyer, must get a truthful answer to any relevant question. You are legally entitled to a straightforward answer to this question: "Are there any hidden defects in this property I should know about before I decide to buy?" Make sure you ask that question before you buy. Make sure you get an answer in writing.

A growing movement across the country is the emergence of buyer's brokers. Buyers pay them a retainer and a flat fee. They are obligated to put the interests of the buyer first. Such brokers must make their position clear to all parties. They usually don't share in the seller's commission. Consider hiring a buyer's broker if you are a first-time income property buyer.

Locate a broker who specializes in income property. He will have a more exclusive file than an ordinary broker. Try to deal directly with the listing broker as he has more influence over the seller. If you make an offer to a broker with an open listing, you run the risk of having the seller use your offer to increase the price another interested prospect may have submitted. You can get a good idea of what agency to use by driving around the neighborhood. If you see a lot of "For Sale" signs belonging to a particular firm, that agency is probably having the most success in that area.

Observe certain standards of conduct when dealing with a broker. While you can consult more than one broker, it's unethical to let another broker show you a property that you've already visited with a competitor. Once a broker shows you a property, he has the right to the commission if you buy.

If matters get to the point where you are bickering over terms, keep the broker informed as to what you have been discussing. Reject any suggestion that you and the seller collude to dupe the broker out of his commission, splitting the difference between you. The broker can sue for his commission. Most brokers won't hesitate to do so.

Buyers should be quiet as to how much money they have and how much they are willing to spend. If the broker knows you have a lot of loose cash, the owner won't do you any favors on the price. The broker will try every sales trick in the book to pressure you into meeting the seller's price. Perhaps the best way to keep your interests paramount is to keep in mind these aphorisms:

We are most credulous when we are most happy.

There's a sucker born every minute.

If You Are a Seller

A listing broker is the broker the seller hires to represent him through the listing agreement. A selling broker is the broker who produces a buyer for the property. He divides the commission with the listing broker at settlement.

Discount brokers charge less than conventional brokers. The discounter appraises the property, lists and advertises it, shows pictures of it to prospects, and helps arrange financing. The homeowner does the showing.

Good brokers are vital to a quick sale. Their services include the following:

1. Knowing how to sell a property.
2. Knowing how to identify a potential buyer in contrast to a "looker."
3. Knowing how to price the seller's property in light of current market trends.
4. Producing a qualified buyer, generally within the time frame dictated by the seller.

The seller should provide the following information to the listing broker, in addition to the property and income specifications:

1. Pay-off notice. Notification by the seller to the lender of the seller's intention to pay off the mortgage. This notice should include the lender's address, loan balance, years remaining on present mortgage, and PITI.
2. Utilities. The seller should provide a record of the past year of gas, electric, sewer, water, and trash-removal bills.
3. Items to be conveyed. The seller should provide the listing broker with a specific list of personal property that is to be included in the real-estate

property for sale. These may include draperies, drapery rods, firewood, washer, dryer, refrigerator, stove, microwave, disposal, storm doors and windows, screens, shutters, antennas, and shrubs. The seller should tag or remove items not to be conveyed.

4. Miscellaneous. The property seller should also try to provide the broker with a schedule of rents and expenses, copy of leases, a termite inspection report, well and septic inspection report, records of property taxes and special assessments and easements, surveys, appraisal, subdivision plat map, floor plan, previous title search abstracts, legal description of the property, warranties, and insurance policies.

The listing broker is spreading the word that the property is available. The listing is generally promoted to two groups: the real-estate community and the buying public. About 60 percent of all buyers come from referrals between buyers and their network of contacts. About 20 percent of the sales come from advertising. The remaining 20 percent are stimulated by "For Sale" signs in yards. Thus, the most productive source of buyers is through other brokers. The multiple listing service (MLS) computer can make your property's description available to the entire MLS membership. Reciprocal agreements with memberships in other territories expand the potential audience even further. Signs in the yard, window, or on the building provide additional exposure. They often create high-quality inquiries because prospects like the location and have seen the property, rather than just a photograph. Some communities don't permit signs on residential property.

THE APPRAISER

An inspector tries to answer these questions:

1. Is the structure sound?
2. Is the structure safe?

An appraiser may address those questions, but his primary concern is value. He tries to answer these questions:

1. What is the property worth?
2. What could the property sell for?

An appraiser will examine the structure and all its equipment. He will get data about leases and rents and investigate sales of comparable properties. The appraiser will usually state three values, one for the land, one for the structure, and finally one for the combined market value of the property. Every buyer should be protected by a professional appraisal of the building he intends to buy. This doesn't mean a seat-of-the-pants guess by a broker. It means a careful, scientific appraisal made by a qualified independent appraiser.

Except when insured by the FHA and VA, few banks will make loans in excess of 80 percent of the house's value. And the value they use isn't the sale price but the value the appraiser sets. Don't be surprised if the appraiser sets the value of the property many thousands of dollars below the price you had agreed to pay. The seller hasn't necessarily bilked you. The standards the appraiser used to judge the property probably diverged from your standards. The actual sales price rarely coincides with the fair market value of the property for these reasons:

1. Buyers and sellers often act under constraints of time or other pressures and thus may not be in a position to accurately evaluate the property.
2. Buyers and sellers are often ignorant of the replacement value of the improvements and may know even less about how to measure depreciation.
3. Brokers eager for a sale may try to sell a property too quickly at too low a price. They may also try to snap it up themselves if they can wheedle it from an owner at a price below value.

Market Value

The price of a property should equal its "fair market value." Appraisers define that as the highest price a buyer is willing to pay and the lowest price a seller is willing to accept when both are operating in a free market, with full knowledge of all the facts, and acting voluntarily without compulsion. An alternative definition is that it's the highest price that a property will bring if exposed for sale in the open market, allowing a reasonable time for finding a purchaser who buys with knowledge of all the uses to which it's adapted and for which it's capable of being used. Both these definitions assume an open, efficient marketplace. Ignorance, fraud, and a number of external political and economic factors can distort the determination of market value. These factors include inflation and rent control.

The Market Approach

In arriving at a conclusion on the value of the subject property, the appraiser makes a survey of properties that have sold recently within the general area. These properties are within an adjustable price range and are compared feature for feature with the property under consideration. Consideration is given and adjustments are made on each comparable sale as to time of sale, size, location, age, and other factors that might affect its value. Terms of sale, price, and interior appointments are verified by examination or consultation with other brokers. As it's impossible to find an identical property to that of the subject, since no two buildings are identical, the appraiser must make adjustments to each comparable. This approach is the most reliable because it reflects the reactions of typical buyers and sellers in the market. For most commercial property and idiosyncratic houses, this approach may have limited value.

The Cost Approach

The cost approach is the reproduction cost of all improvements in new condition, less accrued depreciation, plus the value of the land. The appraiser has gathered current costs from local contractors engaged in building similar properties in the area. He has compared these costs to known costs published in cost manuals and by the Society of Real Estate Appraisers. The value of improvements is based on the square footage of the structure. To determine the area of a house, multiply outside measurements above the foundation, length by width. Square footage includes all heated interior space, even stairwells and closets. Excluded are basements, garages, and attics. If a two-story house measured 40 by 20 feet, it would have 800 square feet on each floor, for a total of 1,600 feet. A finished basement would be measured inside and listed separately. Different appraisers have their own standards for the upper floors of Cape Cods, heated porches, basement rooms with windows above grade, walkout basements, heated garages, and lower areas on split-level houses. The goal is to measure usable living space.

The cost approach will result in a fair estimate if all elements are figured accurately, for no reasonable buyer will exceed the price of a substitute property that offers the same amenities. Distortion occurs when the building has structural elements that are difficult to duplicate. Appraisers also tend to underestimate the cost of a new replacement. A new building may cost $60 a square foot to build. The appraiser may set a baseline figure of $30. Make sure you check all the appraiser's assumptions as to the amount of depreciation that is deducted.

Depreciation must be subtracted from the replacement cost new to adjust the property's value because of age. As time goes by, the building will deteriorate. However, the owner will also maintain or improve the building. The appraisal should reflect this dual process of deterioration and rehabilitation. Depreciation represents the loss in value that may come from age, the presence of undesirable factors, and other circumstances.

Depreciation can be of three kinds. More than one kind of depreciation may be present.

1. Physical depreciation is the physical wearing out of the structure. If a building needs painting or has broken windows, it suffers physical de-

preciation. Some physical depreciation is curable, such as a leaky roof. Some is incurable, such as inherent bone structure deterioration.

2. Functional depreciation is the result of undesirable layout, design, or other features, as compared to a new property. Some functional depreciation is curable, such as an old kitchen. Some is incurable, such as inadequate hallways or space.

3. Economic depreciation is the loss of value from causes outside the property itself. Zoning changes, proximity to nuisances, and changes in land use are causes of economic obsolescence. Economic depreciation is almost always incurable.

To the value of the structure is added the value of the lot, garage, sheds, and the like. The total indicates the fair market value of the property. Land value is usually estimated from recent comparable land sales in the area by the square-foot or front-foot method.

The Income Approach

The income approach is the third approach used to estimate market value. It's most effectively used with properties that are intended to produce income. To apply the income approach to the single-family residence, the appraiser will consider the monthly rent in relation to the sales price and arrive at the gross rent multiplier. The gross rent multiplier is the number arrived at by averaging how many times more than their gross monthly rental value houses are selling for in your area. This multiplier is abstracted from the market by taking rented properties that have sold and by dividing the sales price by the assumed monthly rent. The economic rent is estimated by comparing other comparable rented properties. The gross rent multiplier is then multiplied by the estimated economic rent to arrive at an estimate of value for the subject property.

Correlation

Correlation is the bringing together of parts in a proper relationship. Sometimes the different approaches will be averaged. Sometimes only the market approach is used or modified.

Always buy on the lowest appraisal, not the average. Never pay more than a property's market value. Most properties, market conditions notwithstanding, sell for a realistic price. Most properties sell for slightly less than the original price, rarely more than 10 percent.

The American Institute of Real Estate Appraisers, the National Association of Realtors, and the Society of Real Estate Appraisers will have names of qualified appraisers. Look for the designations M.A.I. (Member of the

Appraisal Institute), R.M. (Residential Member), or S.R.A. (Senior Residential Appraiser) following the appraiser's name in the Yellow Pages.

THE INSPECTOR

Make sure the building is sound. Pay to have the building inspected for water damage, termites, and dry rot. Make such an inspection a condition for buying. Insert a clause like this in your purchase agreement: "Seller warrants that grounds and improvements will be maintained, that roof is watertight, that all appliances, heating, plumbing, sewer, and electrical systems shall be in working order at close of escrow. Seller furthermore agrees to permit an inspection thereof prior to close of escrow and pay for any necessary repairs." If you enter into a contract that is to close 2 months hence, many things can go wrong in that period. Thus, a last-minute inspection a few days before escrow is to close is critical. Don't wait until after you close escrow. Sometimes the terms of the sale can be renegotiated because of what an inspector finds. However, beware of inspectors who may be in bed with the seller's broker.

Obtain the name of a professional inspector who will inspect the building for any defects. Such firms are found in the Yellow Pages under "Building Inspection Services." The fee is well worth the investment. The cost is trivial compared to knowing the real condition of the property. The inspector should belong to the American Society of Home Inspectors, a national, not-for-profit organization of professional home and building inspectors. The society was established to protect the buyer's rights and interests through property inspections by competent people and to minimize unpleasant surprises after closing.

Inspectors hired by the government are neither architects nor engineers. FHA appraisals simply determine a building's worth for mortgage purposes. They don't guarantee that a structure is free of defects.

The inspector should write a report covering the structural condition of the building and heating, electrical, plumbing, and mechanical equipment. It should point out safety and health problems. The report should review the following:

1. Heating. The inspector should check the heating system, condition of electrical and mechanical components, and maintenance requirements. He should check air flow and carbon monoxide leakage. The inspector should report on the condition of smoke stacks, pipes, and the chimney.
2. Electrical. The inspector should check the electrical system for age, capacity, and equipment. He should also check fuses, grounds, circuits, switches, and receptacles.

3. Plumbing. The inspector should check faucets, showers, sprays, tanks, and bowls. He should check for leaks and clogs. He should check the water heater, sump, sewer lines, and fittings.
4. Basement. The inspector should check walls, foundation, floor, beams, supports, and joists for defects, settling, cracks, and water penetration.
5. Roof. The inspector should check its condition, including wear and expected life expectancy. He should report on flashing, gutters, and downspouts.
6. Interior. The inspector's report should discuss walls, ceilings, floors, doors, windows, stairs, traffic flow, and layout.
7. Exterior. The report should discuss the overall structure, walls, foundation, windows, doors, frames, patio, walks, pool, and driveway. The report should determine the repairs and estimate the cost.

An inspection is required by most lenders. It's not usually required for condos, assumptions, and wraparounds. Who is to pay for the inspection is something that can be negotiated between buyer and seller. The seller should be responsible for all repairs. Beware of buying any "as-is" building.

THE LAWYER

One way to get burned in a deal is to buy or sell without the advice of a lawyer. Don't enter any agreement, informal or formal, without your lawyer's guidance. Don't retain a lawyer provided by the seller or broker. Don't even put a mark on a piece of paper without his approval. Consider your lawyer's fee as an integral part of the piece of the property. Better to spend $1,000 for a lawyer and not go through with the deal than spend $1,000 a month for the next 30 years on an ill-advised deal. A well-known tenet of real estate is that the lawyer should be involved in a property purchase from its inception. The lawyer should be with you at the close, even at an escrow closing. It's difficult to extricate yourself from your mistakes if you fly solo at the outset of the realty transaction. Moreover, a lawyer is an excellent intermediary, or shock absorber, in the bargaining process. He can speed it up or slow it down, depending on the progress of your own deliberations. Even while the appraisal is being made, your lawyer can check into the status of the mortgages. For title work, your lawyer should be looking to take advantage of any special endorsements. And he should try to negotiate the best possible rates with the company.

Many buyers think that they don't need a lawyer because the lender and title company will look out for their interests at the closing. But the lender is interested only in making sure its mortgage will be a valid first lien on the property and that you'll pay the mortgage. Likewise, the title insurance company is interested in making sure the title is in order. Too many buyers sign a contract and then call a lawyer. However, once the contract is signed, it's too late to change clauses that might work against your interests. Most aspects of the real-estate transaction are best negotiated in the preliminary sales contract. You would be foolish to sign one without first consulting an attorney.

The attorney's role in real-estate transfers varies throughout the country. In some areas, a lawyer never gets closer to the actual proceedings than drawing up a one-time standard contract form. You may encounter a lawyer representing the seller as soon as you start to negotiate terms for the preliminary agreement. Some attorneys will orchestrate the entire settlement process, including holding escrow monies and certifying title records.

Don't sign contracts the broker or seller provides unless your attorney accepts those contracts. Insist on a contract that will stand up in court. Make sure you understand the boilerplate. Don't hesitate to ask questions about anything you don't understand. Note all deadlines, qualifiers, amounts, and obligations.

You can rely on lawyers too much. They tend to be pessimistic and conservative by nature, perhaps from defending actions from deals that went awry. Listen to your lawyer. But trust your instincts. Lawyers are also expensive. Eighty dollars an hour isn't unusual in major cities. Yet most of what they do is done by people who have never seen the inside of a law school. Paralegals and secretaries do most of the work. They follow directions and fill in the blanks.

Shop for a lawyer carefully. Not all attorneys are skilled negotiators. Nor do they have the same detailed knowledge of real-estate practices. Ask your prospective lawyer if he owns income property. If he does, he will have a better understanding of your expectations.

Make it clear to your attorney that you expect him to represent you at every stage. He must be an aggressive advocate of your viewpoint, not a passive clerk or accountant. You don't want a lawyer who will merely "look over" the contract the seller gives you. He must fight for you. You will determine what type of terms, guarantees, protections, and advantages you want in the contract. Instruct your attorney to negotiate with the seller about these arrangements. He will be responsible for negotiating a price, constructing a compromise on both the preliminary and actual sales contracts. He will also protect your position with the lender and expedite the title search. In summary, he represents your general interests.

THE BANKER

It may be difficult for first-time credit users to get a loan. A lender has no way of knowing how responsible you will be in repaying the loan. The first-time borrower may need cosigners. A cosigner must agree to pay off the loan if the borrower does not. Once the borrower makes regular payments, he has started to build a good credit record. Even if you don't need a loan, you should try to establish a credit reputation by taking out a short-term personal loan. The money from the personal loan could go into a money market fund. The interest from the deposit in the money market account will cover most of the interest that you'll have to pay for the loan. Meanwhile, you're demonstrating to the banking community that you're a good credit risk. By the time you pay off the loan, you'll have enough for much of your down payment. This nest egg will be the foundation of your future prosperity.

Always apply for a percentage mortgage loan, say 80 percent of the property's appraised value, rather than a specific amount, say $60,000. The bank will want to establish that the loan is covered by the property's value, so they will require an appraisal. A percentage loan is insurance you're not paying more than the market value of the property.

The loan officer wants to make a loan that is both secure and trouble-free. For the latter, he will want to look at your financial status, your credit history, and all those aspects of your life that will affect your ability and willingness to meet your monthly payments. He will design and limit the loan to "fit" the property, based on how he views the property and the neighborhood in which it's located.

There are really two basic questions at issue in the mortgage loan process. First, can you come up with the down payment? And, second, can you afford the mortgage payment? That payment will usually include principal and interest and sometimes one-twelfth of the anticipated real-estate taxes and insurance premiums for the forthcoming year. Brokers abbreviate this as PITI. A more realistic abbreviation is PITIMS—principal, interest, taxes, insurance, maintenance, and supplies. Any lender must view the purchase in light of your ability to make these payments. Other questions have no relevance unless they shed light on facts relating to the primary inquiries. Questions may include the following:

What is your gross income?

What is your bank balance?

What is your net worth?

Have you any outstanding judgments?

Have you been declared bankrupt in the last 7 years?

Have you had property foreclosed upon?

Are you a comaker or endorser on a note?

Are you a party to a lawsuit?

Are you obligated to pay alimony?

Is any part of the down payment borrowed?

In the end, you will get the money to buy a property only if the lender considers you an acceptable risk and only if he can afford to lend the money.

Most follow a set of traditional formulas. Some common measures include length of time at present address, length of time at present job, car ownership and age of car, current expenses, current debts, and the ratio of savings to debt. Any record of arrest for misconduct may kill your chance of getting a loan. The lender must consider all steady income from part-time jobs, alimony, and child support. Many banks use the 28–36 formula in figuring qualifications for a mortgage loan. They let you spend up to 28 percent of your monthly gross income for the PITI or 36 percent for the PITI plus all other long-term debt payments.

If your monthly income doesn't match the bank's calculations, try the following:

1. Take care of other loans. The less you're paying out, the more you'll have for mortgage payments.
2. Stretch the term. The longer the mortgage term, the less the monthly payment.
3. Increase the down payment. If you borrow less, your monthly bill will be smaller.

Taking all variables into consideration—credit record, income, savings, condition of the property—the lender will look at a loan as a two-way financial street—money coming in and money going out. If he thinks you and the property qualify, he will send you a loan commitment, a guarantee that a certain amount of cash will be offered to you for a specific period of time under certain conditions. If you don't take him up on that offer, the commitment expires. Don't sign the commitment until the seller has lived up to the terms of the contract—showing records and making repairs and the like. At the settlement, the banker will give you the money to pay to the seller in exchange for the deed and the transfer of title.

In return for the banker's written commitment and the money at settlement, he will want you to sign a personal note and the mortgage instrument. The personal note acknowledges that you owe him a certain sum of money and will repay it according to a specified schedule. The mortgage is a formal document that can be recorded in the appropriate public place of record. It says that the real estate is yours subject to your agreement with him. If you violate your promises, he can sell the property and take the money that you still owe him from the proceeds.

THE CONTRACTOR

After the sale, you may find you need a contractor to make repairs or renovation. Before you contact a repairman, figure out the kind and quality of the repairs needed. This will improve communication and reduce misunderstanding. Contracting for work, having it done, and getting satisfactory results can be a trying experience, even with the most reputable repairman. For your benefit and his, put your agreement in writing. Don't rely on "reputation of honesty," "word of honor," or "verbal understanding." Trust must be earned. To reach a clear and binding agreement, write down in detail what you expect for the money you're paying. The specifications should be brief and clear. They should include the following:

1. The location, nature, and extent of the repair.
2. Type and quality of materials to be used.
3. Color and sizes of materials.
4. If painting, number of coats to be applied.
5. Agreement that the work shall conform to local and state codes.
6. When the job is to start and end.
7. Who cleans up the mess that results from the job.
8. The amount for which the repairman shall assume responsibility for damage to your property or that of your neighbors.
9. That the agreement frees you from all liens that may be placed against the job for failure of the repairman to pay for material, labor, or equipment.
10. A schedule of how and when payments are to be made.
11. A right-to-rescind clause. This gives you the right to back out of the agreement within a certain time, such as 3 days after it was signed.

Avoid signing one-way contracts. Never sign a blank contract. Obtain a copy of everything you sign. Never sign a completion certificate until the job is finished and you are satisfied. Work out a procedure to amend the contract. If an unforeseen problem crops up or if the contractor honestly underestimates his costs, it will be necessary to renegotiate terms. If you try to hold a contractor to unreasonable terms, he will cut corners, stall, or walk off the job. The contract should show the cash price. If you aren't paying cash, it should show the cash down payment, the unpaid balance, the amount financed, and total number of payments. This will show you the amount of money you are paying for financing, above the cost of the work. Make sure you see how the work is warranteed. The key to protecting yourself when hiring a contractor for major alterations is thoughtful contract negotiation. Even contractors with good reputations sometimes get in over their heads. Consider an attorney when the job is complicated or expensive, modifications to an existing house will require the structure to be open to the weather for an extended period, and the nature of the property (swampy, rocky) makes unforeseen difficulties likely.

Make sure the contractor obtains all necessary permits and has the proper licenses.

Make sure the contractor has proper liability insurance.

Seek at least three bids before you choose a contractor.

You may wish to check on the work in progress. However, stay out of the way. Interference will cause delays, affect the quality of work, and create disagreements.

Inspect the project with the contractor when the work is done. If there are questions, refer to the contract. Sign off and make final payment after all work has been completed to your satisfaction.

SUMMARY

Here are some of the main points from this chapter:

1. Retain legal counsel before you sign anything.
2. Have the property appraised before the offer.
3. Have the property inspected before you buy.
4. The broker generally works for the seller.
5. Put all verbal understandings in writing.

4

WHAT TO BUY

The purpose of this chapter is to evaluate different types of income property.

THE SINGLE-FAMILY HOME

The single-family rental unit is usually a small or older home in a residential neighborhood. As a rental, it has several advantages. First, the tenants are responsible for their utilities. The investor doesn't have to figure the fluctuating costs of utilities into the rent payment. Another advantage is the absence of tenant–tenant problems. Since other tenants aren't having late parties upstairs or using too much hot water downstairs, the landlord isn't called to mediate. Also, single-family homes tend to appreciate faster than commercial or apartment property. It represents the epitomy of the American Dream, and from this comes the demand for a lot and a house that you can call home. Smaller, more modestly priced units are rising in resale value faster than larger, more expensive units. Energy-conserving houses also have good resale value. Finally, a single-family rental is easiest to sell. It appeals to buyers who want it as a private residence or a rental. When investment money is scarce, loans are usually available for owner-occupied dwellings. The single-family rental usually attracts long-term renters.

However, it's more difficult—usually impossible—to rent a house to carry itself. A vacant house in January will create an intolerable flood of red ink. An apartment complex generates at least some income. With a house, you're "putting all your eggs in one basket." Nevertheless, houses can outperform alternative real-estate investments dollar for dollar. Even in markets when house prices are flat or declining, investors can get impressive returns by following these rules:

1. Buy at least 10 percent below the market price.
2. Never pay more than 10 percent on the money you borrow.
3. Keep the down payment under 10 percent of the purchase price.

Getting a seller of a house listed for $90,000 but worth $80,000 to take a $70,000 price, a $5,000 down payment, and a 9 percent interest note for the balance is hard, but not impossible. Here are some tips:

1. Concentrate on empty houses. They are a drain on someone. But ask yourself why the house is empty. Local nuisances or structural hazards may make the building unlivable.
2. Seek out little deals that make economic sense, rather than tax shelters designed to lose dollars. Avoid buying a house with a negative cash flow.
3. Look for lower- to middle-priced houses in neighborhoods that make sense to future homeowners. Those houses almost always appreciate faster than the overall market. They also attract long-term tenants who sometimes buy the house. Consider writing a lease that gives the tenant the option to buy. After you've wrung the property for its tax benefits, you can unload it on the present tenant.

THE APARTMENT BUILDING

Most income property investors buy apartments. This investment is generally safer and more profitable than other types of real-estate investments. Many successful real-estate investors launched a fortune with a little money machine—a two- or three-flat apartment building. When you think of all the risky investments that are available—stocks, commodities, and real-estate syndications to name a few—the unglamorous small apartment building can be a winner. Ways to win include appreciation, equity buildup, cash flow, and tax benefits. An apartment on a good block in an improving area is bound to mean hefty appreciation. The biggest lure to most investors is the tax-shelter benefit. They can deduct operating expenses and mortgage interest and take advantage of accelerated depreciation.

Demand for apartments is strong. It's growing stronger. This demand is related more to changing life-styles than to changing population figures. Young people are leaving their homes. The wave of condominium conversions in the late 1970s took many rental units off the market. Few new apartments were constructed to take their place because high interest rates and relatively low rents worked against development. The same high interest rates priced would-be home buyers out of the market, forcing them to stay renters. But economic recovery puts additional apartment seekers into the market who previously doubled up or lived with their folks. These factors have pushed occupancy levels toward 100 percent.

As with all investments, there are elements of risk. The neighborhood could take a turn for the worse. Typical landlord headaches include rising utility costs, boiler breakdowns, leaky roofs, and tax increases. Tenants may cost money. Some renters will damage the property and skip out on the rent. These woes can wreak havoc on your budget.

In most parts of the country, you should be able to buy apartments for six to eight times gross annual revenues. Before you invest in apartments, consider buildings that have these qualities: paved parking lots, pitched roofs, a nonwood exterior, and floors made from lightweight concrete. Financing small residential rental properties used to be more difficult than financing single-family homes. But that problem is less important today than in the past, especially if you plan to occupy one of the units. Single-family homes generally go up in value faster than do small rental properties. However, in areas undergoing renovation and where there's a strong demand for rental buildings, their appreciation has kept pace with single-family homes.

A duplex is two rental units in the same building. These apartments may be arranged one above the other or side by side. Duplexes are often large, older homes that have been converted. These units often have a double garage and feature individual basements and yards. Duplexes are proportionately more expensive than other rentals and may show a loss for several years. They usually appeal to an investor who needs to lighten his mortgage load or wants a retirement home. Although a landlord cannot get depreciation deductions from the unit he is living in, he is building equity. Duplexes are also easy to rent. Many renters prefer duplexes because there are fewer tenants in the building. Duplexes can also be relatively trouble free. Usually, one of the tenants will assume responsibility for the lawn or snow shoveling. Although most older buildings have one furnace and one electric meter, arrangements can be made so that the tenants are responsible for at least some of the utilities.

An obvious drawback of an owner-occupied building is the lack of privacy. Thus, the investor may decide to live elsewhere. Like single-family homes, duplexes appeal to long-term renters. In a tight money market, they are easier to sell than multiunits because they appeal to people wanting owner-occupied property. The well-kept older unit is one of the best investments in real estate.

One advantage of the multiunit is that it usually costs less to manage and maintain the property on a per unit basis than a single family or duplex. The landlord may find it more convenient to have many units in one location. There may be just one furnace to have serviced, one fuse box to check, one stop to make to collect rent, one bill to write for water and sewer, one insurance payment to make. However, larger properties often require sophisticated, even professional management services. Thus, the efficiencies you get by having a lot of units under one structure may be diminished by additional managerial costs and responsibilities. Finally, if you focus too much of your investment capital in one location, you could put it at risk, either through a sudden catastrophe like a fire or slow degradation because of social, racial, and economic urban transition. A scattering of four- to six-unit apartment complexes in several neighborhoods strikes a good balance between achieving multiunit efficiencies and diversification.

Beware of buying a large apartment complex with a mixture of unit sizes. If the units are of varying sizes and bring varying rents, they will attract people of different economic and social backgrounds. If a building has a mixture of studio apartments and three-bedroom suites, you may have a hard time making it profitable. The Cosmo girl and the blue-haired grandmother may not make good neighbors. The CPA family man and the transient poet may not be the best of friends. Ill-assorted tenants make a building hard to manage and hard to rent.

COMMERCIAL PROPERTY

Commercial property includes offices, shopping malls, and storefronts. Some stores have apartments in the same building. Since the demand for apartment property is relentless while the demand for commercial property fluctuates with the state of the economy, such properties can be desirable as they reduce your risk. Income from the property will always cover some of your costs.

Office buildings have appeal because rents can be raised regularly. Office buildings are in relatively short supply. Because the economy is so service oriented, it's reasonable to expect a continuing demand for office space. In some locations, overbuilding has created a glut, forcing landlords to make rent concessions. Most small- and medium-sized retail and service businesses operate from rented premises. Office buildings fall somewhere between shopping centers and apartments. They will give you more headaches than the latter and fewer than the former. Free-standing office space is essential for such businesses as accounting, insurance, advertising, law, medicine, employment, and engineering.

A modest profit can be boosted by deductions for interest, taxes, and maintenance. You can also take a depreciation deduction. If you renovate a commercial structure that is at least 20 years old, you're allowed a tax credit. Finally, if your building is in a district designated for historic preservation, you can write off renovation costs over 5 years even though the building's useful life is longer.

Commercial property is easier to manage than residential property. Maintenance duties are fewer. Business tenants are more apt to keep up their own premises. They will often improve them. For the most part, they are responsible for the interior of their building. Tenants usually stay longer. They often do their own janitorial work. Tenants also pay more for rent, give a bigger security deposit, and accept tax escalation clauses in their leases.

Leases can run for as long as 20 years. For a small property, a 3-year lease with an annual escalator is typical. Some store leases call for a minimum rent. Higher rents are payable depending on a certain volume of business, with percentages of gross sales above the minimum payable to the landlord. Commercial property leases are complicated. Before you buy a building with leases in effect, have an accountant examine the leases and, if possible, the tenant's income statements. Ask your lawyer to review the leases. Make sure the building is not fully rented to tenants who have long-term leases that restrict rent increases. Long-term leases are like rent control. They keep cash flow down and reduce resale values. Recently negotiated long-term leases can spell trouble for the new owner. It's often better if some of the leases are about to expire. Bad tenants are easier to evict. Local landlord and tenant ordinances are often stacked against residential landlords but in favor of commercial landlords. Many investors prefer doing business with businesspeople. They assume that those who run a business will always pay their rent because they want to keep the location. However, many who run businesses have had lots of practice stiff-arming creditors, and a landlord doesn't intimidate them at all. A business is just as subject to eviction as an apartment dweller, but it's not necessarily easy to accomplish.

However, commercial landlords take bigger risks. When a vacancy does occur, you are hit with substantial renovating costs to suit a new tenant, and the vacancy remains longer than an apartment vacancy. Professional tenants can drive up utility and maintenance costs. Parking requirements are greater than for apartment tenants.

Although new buildings are generally too expensive for small investors, there are existing business properties for many checkbooks. Commercial properties don't always require hefty down payments. A shortage of mortgage money has made bank financing elusive for most small-scale business property investing. In a tight mortgage market, the seller will often finance the purchase, accepting 10 percent in cash or less. Bank financing, if you can get it, generally involves putting up as much as half of the purchase price in cash. A property you like may not even be listed for sale. Don't let that stop you from inquiring about it. The owner may consider an offer for personal reasons. Perhaps it will help him retire earlier than he had intended.

LAND

"Buy land," Will Rogers said. "They ain't making it any more." Speculation in raw land is risky but potentially rewarding. Tax benefits are comparatively few. Real-estate taxes are deductible. Interest is also deductible, if you get a loan. Most lending institutions won't lend money for unimproved real estate. If they do, it's generally a short-term loan, rarely more than 10 years. Other disadvantages are:

1. Soaring property taxes.
2. High interest rates.
3. Illiquidity. It may take months or years to dispose of a property at a price you approve. Raw land is harder to sell than income property. Most people buy property to meet a specific, immediate need, not to hold for appreciation.
4. You must be prepared to commit a sizable sum of money to the purchase. It's difficult to obtain much financial leverage.
5. Some forms of property, such as recreational land, are vulnerable to the economic climate. Farmland, for example, has steadily dropped in value throughout the early 1980s. Negative factors in the farmland market include surplus production capacity, rising production costs, high interest rates, and heavy debt loads on many family farms. Production costs and other expenses are increasing. Debt loans on some farms may increase the supply of land on the market because of bankruptcy, foreclosure, and liquidation of assets. These farms are frequently large and highly leveraged. Their operators were often active land speculators during the years of rising land values. These negative factors will tend to limit any increase in land values. High interest rates may make land less attractive than other investments. This will put further downward pressure on land values. Lot buyers can't always count on the increasing value of their purchase or on the seller to complete promised improvements. While, in general, potentially useful land close to population centers has appreciated over the long term, in the short run and in specific regions land may decrease in value. You may find you're unable to use your lot for the purpose intended, that fees and charges associated with the property rise beyond what you expected, and that problems in getting a valid deed may delay legal title to the property.
6. Fraud. The sale of Arizona desert and Florida swampland has a long, colorful history. As this nation developed, the land speculators followed the explorers and missionaries. But it wasn't until 1968 that the consumer won some measure of protection from fraudulent land sales operators. Congress passed the Interstate Land Sales Act. It's a full-disclosure law that requires sellers to register their offering with the Department of Housing and Urban Development and to reveal to prospective buyers facts about the land. HUD doesn't approve or pass on the merits or value of the development. It does try to protect the consumer by assuring access to all the information needed for a sensible, unhurried land purchase. Whether or not you choose to use that information is up to you. Lots may be marketed as sites for future retirement homes, second-home

locations, or campsites. Sales personnel may stress its investment potential. The act requires land developers, promoters, and brokers who sell or lease certain kinds of property within subdivisions to file a Statement of Record with the secretary of HUD. This contains basic factual and legal information about the property, including:

a. Identity of the people who have an interest in a particular lot.
b. A legal description and map of the subdivision.
c. The probable range of prices at which the lots will be offered.
d. The availability of water, sewage, and other facilities and the presence of unusual noise or safety conditions.
e. Identity of any liens, easements, or encumbrances on the property.
f. A copy of the developer's deed and articles of incorporation or partnership and a financial statement.

If the seller has an obligation to register with the Office of Interstate Land Sales Registration, the seller must give the buyer a copy of the current Property Report before the buyer signs a contract. Otherwise, the buyer has up to 2 years to cancel the contract and get his money back. Furthermore, if the seller has represented that he will provide or complete roads, water, sewer, gas, electricity, or recreational facilities in its Property Report, advertising, or sales promotion, the seller must obligate himself to do so in the contract, clearly and unconditionally (except for acts of God and impossibility of performance). The prospective buyer also has the right to void the contract and get a refund of his money if the subdivision has failed to register with HUD or supply a Property Report. The developer may still be liable for contract payments to a third party if the contract has been assigned to a financing institution or some similar entity. The buyer may sue to recover damages and actual costs and court expenses if the Property Report contains omissions or lies. HUD isn't authorized to act as attorney in such cases. Finally, the buyer has a cooling off period and can revoke his contract up to 7 days after the date it's signed. If this right is exercised, he should notify the seller by registered mail at the address shown in the Property Report.

The Office of Interstate Land Sales Registration (OILSR) is the HUD unit that administers the law, examines the developer's registration statement, and registers the land sales operator. This office isn't concerned with zoning or land-use planning and has no control over the quality of the subdivision. It doesn't dictate what land can be sold, to whom, and at what price. It cannot act as a purchaser's attorney. But it will help buyers secure rights given to them under the act. The law authorizes HUD to conduct investigations and public hearings, to subpoena witnesses, and to seek court injuctions to prevent violations of the law. If necessary, HUD may seek criminal indictments.

If you believe you've been cheated in a transaction covered by the Interstate Land Sales Act, write to HUD/OILSR, 451 Seventh St., S.W., Washington, D.C. 20410. Set forth specific details of your complaint and include the name of the developer, name and location of the subdivision, and copies of the contract or other document you signed. Act quickly because there are specific time limits for exercising your legal rights.

The key advantage in buying raw land is the relatively high yield you can achieve over the long term. Land, of course, isn't income property unless its farmed, mined, forested, fished, or drilled. As oil tycoon John Paul Getty reminds us, "The meek shall inherit the earth, but *not* its mineral rights." Buying land, holding it, and reselling it for more money is speculative as the interim cash drain can be considerable. To improve the odds of appreciation, you should try to change the character of the land. This can be as simple as getting a zoning variance or as elaborate as building a subdivision, with new roads, utility hookups, and graded landscaping. The land developer's credo is: Buy acres, sell lots. Current conditions in some areas makes this activity less possible than in bygone days. Many places now have strong no-growth interest groups and environmental controls. Sometimes, in building a road, the developer has to account for every tree. Woe to the investor who must negotiate the resting ground of dead people or live birds. You may win zoning approval for changing the permitted use of the land by donating some of it to the township for park or conservation purposes.

To analyze potential investment land, compile a store of statistics about the undeveloped area, including such basics as the value of industrial payrolls and proximity to highways, major markets, and utilities. Get the names of owners from public assessor records, study county plat maps, and review zoning ordinances. Trudge through the swamps and woodlands. Try to anticipate the path of progress. Employment means development, development means demand for land and housing. Buy property in your own area. Never buy sight unseen. Protect yourself in the contract by making your purchase contingent on financing, a clear title, and local approval. When buying land for speculation, keep the land classified as agricultural, if possible. Tax rates are lower. Make sure the zoning of the land matches your plans for its use. You may want the site as a place to park your camper, but zoning laws may forbid that. Determine the water rights before signing the contract. Water that is visible on the land may not belong to the landholder. Have the lot surveyed. Fences don't always indicate legal boundaries. Make sure your land has the right of way to a public roadway. Places to shop for reasonably priced raw land with profit potential include the following:

1. Areas beyond the suburbs but still accessible to major city facilities.
2. Recreational areas within a 2-hour drive of a large city.
3. Commercially zoned real estate near airports, docks, and railroads.
4. Properties already in the process of change and upgrading by others.
5. Property near highway interchanges and on tollway growth corridors.

6. Lots zoned for light industrial manufacturing or offices on the outskirts of town, in industrial parks with streets, electricity, sewer, water, bus service, gas, and protective covenants.

THE CONDOMINIUM

The condominium and cooperative are forms of ownership that permit multiple ownership of a multifamily building or complex. Individuals own a deed and share with other owners common ownership of public areas. Each owner must pay taxes on a prorated basis and is responsible for upkeep of common areas. Most condos are organized as associations, and the associations through a board of directors provide bylaws with which all owners must comply. Mortgages are extended in the same manner for a condominium as when buying a single-family residence. In a condo, you own your own dwelling plus an undivided interest in the building's common facilities. In a co-op, you own stock in an association that entitles you to a housing unit. When you buy a co-op, you own a share of the association that owns the real estate. The association generally gets a blanket mortgage for the property. Cooperative members contribute toward its repayment, as well as paying a proportional share of operating and maintenance expenses. If a cooperative member fails to make these payments, other members are responsible for his contribution. If a number of cooperative members fail to make their payments, the property could foreclose, causing solvent members to lose their units. Partly for this reason, financial institutions have been reluctant to finance co-ops. Nationally, condos outnumber co-ops three to one. Condos are more popular because they are easier to buy and sell and there are fewer restrictions on the occupants.

As with home ownership, there are distinct advantages and disadvantages to condominium ownership. These should be weighed carefully.

A renter's advantages in buying a condo are:

1. He may deduct mortgage interest payments and real-estate taxes from his gross income in computing income taxes.
2. He builds equity.
3. He may realize substantial appreciation in the value of his unit.
4. He is guaranteed stability in monthly housing payments because his major expense—the mortgage payment—remains constant.
5. He is often given a price discount by the developer.

A renter's disadvantages in buying a condo are:

1. He must produce a large sum of cash for a down payment.
2. His monthly payments are likely to be higher than his rent was.

3. Any problem in the condominium building becomes his problem because a unit owner must share any risk of mechanical or structural breakdowns.

An investor's disadvantages in buying a condo are:

1. Condos give your noninvestor neighbors excessive control over your ability to rent and manage your unit at a profit.
2. Overbuilding and overconverting have created a condo glut in some markets, hurting resale values.
3. It's difficult to rent a condo and still get a positive cash flow.

Investors can often make money by converting an apartment building or hotel to condominiums. The conversion process is as follows:

1. Obtain financing.
2. Select and rehabilitate the building.
3. Comply with government regulations.
4. Sell units, relinquishing control to the owners' association.

Let's look at these four steps in more detail.

Obtain Financing

As with most real-estate development, a combination of equity and debt provides financing for condominium and cooperative conversions. The conversion manager, any partners, and governmental entities supply the equity. It generally finances 20 to 25 percent of the cost. Interim and long-term debt cover the balance. An interim loan finances the hard costs of conversion, such as building acquisition and rehabilitation. Soft costs are also met by the interim loan and include fees paid to attorneys, real-estate firms, consultants, engineers, and government bodies. Long-term mortgage loans are made to individuals buying units in the converted building. The conversion manager is usually responsible for securing both types of loans. Generally, savings and loan associations, mortgage banks, and mutual savings banks provide the long-term or permanent mortgage loans for individual units. Conversion managers frequently pay a particular lending institution from one-half to two points to ensure that the lender will make all mortgage loans.

Financial institutions making mortgage loans usually require that the conversion manager have nonbinding agreements from people representing 60 to 80 percent of all units indicating they wish to buy the units. A small, refundable payment is typically made by potential purchasers when they enter the agreement. Not until this presale requirement is met will mortgage lenders provide individual borrowers with funds to finalize unit sales. Financial institutions request the presale so that unit mortgages may be sold either to the Federal Home Loan Mortgage Corporation (FHLMC) or the Federal National Mortgage Association (FNMA). Each organization has a presale requirement (usually in the 70 percent range) that must be reached before either one will agree to buy long-term mortgages. Loans made by mortgage banks may be sold to FNMA for resale in the secondary mortgage market. In addition to the presale requirement, a converted building must comply with FNMA's building condition standards before individual unit mortgages will be bought. One of FNMA's most important requirements is that a substantial majority of the units in the building be owner occupied. This represents an attempt by FNMA to limit investor purchase and subsequent rental of condominiums, which may have a negative effect on the quality of the project. FHLMC has a role similar to that of FNMA, but FHLMC buys conventional mortgages from savings and loan associations instead of mortgage banks. To determine a converted condominium's likelihood of success, FHLMC inspects the building to be converted and its neighborhood. If FHLMC's criteria aren't met, it may not buy the mortgages for the building.

If developers performing condo conversions are favorably known to local lenders, they usually have no difficulty in getting financing. An exception may occur if the developer is carrying out a major rehabilitation. Lenders may charge a slightly higher interest rate or add points to the cost of the interim loan because of the developer's greater financial risk. For example, the discovery of unanticipated structural defects may delay the conversion and add to the carrying costs on the interim loan and to the overall expense of the project. If these costs are high, lenders fear the developer may default on the interim loan.

Select and Rehabilitate the Building

Selecting a building may appear unnecessary in a landlord- or tenant-managed conversion. However, they should examine a building's location and other features just as a developer would to ensure that it's suitable for conversion. The following six elements are typically considered in selecting a building:

1. Location
2. Quality of construction
3. Number of bedrooms and size of rooms
4. Age of building
5. Amenities
6. Remodeling costs

Let's look at these six factors in more detail.

1. Location.   An appropriate location is one with access to public transportation, business districts, and shopping. Buildings situated in a historic part of the city or in a neighborhood with special ambience are also desirable for conversion. This feature is so important to some developers that they will choose poor-quality buildings if they offer superior locations.

2. Quality of construction.   The conversion manager, engineers, or architects usually make a preliminary inspection of a building to determine if it's sound enough to be converted. If the building is judged suitable, detailed architectural and engineering studies are made of its structural and mechanical elements. Problems discovered in these examinations may eliminate a building from consideration, particularly if the conversion manager plans a rapid, inexpensive conversion process.

3. Number of bedrooms and size of rooms.   The importance of this feature varies with the market. In areas where professionals comprise a major market share, buildings with a high proportion of one-bedroom and efficiency units will sell rapidly. Units with two bedrooms or more are popular in the suburban and retirement communities because buyers have larger households or want extra space for guests or for hobby rooms. Smaller rooms are acceptable if other features—principally location—are outstanding. In other cases, large rooms may be a strong selling point.

4. Age of building.   Buildings less than 20 years old are favored for conversion because appliances, mechanical systems, and structural components are more likely to be in good condition. However, older buildings are selected if they have been well maintained and if regular repairs and renovations have been made by the landlord. These buildings may also have more favorable locations, be better constructed, or have more architectural appeal than new buildings.

5. Amenities.   Again, the particular market determines the importance of features such as swimming pools, party rooms, putting greens, health spas, and saunas. Marketing campaigns are often built around such amenities.

6. Remodeling costs.   Conversion managers carefully consider the extent of rehabilitation needed so that the sale prices of units won't be prohibitive to their intended purchasers. Developers who specialize in major rehabilitations may choose buildings that other converters would reject. They often select small, vacant, abandoned, or dilapidated buildings that can be bought cheaply. However, developers ensure that the buildings or their neighborhood offer some distinctive feature that will justify the expensive renovation. Many buildings chosen for conversion need only minor rehabilitation. Usually, sub-contracting firms under the direction of a general contractor carry out the renovation. Interior and exterior designers sometimes create a more homelike atmosphere by placing furniture, plants, and colorful paintings in lobbies and patio furniture around swimming pool areas. In garden-style and townhouse complexes, exterior work sometimes includes minor architectural changes, such as varied doorways, to give each unit an individualized appearance. Although renovation is an important part of the conversion process, purchasers are sometimes given the option of having little renovation done to reduce the unit's selling price. The exterior is refurbished, but individual units are re-paired only to meet local building code standards. Purchasers decide what improvements they want and pay accordingly. The speed and care with which rehabilitation is done is important to conversion managers, to tenants (whether buying or moving), and to outside purchasers. If rehabilitation is accom-plished rapidly and well, units can be sold sooner, thus reducing the carrying cost of any interim financing.

Complying with Government Regulations

The degree to which condominium and cooperative conversions are reg-ulated varies across jurisdictions and states. All states have adopted laws re-lated to condominiums and about one-half impose additional regulations on conversions. State laws generally also govern the formation of cooperative corporations, although few states or localities regulate cooperative conver-sions.

Conversion managers generally hire an attorney to ensure that proper legal documentation is filed and that all legal requirements are observed. To legally convert a building to condominium ownership, a state or jurisdiction usually requires that a master deed or declaration be recorded. A record plat, which describes and depicts the way in which the property is subdivided, and the bylaws for the condominium association generally are filed with the master deed. Other legal documents that will be needed at various stages of the con-version process are as follows:

1. Purchase agreements for those buying units.
2. Individual unit deeds.
3. A management agreement with the firm operating the building during and after conversion.

Many jurisdictions and states have enacted measures that attempt to re-strict condominium conversions or to protect existing tenants and purchasers of units. To comply with these laws, conversion managers often must get var-ious government approvals before proceeding with a conversion. It may also be necessary to file a registration statement, offering plan, or disclosure statement before converted units may be sold. These documents are provided to unit purchasers and sometimes to existing tenants as a form of buyer protection. The most common form of tenant protection offered by law is a notice to tenants that their building is to be converted.

The conversion manager must provide all legal notices in writing. And, although not required by law, many developers follow such a notice with a meeting for tenants. During these meetings, a tenant's rights regarding the unit and any legally mandated form of relocation assistance or financial aid are explained.

State or local laws sometimes require a conversion manager to provide relocation assistance to tenants moving from a converted building. For example, in the Los Angeles marketing area, conversion managers comply with ordinances of some municipalities by providing monetary payments to tenants who move or by helping them find new housing. When relocation assistance isn't legally required, some conversion managers voluntarily provide this service to tenants. Local ordinances provide additional protection. Tenants, finally, are protected by common law. For example, a landlord cannot break a lease because he wants to convert the building to a condominium. Therefore, a landlord should make sure his tenants are on month-to-month agreements if he is thinking about converting.

Marketing Units and Relinquishing Control

Many conversion managers aim at a high rate of tenant purchase and market units accordingly. If a large proportion of tenants buy units, the presale requirement often needed for financing will be easier to meet. Units may be sold faster, reducing the length of the conversion process and the overall carrying cost of any interim loan. Also, tenants will be less likely to oppose the conversion and take actions that could delay and add to the cost of the conversion process. To ensure high rates of tenant purchase, developers and landlords frequently offer discounts ranging from an average of 10 to 20 percent. Tenant discounts have benefited many tenants by allowing them to buy units at below-market prices and realize substantial appreciation in the unit's value quickly. Marketing strategies also differ between individual buildings and townhouses or garden-style complexes. In a single structure, all units usually are marketed simultaneously and sold over a short period, say 1 year. Garden and townhouse complexes are generally converted and marketed in several phases, with the overall process sometimes spanning 5 years or more. Often several units in the complex are renovated and advertised as models to test public acceptance of the conversion.

As part of the marketing strategy, most developers open a sales office on the premises immediately following the announcement of the conversion. They also use meetings and social gatherings with tenants as an opportunity to sell units. Emphasis is placed on tenant discounts and the tax advantages of homeownership, while discussion of increased monthly housing costs is minimized. Salesmen generally use low-key approaches, but may resort to more forceful tactics, such as repeated telephone calls, if sales are lagging or if the developer wants a rapid sellout.

Marketing problems are more likely to occur in a major rehab project than in a conversion requiring only minor repairs. Unforeseen rehab expenses can push the planned sales price beyond the cost of comparable housing, and it's difficult to show and sell individual units before most renovation is finished. However, in markets with a heavy demand for totally rehabilitated units, people wanting to buy condos often drive through neighborhoods looking for newly begun conversions. When a building is located, interested parties follow its progress and often make bids for a unit before a firm price is set.

State and local condominium laws specify the time at which the conversion manager must relinquish control of a building to the condominium owners' association. However, the turnover generally occurs when at least 70 percent of the units have been sold and most of them have gone to closing. These same laws also indicate organizing principles for the association, such as the duties and responsibilities of the board of directors. The directors usually have the discretion to determine if households renting in the converted building may join the association, as well as their voting powers.

Multifamily rental buildings are converted to condominium or cooperative ownership in a process that involves these four steps. Each conversion venture is a unique project, influenced by elements external to that process. Variations within each phase of the process may result from the ownership arrangement, the extent of renovation, and the individual or organization managing the conversion.

THE TIME SHARE/INTERVAL OWNERSHIP

Time sharing, or interval ownership, is a vacation program that allows you to buy or lease a resort condominium for a limited time during the year. The unit often has two bedrooms. The time period is typically 2 weeks in a year. The advantage is that you have a luxury place to spend 2 weeks a year that will cost you relatively little after you've paid off the unit, usually within 5 years. With your one-time outright ownership purchase at today's prices, you won't be affected by skyrocketing resort costs. The settings are often attractive and offer activities such as skiing, horseback riding, rafting, hiking, swimming, and dancing. You are also entitled to exchange your unit with other units in luxury resorts around the world. The unit itself is well-appointed, with amenities such as a Jacuzzi and maid service.

This sounds appealing, but one fact needs to be stressed. Time sharing isn't an investment, except perhaps for the developer. Most resorts don't have a resale program. Most real-estate agents won't handle time shares. Most time shares are hard to rent. Hence, time shares have questionable investment value. However, because it's often promoted as an investment, I've decided to include time sharing in this chapter.

If you took the money you spent on the time share and invested it instead, you could use the profits for a vacation at accommodations as posh as any time share without being locked into a fixed program. The full cost of the time share includes its initial price, cost of financing, maintenance costs, and cost of lost interest from an alternative investment.

Buyer dissatisfaction often stems from unrealistic expectations, misinformation, misleading sales practices, and false promises by time-share salesmen. Many buyers are initially lured into making the trip to the resort with an offer of an "investment seminar" or "sweepstakes prize." Free vacations, paintings, luggage, savings bonds, trading stamps, "conversation pieces," and other sorry "gifts" are used to draw people to sales presentations or development sites. These treats may never materialize. Sometimes special conditions are attached to the lure or a customer is advised that gifts only go to unit buyers. A free vacation may be the means of delivering the innocent to a battery of high-powered salesmen in a lonely place. Buyers inevitably have to sit through a somewhat evangelistic presentation featuring slides, movies, and testimonials before the gifts are distributed. The buyer may be lured to the resort with a certificate entitling him to a "free" unit. The certificate may bear a face value of $500 to $1,000 dollars. That amount is simply included in the inflated price of the unit they choose. Some salesmen drive prospective customers around the resort in cars equipped with CB radios that provide a running commentary of sales presumably in progress. More offensive is abusive language used to embarrass customers who delay making an immediate decision to buy. In some instances, hesitant buyers have been isolated in remote places where transportation is controlled by the selling organization.

Most time shares feature the right to exchange their unit for another unit in another resort. Some people buy solely to exchange. But exchanges are often difficult. It may be hard to switch a week at Ocean City in the fall for a week in Paris in the spring or a week in Florida in August for a week in Colorado at Christmas.

If you like the idea of having your vacations programmed for you for the next few decades, time sharing is probably for you. But, before you buy, consider these tips:

1. Take the time to do some math. The cost of the time share may seem reasonable, say $5,000. But to that you must add the cost of financing, the cost of lost interest on your down payment, and the annual maintenance cost. Many resort-type time shares have additional expenses.

2. It's much easier to sign a contract than to get released from one. In most cases, it's a long, difficult, expensive business. Think before you sign.

Have your attorney review all papers. Beware of making significant, long-lasting commitments without adequate reflection. Shun salesmen who insist on your making "on-the-spot" decisions. Wise decisions will stand the scrutiny of in-depth study and the criticism of others.

3. Don't rely on the developer's oral promises. A future golf course, swimming pool, or marina may never materialize. Get all verbal promises in writing.

4. Ask about the financial soundness of the time-share company. If the firm goes out of business, your chances of getting a refund are slim.

5. Determine if you will own the time share or just have the use of it, as in a lease.

6. Check to see if you have a certain number of days to cancel the contract. See if cancellation can be made without penalty.

7. Make sure the amenities listed in the contract exist in the unit.

8. Investigate all laws regulating time shares. Verify that the developer has complied with them.

9. Find out the amount of the annual maintenance fee and how often and how much it has increased in recent years.

10. Think twice before you buy.

PARTNERSHIPS

A real-estate limited partnership (RELP) is a method to raise money for real-estate purchase. The syndicator or developer gathers together a group of investors. These are limited partners who buy interests or units in the partnership. The general partner directs the partnership's affairs and decisions. Limited partnerships can be private placements put together by a developer with some of his friends. He finds a building, prices its acquisition and rehabbing, and then asks a group of people with some spare change to join him in a partnership venture. As general partner, he provides the expertise. As limited partners, they provide the cash. Most limited partners are found through word of mouth. Publically placed partnerships are large offerings registered with the Security Exchange Commission.

In both cases, state and federal security laws regulate what the syndicators must disclose and the types of fees they can collect. In public offerings, partners will get a prospectus detailing the risks, fees, and plans for the partnership. If developers don't do this and the investment sours, they leave themselves open to a lawsuit from disgruntled limited partners. The prospectus is basically 200 pages of why it's a bad deal. The SEC requires such prospectuses, but the agency doesn't rule on whether the specific deal is good or bad or if the developer is lying. It merely rules that the general partner has provided all the information required by law. Private placements should also have prospectuses, but many do not.

The SEC limits the size and types of fees the general partner can collect, as well as his method of collecting them. But each partnership has its own way of structuring fees. The developer usually collects three types of fees. He can collect acquisition fees for finding and buying the properties, a management fee for running the partnership, and a share of the profits when the partnership is dissolved, as well as brokerage fees if he sells it. The "load" on your investment is a significant factor in determining your return. In public offerings, the developer or syndicator usually subordinates his interest to those of the limited partnerships. They must receive all their capital back, as well as some fixed annual cash flow, before the developer can skim his profit.

There are three ways of getting a return on a RELP. First, you will get a tax shelter from depreciation and interest write-off from the property. In the first few years of the project, limited partners get the benefits of the project's high initial costs. As in most real-estate purchases, a partnership may only put down 20 percent on the building, yet claim a depreciation based on 100 percent of the building's cost. Then, you will get cash flow from the property itself. Most deals are at best break-even. Finally, you'll make money when the project is sold at a profit. Aside from leverage, tax advantages, and cash flow, RELPs also offer a hedge against inflation. Since replacement costs inevitably run higher than those of existing structures, market prices of old buildings tend to rise at roughly the same rate as construction costs. But it's foolhardy to believe that inflation—down dramatically in the early 1980s—will be sufficient to ensure high prices. On Wall Street, investors are warned against being the "greater fool." The greater fool theory basically says that the price you pay for a commodity is irrelevant as long as you can find a greater fool to take it off your hands for more money. From this idea arises chain letters, Ponzi schemes, multilevel distributorships, and, in some cases, limited partnerships. You would do well to be skeptical of any RELP in which appreciation is the centerpiece of the partnership's marketing thrust.

Most public offerings are blind pools. This means the money is raised before the properties have been purchased. This makes fraud potentially possible and knowledge of the syndicator all-important.

Syndications are relatively illiquid. You may lock up your money for 5 to 12 years until the individual properties have been sold off. Unlike for stocks and bonds, there's little market in syndication interests. Some distressed sellers can sell their interests. These transactions usually involve a loss of up to 40 percent of an interest's market value, high compared with the commissions involved in stock or bond sales. The syndicate picks the year in which to sell. The resultant income may complicate your taxes.

RELPs are a good way to invest small amounts of money in real estate. But you must be careful. Some tips follow:

1. Only give your money to a group headed by a general partner you know and trust.
2. Read all the fine print and discuss it with your tax advisor or accountant.
3. Scrutinize the RELP's operating document. Have your attorney verify that it complies with regulations.
4. Stay abreast of tax law changes that could have a negative effect on RELPs, either by reducing your tax benefits or the benefits of potential buyers of partnership properties.
5. Make sure the property makes economic sense. Check:
   a. Amount of leverage.
   b. Financing on the balance.
   c. Kind of property.
   d. Economic conditions, such as inflation, interest, and tax changes.
   e. The local market, such as vacancy rates and retailing shakeouts.

How can you find out what your interest in a partnership is worth? There's no quick answer. Adjusting the original cost for inflation and a price–earnings or income multiplier valuation can be misleading. The property's value will depend on external factors, such as the energy situation, changes in location desirability, rent restrictions, financing, and the quality of maintenance and management.

For further information, read the section on tax shelters in the forthcoming chapter on taxes. I also recommend these publications:

Craig Hall. *Craig Hall's Book of Real Estate Investing: How to Beat Inflation and Taxes through Partnership Investment for High Returns at Low Risk.* New York: Holt, Rinehart and Winston, 1982.

The Real Estate Syndication Alert. Warren, Gorham & Lamont, Inc., 210 South Street, Boston, Mass., 02111.

SUMMARY

Here are some main points from this chapter:

1. Single-family homes are easy to finance and quick to sell.
2. Apartments provide safety, income, and tax benefits.
3. Commercial property is easy to manage and commands high rents.
4. Land, condominiums, and time-share programs are generally inappropriate properties for the small investor.
5. Limited partnerships provide high-tax-bracket investors with most of the advantages of active real-estate investing, but can be speculative.

5

ACCOUNTING

OVERVIEW

In a nutshell, the process of successfully managing income property follows this sequence:

1. Evict problem tenants and fill vacancies.
2. Have tenants sign written leases and make security deposits.
3. Renovate the property and upgrade services.
4. Raise the rent.
5. Turn the property over to professional managers, and have them do the preceding steps when necessary.

Managing income property involves two kinds of management—financial management and tenant management. The next three chapters cover financial management—accounting, insurance, and taxes. Chapter eight deals with tenant management.

RECORD KEEPING

Keeping careful books is one of the most important jobs of successful landlording. The biggest error you can make is to keep careless records. Landlording is a business and should be conducted as you would any business. So, as in a business, you must keep meticulous records. Yet the need for an effective bookkeeping system is frequently overlooked. One detailed study of ten small, unsuccessful manufacturing enterprises revealed that all maintained imprecise books. In contrast, a similar study of ten prosperous organizations showed that each had a complete accounting system and well-informed managers who made complete use of financial information in guiding the firm. Misleading financial records leads to serious problems in every aspect, from collections to insurance, from taxes to inventory control. Accurate books are essential for tax accounting, rent and security disputes, and vendor disbursements.

BOOKKEEPING

Even if an accountant keeps your books, some knowledge of bookkeeping is useful. Simplified bookkeeping textbooks and introduction to accounting books are useful self-instructional tools. Junior college or adult education courses could be taken to learn the basic principles. This section will introduce you to some of these principles.

Bookkeeping comes before accounting in the alphabet of business management. Bookkeeping can exist without becoming accounting. But to do an effective job, you may need more than bookkeeping. Bookkeeping is a history of the financial transactions of the organization. It's a chronological record without any integration. Accountants relate these records with manager's goals, plans, and budgets. Money that is received and spent needs to be recorded in a more sophisticated way than do personal cash, checking, or credit-card transactions. You may have to report on your finances to government, partners, or future investors. Consequently, systems have been designed to organize the transactions.

The type of accounting system you will use depends on the size of your operations. A computer service bureau may be helpful if you own many properties. On the other hand, a diary with a blank page for each day will suffice if you only own a two-flat. Use the diary to record all expenses and the rent. At the beginning of each month, print on the top of one page the word "income" and on the other page the word "outgo." Enumerate by check number and date every expense and by apartment number and date every rent. On the other pages, paste canceled checks, bills, and receipts for each day the transaction took place. Most people throw receipts away after making the ledger or diary entry. But these receipts contain valuable information. They often list specifications, telephone numbers, part numbers, and brand names. By keeping invoices in a diary, you create a storehouse of information for future reference, a kind of corporate memory. The diary will provide a history of income and expenses and proof to the IRS for all property-related deductions. Keep the diaries for as long as you own the property.

The Double-entry System

If you are renting out a part of your house, vacation property, or a condominium, a diary will do. If you own more properties, a more reliable accounting system is desirable. The best method for keeping an accurate accounting record is the double-entry system. Double entry describes the principle that one transaction has an effect on two different groups of financial accounts. The groups of accounts are assets, such as cash, liabilities, such as loans payable, income, such as rent, and expenses, such as utilities. The double-entry system requires that each transaction be recorded in two accounts, because the enterprise is described by the accounts from two viewpoints—assets and liabilities. Each transaction involves at least one increase and one decrease. The kind of account determines on which side an increase is recorded and on which side a decrease is recorded. Asset accounts record increases on the left or debit side. Liability and net worth accounts record increases on the right or credit side. Decreases go on the opposite side from increases.

Asset Accounts		Liability and Net worth Accounts	
Cash		Accounts Payable	
Debit	Credit	Debit	Credit
+	−	−	+
Land		Net Worth	
Debit	Credit	Debit	Credit
+	−	−	+

Once the original transaction is properly recorded, the effect of the transaction on the enterprise can be traced through the accounting records. The accounting records are obtained through the following process:

1. Record all invoices. This includes rent receipts and check payments.
2. Transfer each item in a transaction into its own journal, cash received into a cash receipts journal and cash payments into a cash payments journal.
3. The bookkeeper then posts the information in the journals to the various ledger accounts. This system of accounts is called a general ledger. Each account is usually recorded on a separate ledger page. The general ledger classifies the transactions to accumulate the total effects of the transactions on the accounts for a specific period of time. Ledgers can be organized in terms of balance sheet accounts (cash, accounts receivable, inventories, real property, equipment, etc.) and income statement accounts (rental income, operating expenses).
4. At the end of each operating period (day, week, month, or year), the net amount or new balance in each account is found by a trial balance in

each ledger account. It tests to make sure that all double entries have been made and that the general ledger is in balance. The trial balance is a ledger listing that shows all accounts by name and number and gives the appropriate amount in either the credit or debit column.

5. Finally, if the trial balance is accurate, the bookkeeper can derive the financial reports.

These reports are as follows:

1. Operating statement
2. Balance sheet
3. Accounts payable reports
4. Accounts receivable reports
5. Inventory control
6. Payroll
7. Fixed-assets reports

Let's look at each of these reports in more detail.

Operating Statement

The operating statement displays your cost of operations and your retained earnings. The total revenues are adjusted by subtracting direct expenses to find your gross profit. The general and administrative expenses are subtracted to determine your net profit or loss. Retained earnings from the beginning of the period are compared with the current retained earnings figure. This difference may then be posted to your retained earnings ledger account. The operating statement may be made as often as you like, even daily. It's sometimes known as the P and L (profit and loss) report. For example:

```
Income Ledger
  Building A
    Apartment 1
    Apartment 2
  Building B
    Apartment 1
    Apartment 2
  Total income
Expense Ledger
  Payroll
    Resident manager
    Gardener
    Janitor
```

Utilities
  Electricity
  Water
  Gas
  Telephone
  Cable
Administration
  Advertising
  Legal
  Accounting
Cleaning
  Apartment
  Carpet
  Curtains
Contracts
  Management fee
  Pest control
  Rubbish
  Pool
  Security
Supplies
  Electrical
  Plumbing
  Cleaning
  Office
  Grounds
Repairs
  Furniture
  Building
  Plumbing
  Electrical
  Appliances
Insurance
  Property
  Employee
Taxes
  Payroll
  Property
  Local
  State
  Federal
Capital expenditures
  Furniture
  Equipment
  Buildings
  First mortgage principal
  First mortgage interest

Second mortgage principal
Second mortgage interest
Total expenses
Net profit

For most small operations, you can get by with fewer accounts. Keeping books with an eye on transferring ledger entries to an income-tax return can transform a major headache into a simple chore. Some bookkeepers enter all expenditures in chronological order in one general account book and then sort out the various breakdowns at the end of the year. A simpler method is to prepare a separate ledger account, composed of one or more pages, for each entry that will later be made on the income-tax statement. The accounts you use should reflect the structure of Supplemental Income Schedule E. Thus:

Account Number	Description
4	Advertising
5	Auto and travel
6	Cleaning and maintenance
7	Commissions
8	Insurance
9	Legal and professional fees
10	Mortgage interest paid to financial institutions
11	Other interest
12	Repairs
13	Supplies
14	Taxes
15	Utilities
16	Wages and salaries
17	Other
17.1	Snow and lawn
17.2	Pest control
17.3	Rubbish
etc.	

The IRS may change the form, so the line numbers may change. But the categories will probably stay the same.

For each expenditure, enter the account number and use it to flag all expenditures within each account. An item in your expense ledger might look like this:

Account	Check	Cashed	Description	Amount	Date
12	311	Y	John Doe Plumbing	$1,210.00	MM/DD/YY

To complete your tax return, add each ledger account, list each total as an entry under the appropriate major category on your income-tax return, and total the various major accounts.

Balance Sheet

The balance sheet summarizes the assets and liabilities of your enterprise. It can only be obtained immediately following a monthly closeout.

A. Assets: What the business owns.
   1. Current assets: Assets in varying states of being converted into cash within the next 12 months.
      a. Cash: Currency, coins, checking accounts, savings deposits, money orders, traveler's checks, credit-card receipts.
      b. Accounts receivable: What the customer owes the business for services already received.
      c. Notes receivable: Fund debts owed to the enterprise.
      d. Inventories
      e. Prepayments, such as for insurance and utilities.
   2. Fixed assets: Assets used in the operation of the business, not intended for resale, or not to be sold within the next 12 months.
      a. Real property: Land and improvements, buildings and fixtures. The amount stated is the original cost plus improvements minus depreciation.
      b. Machinery, equipment, vehicles, furniture: The amount stated is the original cost minus depreciation.
B. Liabilities: What the business owes.
   1. Current liabilities: Debts owed by the business that will be paid within the next 12 months, used to acquire current assets.
      a. Notes payable: Fund debts owed by the business to financial institutions.
      b. Accounts payable: Debts owed to trade creditors/suppliers.
   2. Long-term liabilities: Debts owed by the business that are used to acquire fixed assets and aren't payable within the next 12 months.
      a. Mortgage loans: Debts owed for land, buildings, and improvements.
      b. Long-term loans: Debts owed to financial institutions to acquire machinery, equipment, vehicles, and furniture. Generally, the current portion (to be paid within 12 months) can be deducted from the outstanding amount to reflect true long-term liabilities.

The operating statement and the balance sheet are essential to monitoring the financial progress of any business enterprise. You can use and expand on the data that make up these two reports to derive supplementary reports. These reports deal with accounts payable, accounts receivable, inventory control, payroll, and fixed assets. For large real-estate enterprises, such reporting is critical. Managers of these organizations will need these reports for allocating resources, strategic planning, and tax requirements. Such reports are of lesser use to those who own a few properties or whose properties are managed professionally.

Let's look at some of these reports.

Accounts Payable

The accounts payable function monitors money you pay out. It can be helpful in maintaining a good credit standing since it produces reports of whom you owe, how much you owe, and for what time period. The accounts payable report shows the aging on the balances you owe each vendor, along with the vendor name, number, purchase order number, and amount of each active invoice. The report should be produced after all transactions have been completed for a month, but before the month is closed.

Accounts Receivable

The accounts receivable function allows you to set up initial tenant payment files. The accounts receivable report will show you what tenant has paid his rent, when he paid, how much he paid, and how much he should have paid.

Inventory Control

The inventory control function keeps track of items that are frequently used and need to be restocked in the course of maintaining the properties. The inventory status report should consist of the item number, description, cost, price, quantity on hand, minimum amount, and maximum amount. Items to be monitored in inventory might include certain kinds of hardware, office supplies, and utility products.

Payroll

A personnel report should list all employees, including pay status, rate of pay, date of last raise, and personal data. The report may also include deductions for each individual. The report should be made weekly, monthly, quarterly, and annually.

Fixed Assets

The fixed assets function maintains current records of your fixed assets and determines depreciations for you. Depreciation has the effect of lowering the value of the asset, creating a "book value" for the asset. Fixed assets reporting should be made for improvements, machinery, equipment, and furniture. The report should consist of the item number, description, serial number, date of purchase, cost, life, depreciation method, salvage value, and depreciation taken in previous years. Land values should be kept separate from the value of buildings and other improvements.

OTHER RECORDS

You can discard rental and job applications from people who have drifted away without renting an apartment or taken a job after 1 year in most states. Keep the records of residents and employees indefinitely. Questions could arise about Social Security, an injury claim, or some other matter. Other records to keep include a history of each unit, who occupied it, for how long, what damages were done, what appliances were installed or repaired, dates of painting and decorating, the date you informed a tenant his rent would be raised and the date he began paying the increased rent, the date a tenant said he was moving and the date he moved, the date and check number of the tenant's security deposit, and the date you sent him an eviction notice.

FINANCIAL CONTROL

Many real-estate enterprises are in a state of permanent marginal operations. Some fail within a short time. The major ailment in most cases is difficulties in financial management. The inability of an entrepreneur to pay his debt as it becomes due shows a lack of sound financial control. Cash crises due to undercapitalization are common in real-estate investing. Why? Investors are suckered into buying real estate for noneconomic reasons, either out of speculation or tax evasion. They confuse ownership with control. If the cash is flowing the wrong way for any length of time, you have no control and you'll soon forfeit ownership.

Some investors talk blithely of building a real estate empire using double mortgages and 120 percent financing. They aren't quite so blithe when it comes to meeting the interest payments or the balloon. Investors tend toward optimism, but prudence requires that you anticipate failure—or at least hard times. Everything will cost more than you thought and will take longer than you thought. "The bills come in promptly, only the rent doesn't" is the landlord's lament.

Even if you cannot raise the rent or even collect the rent, you'll still have to pay the property tax and utility bills. Losing sight of the importance of maintaining a healthy financial position is a grave error. When a shortage of funds afflicts you, you'll have no choice but to try to appease your creditors. Running out of money is a major cause of landlording failure. Many independents allow capital to dip to dangerously low levels. They forget that cash alone—not equity nor leases—pays the bills and provides funds in an emergency. In the introduction, I recommend that the beginning investor save 6 months of income and an additional $1,000 per unit and put down 20 percent on the property. These requirements are tough, but realistic, based on what I've seen. If you're not prepared to meet these requirements, I question whether you're suitable to invest in income real estate.

William of Ockham, a Franciscan monk of the fourteenth century, formulated a maxim that came to be known as Ockham's Razor or the Principle of Parsimony: "Entities should not be multiplied beyond necessity." Basically, he was calling for philosphers to examine any question, as with a knife, slashing away the peripheral and the secondary. A common failure among real-estate investors is the tendency to overextend. Properties are overfinanced and undermanaged. Ockham's Razor forces the question: Do I really need that extra property? According to business theory, administrators can manage about eight people before losing control or needing to create a second level of management. If you have a salaried job, you won't be able to handle by yourself more than ten units and do justice to your career and family. You'll be running around like the proverbial chicken with its head cut off. Even if you use a professional manager, I would urge caution before buying that next property. The key is to move slowly but surely.

Profits from your rentals should be plowed back into the enterprise, to remodel or to buy additional property. Don't consider profits personal income. By placing profits back into your properties, you maintain their value and keep taxes low. Net profit is meaningless. Growth and cash flow are everything.

To control the use of credit and make sure that growth is properly paced and not too much credit is tied up in fixed assets, the investor must act like a controller. The corporate controller is a person who gears the firm's operations toward planned goals of profitability, eliminating overspending and waste. His duties are:

1. To keep accurate accounting records.
2. To manage the enterprise's cash position and provide the means of meeting current liabilities.
3. To determine the financial needs of the enterprise.
4. To prepare financial reports from accounting records, including the balance sheet and operating statement.
5. To exploit appropriate external sources of funds when necessary.
6. To allocate and account for these funds.

As a property manager, you should be able to assume these responsibilities. You can master the skills of controllership. For example, a controller routinely thinks in approximations and significant digits. At the highest level of deliberation, you aren't concerned with dollars-and-cents precision. Get into the habit of truncating and rounding. For example, translate in your mind $2,745.12 to $3K. "K" means kilo, or thousand. Three is an easier figure to hold in your mind, to contemplate, to manipulate than $2,745.12.

There's a time for precision. But in making broad managerial decisions, you're more interested in trends and variations from the norm. What is the norm? In the case of real-estate income, it's market rent caused by supply (usually limited), demand (usually great), and ability to pay (always judgmental). In the case of outgo, it's expenditures compared by category over time—monthly, quarterly, and annually. Your accountant should design reports or memos so that these critical facts are available to you.

Graphs, charts, and other visual means of reporting financial data should be a regular part of your financial reports. Graphs show trends and projections effectively. Focus on the year-to-date amounts as compared to budget, rather than just the current-month amount. Columns for "actual," "budget," and "difference" on your expense reports are helpful. Comparisons to the prior-year amounts may also provide useful information for decision making. Experience indicates that at any one time most of us can absorb up to ten critical facts. To prevent mental overload and enhance clean decision making, you should evaluate reports for simplicity and accuracy. You want information to enlighten you. You don't want data to paralyze you.

Financial ratio analysis of liquidity, profitability, and efficiency provides the principal tools for analyzing and controlling the flow of funds within an enterprise. It can tell you if your business is overstretching itself. Some common ratios follow.

1. Current ratio.   Company's ability to pay current liabilities:

$$\frac{\text{Current assets}}{\text{Current liabilities}} =$$

A current ratio of 2.00 and above is considered, in general financial circles, as a symptom of healthy, sound current accounts management. If the current ratio is 1.00, the current assets equals the current liabilities. At such a ratio, the business is merely paying off its current liabilities with its current assets and there is no working capital left over for expansion of the business or a reserve for future expenses.

2. Profitability ratio.   Company's ability to make a profit:

$$\frac{\text{Net profit after taxes}}{\text{Net worth}} =$$

There must be a financial justification for going into or owning a business. If the net profits after taxes are less than the wages that can be earned in alternative employment or the benefits are less than can be earned in an alternative capital investment, then the business is a failure.

3. Leverage ratio. Company's ability to meet long- and short-term debts:

$$\frac{\text{Total debt}}{\text{Total assets}} = \quad ; \frac{\text{Total debt}}{\text{Net worth}} =$$

A constant ratio of 2.00 or less is desirable. At that ratio, the owners of the business are providing one-third of the funds used in the operation of the business. A ratio close to zero is undesirable, because it shows that the investor is unwilling to assume some level of financial risk and that the enterprise isn't using its sources of funds to optimal advantage. A ratio value higher than 4.00 is undesirable because it shows that the business is subject to insolvency if it should suffer a slight setback. If external sources of funds are misused (over-leveraged), the business could suffer insolvency and bankruptcy.

4. Acid test. Ability of liquid assets to cover current liabilities:

$$\frac{\text{Cash, marketable securities, and receivables}}{\text{Current liabilities}} =$$

The acid or quick test will show if you can cover your short-term debts. The ratio should never fall below 1.00.

Too many investors think that extra cash will solve every problem. But good management—not money—is the key to whether your enterprise will succeed or perish. Here are five common managerial errors:

1. Bad advice
2. Reckless spending
3. Rents too low
4. Failure to plan
5. Underinsurance (covered in the next chapter)

SUMMARY

Here are some of the main points from this chapter:

1. Keep accurate records.
2. Save physical documentation of expenses.
3. Assume the duties of a financial controller.
4. Maintain files of nonfinancial rental information.
5. Cash, not equity nor leases, pays the bills.

6

INSURANCE

"Observe always that everything is the result of change and get used to thinking that there is nothing nature loves so well as to change existing forms." Emperor Marcus Aurelius wrote that nineteen-hundred years ago, but the principle still is true. Change is the one constant of life. As a prudent landlord, you will set up reserves to handle slow changes, such as decay and wear. But you must protect yourself against sudden change. That's the purpose of insurance, and the subject of this chapter.

TITLE INSURANCE

Once you and your lender have decided to do business, your lender will make sure that no one will jeopardize his right to a first lien on the property as long as you owe him money. Title insurance firms will provide this security in the form of insurance. It protects against loss and covers legal expenses required to defend against adverse claims.

Title insurance is generally needed for anybody who is buying real estate. In fact, the FHA won't insure a mortgage unless there is title insurance on the property. Banks often refuse to extend a mortgage unless there is title insurance. You will pay a one-time premium at the time of closing. Insuring the title doesn't mean it can never be lost. It does mean that if you lose title you will be compensated, usually for the price of the property.

In some states, it's customary for the seller to give a warranty of title. It's only as good as the financial condition of the seller. In others, a quitclaim deed may be executed, giving the buyer the rights of the seller. This provides no guarantee that the seller actually possesses a clear title. You must discover the extent and nature of your coverage to make sure you're fully protected.

A title insurance policy specifically insures against any loss resulting from an error or omission in examining the title. It also insures against losses due to "possible defects against a clear title, which would not be revealed by the most thorough title examination." These include:

1. Acts of incompetents, such as the insane or feeble-minded.
2. Acts of minors.
3. Community interest of spouse not exposed by records.
4. Documents void by reason of lack of legal delivery.
5. False court affidavits, as in the settling of an estate.

That's the tip of the iceberg. Hundreds of possible claims could be made against your ownership of the property, including forgery, claims by missing heirs, and vendor claims.

If you own a single-family home, you are already aware of personal property insurance and homeowner's insurance. Since both forms of insurance are applicable to the small income property landlord, they are included in this chapter. Types of insurance may vary according to where you live and what kind of property you own. These sections introduce the subject. Your agent will be able to discuss the types of insurance you specifically need in greater depth.

PERSONAL PROPERTY INSURANCE

Landlords should encourage their tenants to carry adequate personal property insurance. Thousands have lost their belongings to such disasters as hurricanes, fires, and storms. Did they have enough personal property insurance to offset those losses? Almost surely, no.

Many homeowner policies are written so that the dollar amount of coverage on personal property is about 50 percent of the amount on the building. If the home is insured for $60,000, personal property is covered up to $30,000. This may be adequate if a burglar takes only a few of your things or if a fire destroys only a few possessions. But suppose a storm destroys everything. How do you determine whether your personal property coverage is adequate and, if it isn't, how much more you need? There's only one way. Take a detailed, room-by-room inventory of your property, including factual descriptions of the appearance, type, and condition of each item of value. Keep a copy of this inventory in your safety deposit box and with your insurance agent to support any insurance claim you may make later. If the combined value of your personal belongings exceeds the personal property insurance coverage in your homeowner's policy, consider insuring them separately. You may have to insure them separately anyway, because property such as stamp collections and stereo equipment is often classified "high risk" and assigned only nominal coverage unless extra premiums are paid.

If you can, note how much you paid for each item and when it was acquired. Look into replacement cost coverage on personal property. If you don't have this kind of coverage, your personal property losses will be paid for on an actual cash value basis—the cost of replacing them less the depreciation that has taken place since they were new. If you bought a sofa with an estimated useful life of 15 years 10 years ago for $300, its actual cash value would be close to zero. If that same sofa would cost $750 today, the insurance company would pay $250 under an actual cash value policy. Only one-third of the old sofa's useful life remained, so it will pay one-third of its cost at today's prices.

HOMEOWNER'S INSURANCE

As a property owner, you not only have a valuable asset, but you also have new risks of loss and potential liabilities. You must not only protect yourself against the physical loss of your income property. You must protect yourself from liability in the case of a suit for injury. Therefore, you will need to carry fire and extended coverage. You should acquaint yourself with the available coverages and rates about a month before closing. In most cases, you must have bought your insurance before closing. You should name your mortgage lender as the insured. This will be certified in the form of an insurance binder, a form from your insurance company stating the essential facts about your insurance coverage.

The type of insurance you will get will depend on your property's zoning and construction. Most apartment buildings are protected by a commercial business owner's policy. This policy may consist of fire, loss of income, and liability clauses. A deluxe or special version of the policy may cover many more risks, much like the gradations found in homeowner's insurance policies. Homeowner's insurance protects the purchase of a rental house or two-flat in residentially zoned areas. Although the names of the clauses differ with commercial apartment policies, the coverage is essentially the same.

As a rule, a homeowner's policy covers the property against a variety of perils, including fire, lightning, windstorm, tornadoes, explosions, and riots. The "broad form" policy adds to this list such perils as falling objects, weight of ice and snow, and electrical damage to appliances. The more expensive "all-risk" policy covers you against every possible threat to your property, except earthquakes, volcanic eruption, landslides, floods, tidal waves, sewage back-ups, nuclear radiation, war, and some other possibilities.

Basic Form, or HO-1

Eleven risks are covered, including loss by fire, smoke, or lightning, windstorm or hail, explosion, aircraft, vehicles, vandalism, theft, and glass breakage.

Broad Form, or HO-2

This covers 18 risks—all of those in the HO-1 policy, plus damage from ice and snow, accidental water or steam leaks, frozen plumbing, and injury from electrical appliances and wiring.

Comprehensive Form, or HO-3

Probably the most popular homeowner's insurance, the HO-3 covers the 18 risks and all other perils except such disasters as flood, earthquake, war, and nuclear accidents. HO-3 provides "all-risk" type coverage to your home and other structures, unless specifically excluded or limited.

Special Form, or HO-5

This policy gives the homeowner the same broad coverage as the comprehensive form for a dwelling, but cuts costs by covering personal property for the smaller number of perils included in the broad form. Homeowners should buy either the comprehensive or the special form.

Additional Coverages Included in the Homeowner's Policy

1. Property damage. For minor damage, such as a broken window. (It doesn't make sense to make a claim under this provision if the deductible exceeds the damage.)
2. Living expenses. Covers motel or hotel and restaurant meals if your house is damaged and you have to live elsewhere.
3. Debris removal. Pays the reasonable cost for cleanup of property damaged in an insured loss.
4. Removal of property. Coverage is for possessions damaged while being removed from your house to protect them from an insured peril, such as fire.
5. Fire department service charges.

While this coverage seems generous, you should be aware of what a typical policy doesn't cover:

Outdoor swimming pools
Fences or retaining walls
Walks or roadways
Underground pipes
Trees and shrubs
Outdoor signs
Mechanical breakdown, wear and tear, rust, dry rot, inherent defect
Floods, overflows, sewer backups
Vandalism in vacant units beyond a period of 30 days
Faulty design, workmanship, or construction materials

The effect of these and other fine-print exclusions and high deductibles is that you will only be able to make a claim if there is the most obvious catastrophe.

Seek the broadest coverage possible within your budget. Some homeowner's policies are little more than fire-insurance contracts. No homeowner's policy covers flooding. Flood coverage must be obtained separately. Flood insurance is available through the National Flood Insurance Program. It's offered only in communities that have passed and enforce federally approved zoning restrictions on future floodplain development. Your agent can tell you how to buy this coverage.

Fire insurance should cover the premises immediately, certainly no later than closing. It's also necessary to satisfy the lender with an insurance binder to provide coverage from closing until you get the homeowner's policy.

Most standard homeowner's policies will pay the full value of the policy only if that value is 80 percent or more of the replacement value of the house. If coverage is below 80 percent, the maximum payment is limited to the replacement value minus a depreciation charge (usually quite large) based on the age of the house. Most insurers will increase your annual premium to keep up with inflation. All-risk policies are the best policies. They cover nearly everything and take the burden of proof of coverage away from you. These policies make the insurance company prove the risk was excluded from the contract. Look for credits for higher deductibles, particularly percentage deductibles. Look for credits for burglary and fire alarms. Look into firms that pay dividends.

Since insurance is a form of bet, you should only cover what you cannot afford to lose or replace at reasonable costs. The deductible is a dollar amount that the insured party has to pay. It should be equal to the amount you can afford to lose. Deductibles also reduce the amount of premium payments since they exclude small losses that are costly to adjust and that are frequent. Insurance isn't a good device to handle small, frequent losses that you can afford to assume.

Obviously, the more risks you insure your property against, the more your coverage will cost you. Decide realistically which risks are a significant threat to your property. Buy the coverage that is suitable, but don't overinsure by basing your coverage on an inflated appraisal of its value or by including the value of your building site, foundations, or underground pipes and wiring in your valuation. Undercoverage or overcoverage is a sign of poor planning. Get enough insurance to pay off all outstanding bills in case there is damage, accident, or loss.

Your lawyer is a good source of advice on reputable insurance agents. Get estimates for coverage from an independent agent who represents several insurance companies. He will offer a larger menu of coverage alternatives than a direct writer, an insurance salesman who is employed by one particular insurance firm. Ask the previous owner of your property what kinds and amounts of insurance he carried. Use this as a starting point only, for it's more than likely he was underinsured. Also, ask which major additions or improvements, such as a new garage or a new wing, were made since the policy was last reviewed and updated. Fill in your insurance agent on the details and costs of such additions and ask that he revise your coverage. Finally, shop among insurance companies. If you don't have time to shop when you buy your house, do so when it's time to renew your coverage. Rates can vary widely for the same coverage.

LIABILITY INSURANCE

Liability insurance protects you from suits for bodily injury due to negligence or noncompliance with community health and hazard codes. "Reasonable care and nonnegligence" on your part don't constitute a legal defense. "Due care and vigilance" are required.

Traditionally, the landlord had limited liability for injury or damage that occurred on the rented premises. Because the landlord has no general duty to repair premises that are in the tenant's possession, he cannot be held liable for damage resulting from the condition of the premises.

Both the landlord and tenant have a duty of reasonable care to people in the portion of the leased premises under their control. The landlord must inform the tenant of concealed defects that could endanger the tenant. If he fails to do so and the tenant is injured, the landlord is liable. This liability for concealed defects extends to nontenants as well.

Usually, leases provide that the landlord isn't liable for personal injuries or property damage. So far as third persons are concerned, such provisions have no effect. Such third persons haven't signed the lease and aren't bound by its provisions.

Where the landlord retains control over common areas, such as hallways, stairways, porches, sidewalks, and elevators, he must keep such parts of the building in a safe condition. If he fails to do so, he is liable for injuries caused. However, there are also cases where the tenant is also liable if some third person is injured. In those cases, the third person may sue either the landlord or the tenant or both.

If the landlord has made no agreement to repair and the premises were in safe condition when rented, and if the defective portion is in the exclusive possession of the tenant, the tenant is liable. Suppose the tenant on an upper floor leaves the water running and the water drips through the ceiling and ruins rugs in the apartment beneath. The landlord isn't liable, since the tenant is in exclusive possession of his apartment.

Despite the theoretical rights of the parties, in any suit for personal injuries it's unlikely a jury will give a landlord sympathetic consideration. Also, people sometimes make a business of instituting litigation against property owners on unfounded claims of injuries. Even a successful defense of such litigation will prove costly. Hence, the prudent owner should protect himself by taking out owner, landlord, and tenant's public liability insurance. OL&T provides coverage against liability for accidents arising from ownership, occupation, or use of the premises. This policy doesn't cover employees.

Insurance provides compensation to victims of a calamity. But it rarely provides full compensation. How can you compensate for the loss of years of family letters and photographs in a fire? How can an insurance firm make up for the terror you feel as a victim to a home invasion? Insurance is also an after-the-fact remedy. For example, most brokers take out errors and omissions insurance to protect them from a lawsuit for misrepresentation. But, if the broker loses the lawsuit, the insurance firm may decline to renew this insurance. Insurance may provide financial compensation in the event of harm. But it won't protect you from harm. The following sections are appropriate to our discussion on insurance, as preventive care is indeed the best insurance.

DEALING WITH FIRE

Smoke Detectors

How strange it is that a landlord will spend thousands of dollars on landscaping but nothing on essential protective devices, such as smoke detectors. (Some landlords provide smoke detectors, but complain with some justification that tenants steal the batteries. If that's the case, the detectors should be electrically powered. Also, the landlord must educate the tenants as to the importance of having smoke detectors that work.)

Smoke is the greatest danger in a fire. Most people die because smoke either blocks their escape or disables them. Not only are gases from a fire poisonous, but the stress of an emergency makes you breathe harder, so you take in more of these gases. Some gases affect young children and old people more quickly than healthy adults.

When someone dies from smoke inhalation, it means carbon monoxide suffocated the victim. Fire produces carbon monoxide and that prevents red blood cells from picking up oxygen. Oxygen gets to the lungs, but it can't get into the blood cells. Carbon monoxide sometimes kills before the victim sees flames or smells smoke. The insidious thing about carbon monoxide poisoning is that you don't even realize you're being overcome. You get drowsy and go to sleep.

Another product of fire can be cyanide, often created when flame meets plastic. Like carbon monoxide, cyanide can suffocate. In fires, the amount of carbon monoxide is always overwhelming and much more important than cyanide. Carbon monoxide is the killing agent.

Smoke detectors are important, because people die in their beds without being awakened by the fire. You may think you will awake as the house fills with smoke. But the facts prove differently. A smoldering couch gives off sufficient smoke, heat, and other gases to fill the house silently and quickly so that no one escapes. But it need not be. Special devices can detect small amounts of smoke and sound an alarm while there's still time. Many types of smoke detectors are good, reliable, and inexpensive. Underwriter's Laboratories (UL) or Factory Mutual (FM) tests and labels them. The UL or FM label assures you that the device has been tested for sensitivity and reliability.

Smoke detectors typically operate either on a photoelectric or an ionization principle. Heat detectors are also available. Because they sense the temperature of the fire after it has already reached the flaming stage, they won't give early enough warning. But heat detectors can be used to supplement smoke detectors.

Home fire alarms are needed primarily to alert occupants about a fire that starts while they are asleep. Smoke detectors are essential in mobile homes, small apartments, and small houses, which quickly fill with lethal smoke. A home fire alarm system can range from a single smoke detector outside each bedroom to a complete system covering all rooms. Many detectors are available for easy installation in attractive units containing both a detector and a buzzer or alarm. When a large home or an apartment building is to be protected by detectors, you should use a professionally installed electrically supervised system. You can attach as many detectors as you want to the system. When a detector is activated, it sends a signal to a panel. This sounds alarm bells in various parts of the building. Electrical supervision means that if a wire becomes loose or a smoke detector becomes inoperative a signal will sound. Some systems can even call the fire department or perform security functions. Home fire alarm systems vary considerably in complexity and cost.

Household current or batteries operate the single-station smoke detector. These units are easy to install and require only periodic checking.

Where only a partial system is installed, the areas to be considered first for installation are listed next in decreasing order of importance:

1. A smoke detector outside each sleeping area.
2. A smoke detector at the top of the basement stairs.
3. A smoke detector in the living room, family room, or study if the entrance to the room is more than 15 feet from the bedroom's smoke detector.
4. A smoke detector in the bedroom of the person who insists on smoking in bed.
5. Smoke or rate-of-rise heat detectors in other rooms or spaces.

Smoke detectors belong on the ceiling or high on the wall in the hallway outside the bedrooms, in the stairwell, and on the cellar ceiling. Don't install them near windows, doors, or air registers that could impair sensitivity. Don't put detectors in the kitchen. Cooking fumes can falsely trigger them.

The danger of house fires hits a peak in winter as families spend more time indoors and heavy demands are put on heating and wiring.

After the Fire

Fire losses are deductible from your federal income tax. Get receipts and keep records of the money you spend in repairing or replacing damaged property and in covering your living expenses during the recovery period. These records will be used to calculate the casualty loss on your income tax. A refund within 90 days of filing is possible if you file Form 1045, Application for Tentative Refund, at the same time or in the same year as you file your yearly return.

Your insurance will be the most important single component in recovering from a fire loss.

Actual cash value is the basis for most insurance agreements. The insurer agrees to pay for the property you lose at its value on the day of its loss. Personal property, such as furniture, appliances, and personal effects, are generally valued on an actual cash value basis.

The standard homeowner's form covers buildings at replacement cost without deducting for depreciation if you are 80 percent or more insured. If you aren't 80 percent insured, they'll pay the larger of either the actual cash value of the damage or the cost to replace the damage times your percentage insured.

Loss adjustment is the process of establishing the value of the damaged property. Parties to this process are the owner or occupant and the insurance company and its representatives. The owner is bound by the insurance contract to prepare an inventory and cooperate in the loss valuation process. The insurance company provides the loss or claim adjuster. An insurance agent may act as the adjuster if the loss is small. The insurer may send an adjuster who is a permanent member of the insurer's staff, or the company may hire an independent adjuster. The amount of your settlement won't affect the independent adjuster's income. The insurance adjuster will monitor and assist in the loss valuation process to arrive at a just, equitable settlement.

The insurer may hire a fire damage service company to provide these five services:

1. Securing the site against further damage.
2. Estimating the cost to repair damage.
3. Packing, transporting, and storing household items.
4. Securing cleaning or repair subcontractors.
5. Storing repaired items until needed.

Coordinate with the insurance adjuster before contracting for any services. You may invade the insurer's area of responsibility. This may leave you with bills to pay that the insurer would have otherwise covered.

A general contractor may need to estimate the cost to repair structural damage. The insurance company may send a contractor to estimate the work. However, you may select and pay your own contractor if you want an independent estimate. Pick a contractor familiar with the insurance company's estimating requirements. These can be detailed. The insurer will require a written, itemized statement of all work to be performed, the cost of the work, and interim and final completion dates. Make sure that work, costs, and dates are spelled out. If there's a delay in rebuilding, the insurer should allow additional living expenses.

The value of the loss will be on an actual cash value or replacement cost basis, depending on your policy. The fire may have destroyed receipts for damaged items. Nonetheless, the insurer and the insured must come to an agreement about the value of the damage. Most policies provide for arbitrating differences in the appraisal of goods. Some policies give the insurer the choice of repairing or replacing an item. Other policies give that option to the owner. In either case, after the insurer makes settlement, the property belongs to the insurer and the firm may dispose of it for its salvage value.

You will have between 30 to 60 days to submit a proof-of-loss statement to the insurer. This establishes your claim. The insurer has up to 60 days to pay your claim. Some elements of your claim may drag on longer. For instance, the firm will arrange payments with the contractor for reconstruction. Cashing the payment check indicates you agree with that portion of the settlement.

DEALING WITH CRIME

The wilderness has been tamed, but our cities remain asphalt jungles, where millions have to claw to survive each day. Even in town and country, crime has eroded the stability of the community. We live in a time where uncertainty isn't the exception but the rule.

Fear of violent crime seems to have made this nation helpless, incapable of dealing with the sources of its fear. Fear may be one of the factors impeding our ability to cope with crime. That fear is measurable in the ways we're adapting to the new realities—the gun sales, the karate classes, the rush to buy burglarproof locks.

More than 6 million burglaries are committed in houses and apartments each year. Why? It's profitable. Victims lose more than $1 billion each year. It's easy. Thieves often enter through an unlocked door or window. And it's safe. Burglars are seldom caught. If they are caught, they are usually back on the street before long.

You must face reality, and these are the realities. Don't depend on the police, courts, law, and jails to protect you. You must protect yourself. How? There are two steps. The first step is to develop a proper attitude, a tough-minded way of dealing with potential violence, street smarts. It means recognizing that some of the most vicious criminals appear almost angelic. The little girl with the pink ribbons in her hair is on your front step. She's selling Girl Scout cookies, but is she also casing your living room for a break-in? The little boy with the big eyes is break-dancing on your sidewalk. Is he "innocent youth" or a junkie pyromaniac? These kids often show legal erudition beyond their years. They know their "rights" and the flaws, loopholes, and logjams in the system. They know how to exploit not only the system, but also the feelings and sympathy of people of good will who serve the system as jurors and judges. For the property owner, it's one more indignity that goes with the territory. But there are ways to reduce the threat of harm to person and property.

Step 2 is to develop defensive and offensive procedures of dealing with crime. Defensive procedures include the use of lighting, alarms, sound doors and windows, good locks, and proper landscaping to reduce the threat of crime. Offensive procedures include aggressive attempts to reduce gang influence and sponsor neighborhood watch programs.

Let's look at these procedures more closely.

Lighting

Examine the lighting around your building. Is it adequate? Check the stairwells, parking lot, laundry room, and exterior. Burglars like the dark. Keep porches, patios, and yards well lit. Thieves do most of their work at the rear of the house. Spotlights work, but other types of lights can be more economical and just as effective. Check with your police for more lighting suggestions.

Alarms

Alarm systems range in expense and can cost as much as several thousand dollars. Sometimes there's a monthly maintenance charge.

Three types of systems are available:

1. A local alarm rings a bell or flashes lights if an intruder enters your home.
2. A central station or silent alarm rings at another location, such as the police station or security company.
3. An automatic direct-dial alarm activates a tape-recorded message transmitted by telephone to the police.

Combination systems are also available. Smoke detectors can be attached. Make sure the burglar alarm and the smoke alarm have different warning sounds. Consult local law-enforcement officers about the type of alarm that would be best for you. There may be zoning restrictions on particular types of alarms.

Doors

Install solid-core doors with securely attached strikeplates. Exterior-mounted hinges should be pinned. Locks that can be easily forced, such as key locks in door handles and slip-bolt latches, invite burglars.

Watch for loose pins in the hinges. If a door has windows, the glass can be cut or punched out and the pins removed through the opening, letting the door fall from its hinges.

A lock is only as good as what it's attached to. Doors should be solid wood or metal. When screwing into door and window frames, use 2 to $2\frac{1}{2}$-inch screws to reach into the solid wood studs behind the frame.

Drill a peephole with wide-angle lens to let the occupant see who's outside without opening the door. To install, drill a small hole in the door at a child's eye level. Insert the viewer and twist to tighten.

Windows

Burglars don't want to be seen or heard, so they usually won't risk breaking glass to enter a home. Be sure to use whatever locks are already on your windows.

Burglars like sliding glass doors. Don't count on using a broom handle for security. It can be surprisingly easy to dislodge. Get a slide bolt.

Windows can be secured by screwing them shut. Drill a small hole through the interior frame partially into the exterior frame. Insert a sheet metal screw long enough to reach into the exterior frame. For windows frequently opened for ventilation, drill a hole at a downward angle and loosely insert a nail. For casement windows, make sure the existing locking device works properly and remove the crank handle. Board up all basement windows and fill the outside depression with cinderblocks.

Locks

Most locks are installed with economy, not security, in mind. Take a good look at your house and apartment locks. Just because you cannot get in without a key, it doesn't mean the same is true for a burglar. Sometimes a plastic credit card can open a door in seconds.

A deadbolt lock provides the best protection. The lock mechanism slides a strong metal bolt from the door to the frame. The bolt should extend at least 1 inch from the edge of the door. Install deadbolt locks on all exterior doors. The tenant usually pays for these. Don't master-key your lock to management locks. The key might fall into the wrong hands.

For doors that open inward and that have flat exterior sides, install a metal plate over the lock. This will prevent someone from prying the lock open.

Landscaping

Landscaping near doors or windows is perfect camouflage for burglars. Are there large trees near the house? Prune the lower limbs to prevent burglars from climbing into second-floor windows. Trim bushes and vines so that windows are visible to neighbors. Don't install fences that could hide criminals. Keep trellises from windows and roofs.

Landscaping can be an effective deterrent. A small fence or hedge around the edge of your property has the effect of staking out your turf, of making it clear to outsiders that you're possessive of your territory. This barrier is more psychological than physical, but it can provide resistance to criminal incursion. Show that you'll fight for your land, that you care, and chances are good that thieves and vandals will leave you alone.

Fighting Gangs

Gangs attract kids because gangs provide them with companionship and solidarity. They can also serve as a channel for crime—young against old, gang against gang, gang against establishment, gang against property. How do you deal with gangs? Some ideas follow:

1. Remove graffiti from the walls of your buildings as soon as they appear. By doing so you let it be known that your property won't be turned into a gangland war zone. Also, graffiti writers won't engage in their adolescent artistry if they don't have the chance to admire their work.
2. Evict anyone you suspect of dealing with cocaine, heroin, and other controlled substances. The drug and gang cultures feed on each other.
3. Don't be intimidated. Don't back down because of harassment. At the same time, don't provoke or insult.
4. Treat gang members as members of individual families. Get to know their families. Treat them with respect. They may become friends and allies. But don't get sentimental. Many gangsters have casual or no family ties. Also, no matter how decently you treat some people, they behave psychopathically. They're sick. Nothing you can do will change them.

Know Your Neighbors

Organize to improve security in your building and neighborhood. Many large apartment buildings have tenant patrols. They help police by watching for crime. They also provide escort services for vulnerable people. Some police departments will send an officer to meet with residents to discuss home security and ways to monitor their neighborhood. With guidance as to what they can and cannot do, neighbors can form patrols to check on abandoned buildings and vacant homes.

Know your neighbors. Make it a point to be on speaking terms with every person around you. It doesn't matter if your building is large or small. You can never know enough about the people who live there.

You will attract better tenants if you enhance your property's security, perhaps by replacing the antiquated intercom system or by hiring a private guard. Establish a uniform system for verifying tenancy in your complex. Passwords, showing lobby door keys, and identification cards work well. Devise a system for identifying guests, house-sitters, domestic help, and the like.

Insurance Information

If your insurance company refuses to offer you coverage because you live in a high-crime area, apply for a federal crime insurance policy. This comparatively inexpensive insurance, sold by the government in 28 states, will help you replace stolen possessions or repair property damaged in a break-in. Regardless of the number or size of claims you make, it cannot be canceled. To qualify, you must install approved types of locks on outside doors and windows. For more information, call or write the Federal Crime Insurance Program, Federal Insurance Administration, Department of Housing and Urban

Development, P.O. Box 41033, Washington, D.C. 20014, (800) 638-8780. In Washington, D.C., or Maryland call (301) 652-2637.

SUMMARY

Here are some of the main points from this chapter:

1. Title insurance compensates you if you lose your claim to the title.
2. Know what your homeowner's policy excludes from coverage.
3. The landlord has the duty to maintain common areas.
4. Preventive care is the best insurance.
5. Consider federal insurance if you have property in high-crime areas.

7

TAXES

TAX LAW

The United States has basically four separate tax systems: federal, state, county, and municipal. Including the counties and municipalities, there are thousands of tax jurisdictions. Tax laws are complex and confusing. Thus, the potential for error is great. To properly buy, operate, and sell real estate, you must understand some tax law. But the code is a tangle of laws, regulations, intentions, avarice, footnotes, nuances, and exceptions. Not a year goes by without the addition, deletion, or modification of significant real-estate legislation.

The federal tax code is embodied in 10,000 pages of dense legalese that take up 32 feet of shelf space. Even if you could wave a magic wand over it to make sure it never changes again, the CPAs and tax attorneys would still be securely employed. For every line is subject to contradictory interpretation. Therefore, I would be presumptuous to try to condense the complexities of the tax code into a mere chapter. Rather, I'll review the broad concepts and trust you to consult annual IRS guides and a good real estate CPA to fill in the details (see Appendix D).

The following areas of tax law will probably change in the future. Given the pressure to reduce the federal deficit, most changes will be to the detriment of the real-estate investor:

1. Credits
2. Deductions
3. Record-keeping requirements

4. Depreciation rules
5. Selling and exchange rules

Seek competent tax advice. Either about the time you are buying your first rental or certainly before filing your income-tax return, get with a tax advisor who is thoroughly familiar with real estate.

TAX RECORDS

You should keep a file of tax information about your property, containing:

1. Its legal description.
2. History of the tax rate and data about the valuation of land and improvements.
3. Your tax attorney's name, address, and telephone number.
4. Paid tax bills.
5. Correspondence about protests, appeals, and complaints.

Records concerning fixed-assets depreciation and basis changes are also needed.

You will discover the importance of well-kept records when they are challenged in an audit. When it comes to taxes, "documentation" is the word. The IRS doesn't argue with facts, but with fables. This presupposes that you can generate, store, retrieve, and express those facts through an orthodox management-information system. An exact and complete accounting structure will permit you to pay for debts as they reach term, track expenses, and make the allowable tax deductions.

The IRS has strict rules about what kinds of proof it will accept. For example, the tax agent may refuse to accept a canceled check as evidence of an expense. He may also want to see the work order. IRS auditors know they don't have to allow the deduction in question unless the taxpayer can provide proof. There's more to having proof than throwing all your receipts into a box. Retain all income and deduction records, invoices, canceled checks, and financial statements until the statute of limitations expires. That's usually 3 years from the actual filing date of the return or 2 years from the date the tax was paid, which ever is later. The statute of limitations sets a legal time limit on the IRS for conducting audits and also for making adjustments or assessing deficiencies. Likewise, a taxpayer may not claim a refund once the statute has expired. The 3-year limit, however, doesn't apply in unusual cases. These would include omitting 25 percent of your gross income, whereupon the statute is extended to 6 years. In cases involving fraud, the statute is extended indefinitely.

INCOME

It doesn't make sense to refuse income because of the taxes on it. That could only occur where the tax on the additional income exceeded 100 percent. If your marginal tax bracket is 30 percent, no matter how much money you make, you always keep 70 percent of it. But losses reduce your net worth. This reduction always exceeds the reduction in your tax liability. If you're in the 30 percent bracket, losing $10,000 reduces your tax by $3,000. Since you lost $10,000, you're $7,000 worse off that if you didn't have the loss. The point: Never buy real estate solely for its write-offs. The purchase must make economic sense. That is, after the turnaround phase, the property must generate a consistent profit or be able to be sold for a sure profit. In buying property, the prudent investor will make tax avoidance a secondary consideration.

Rents are amounts you get for granting others the use of your real estate. The accounting basis determines when you report them. If you're on a cash basis, report income as of when you get payment. If you're on an accrual basis, report income as of when you're entitled to receive payment. Don't report this income if collection is doubtful. If you have to sue for payment, don't report the income until the litigation has ended in your favor.

Include advance rents as income in the year received regardless of the period covered or whether you're on the cash or accrual basis.

Security deposits shouldn't be included in income when received. Where a security deposit is to be applied as payment of rent for the last year or month of the lease, it's advance rent and must be reported when received.

Payment received for canceling a lease is taxable and must be included in full. It may not be reported in equal installments over the balance of the term of the canceled lease. This is true whether you're a cash or an accrual taxpayer.

If the tenant makes improvements rather than pays rent, you must include the value of these improvements as additional rents. The improvements aren't additional rents if the tenant improves the property voluntarily.

CREDITS

A credit is deducted from the tax on your income. For example, if you're in the 30 percent tax bracket, a $100 deduction will reduce your taxes by $30. But a $100 credit will reduce your taxes by $100.

You should consider two tax credits: the Investment Tax Credit (ITC) and the Rehabilitation Investment Tax Credit (RITC).

The Investment Tax Credit

IRS Sections 7, 8, 28, and 46 authorize the ITC. If you bought equipment during the year that was used to produce rental income, you may reduce your tax by a portion of its cost based on its useful life. Qualifying property includes machinery, equipment, vehicles, furniture, and fixture. Nonqualifying property includes intangible property, real property, and horses. IRC Section 48(a)(1)(b) says eligible property doesn't include "a building and its structural components." But investors own more than just buildings. A significant part of the property that comes with real estate is eligible for the ITC. Also, property that is used in conjunction with real-estate investing, like vehicles and office equipment, is eligible. If you use a car in the rental business, even if it's only part-time, it's eligible for the ITC. You'll have to prorate the credit if the use is part-time. If 50 percent of your use of the car is for business, you only get 50 percent of the credit.

Other eligible property include the following:

1. Office equipment, such as typewriters, calculators, photocopying machines, computers, telephones, answering machines, refrigerators, coffee machines, and cleaning equipment. Reg. Section 1.48-1(c).
2. Furniture for offices, hotels, motels, industrial buildings, and retail buildings, but not apartments. Rev. Rul. 81-133.
3. Hot-water heaters. Rev. Rul. 69-602.
4. Vending machines, including the plumbing and electrical connections associated with the machines. Coin-operated vending machines, like washers and dryers, are considered a separate business. They're eligible for the ITC even if they're in apartment buildings.
5. Tacked-down wall-to-wall carpet in commercial establishments. Rev. Rul 67-349.

The Rehabilitation Investment Tax Credit

ITC Section 48(g) authorizes the RITC. It permits a credit for substantially rehabilitating income-producing real estate. The credit is 15 percent for buildings at least 30 years old, 20 percent for buildings at least 40 years old, and 25 percent for certified historic structures. The 15 and 20 percent credits are available only for rehab work on nonresidential structures. The 25 percent credit applies both to residential and nonresidential historic buildings. Money spent enlarging a property or replacing more than 25 percent of existing external walls isn't eligible.

The rehab must be more than the adjusted basis of the property 2 years prior. In addition to the RITC, you may also recover the cost of the rehab using the Accelerated Cost Recovery System.

To qualify for the 25 percent rehab, a building must be on the National Register. At least a portion must be used for a commercial purpose, such as a small business or a restaurant. There are no exact figures on the number of buildings listed on the National Register, because some entries include entire city districts. Estimates range from 250,000 to 1 million buildings. Most RITC renovations are being done in New England. Rehabilitation projects outnumber new construction projects in at least two states, Massachusetts and Rhode Island.

DEDUCTIONS

Deductions don't shelter income. They are like a discount. If you're in the 30 percent tax bracket, a $100 deductible expense reduces your taxes by $30. Thus, your after-tax cost is actually $70. All ordinary, necessary, and reasonable expenses attributable to rental property are deductible. Some common deductions are discussed next.

Interest

Interest is often the largest deduction. Some taxpayers may be limited to deducting a portion of interest used for personal or investment purposes. Mortage prepayment penalties are deductible as interest deductions.

Maintenance and Repairs

You can deduct maintenance costs connected with the property. Utilities, gardening, and repairs should be itemized and claimed against the rental income. A repair expense includes the cost of•labor, materials, and other items. The repair must be for maintaining the property in operating condition. An expenditure that adds to the value of the property or appreciably prolongs its life isn't deductible. Such an expenditure is a capital charge. The cost of a capital addition must be depreciated over the improvement's useful life. Although the cost will eventually be recovered through depreciation, this isn't as good as a deduction in the year the expense occurred because of the time value of money.

Materials and Supplies

If records are kept on materials and supplies, the deduction is limited to the value actually used during the year. If no record is maintained on consumption, you can deduct the entire amount expended. Records on expenditures must be kept, but careful records of consumption and use of materials and supplies isn't advised.

Taxes

Taxes are deductible as operating expenses when property is held to produce income. The taxes are deductible in the year that they are paid. The property tax must be apportioned between the buyer and seller for the year of sale, even when the buyer pays all the taxes for the year. You can use either your receipts or the IRS table based on gross income to calculate how much you can deduct for sales taxes.

Insurance

Insurance premiums against fire, accident, and theft are generally deductible.

Trips

Trips made to the property are deductible. Anytime you answer a tenant complaint, pick up rent, and make a repair, make note of that trip. List the date, beginning and ending mileage, and purpose of each trip in a notebook.

Casualties

A casualty is the destruction of property resulting from a sudden unexpected event. Examples are fires, storms, earthquakes, and other acts of nature. The progressive deterioration of property isn't a casualty. Damage or loss of home or personal property entitles you to a casualty deduction, but not to the amount of replacement value. You can only claim the lower of either the actual cost or the fair market value immediately preceding that loss. You won't be able to deduct small losses in relation to your gross income.

Fees and Commissions

Fees and commissions for services that produce current benefits are deductible. These include most legal and accounting expenses. The costs of collecting rent and managing property are deductible in the year paid. If the benefit of the service goes beyond 1 year, it must be amortized over the length of the benefit.

Net Losses

To deduct net losses in a certain year, you must have other income. In other words, you can't end up with an overall loss on your tax return. If you can't take full advantage of a loss in 1 year, you can sometimes carry that loss back or forward to offset income in other years.

Home Office

If you use part of your home exclusively and regularly to conduct your real-estate business, you may deduct a part of your total income expense as a home office expense. The amount of deduction for a home office can never exceed the total amount of income derived from your home office.

Some of these deductions have stringent qualifying criteria. Also, the investor may be able to take advantage of other deductions that I haven't listed. For these reasons, an accountant should review your expense ledger to make sure that you can write off as much as you are able. Particularly in the early years of ownership, these deductions and depreciation will virtually eliminate your federal tax burden.

INCENTIVES

Tax incentives, either in the form of tax abatements or freezes on reassessment, are the most common types of public assistance for revitalization projects, usually at the city level. In several states, cities will grant property tax abatements or exemptions up to 25 years. A program in New Orleans includes up to a 20 percent tax deduction for developers creating public open spaces and plazas. In Missouri, the 1949 State Urban Development Corporation Law enabled cities of over 350,000 people to grant a 25-year tax abatement in blighted areas. Improvements aren't taxed during the first 10 years. Taxes during the next 15 years are based on a 50 percent valuation of the developed property.

The 1975 New York State Property Tax Law allows tax abatements for multiple dwellings. Section J-51-2.5 of the Administrative Code and Section 421-a and 489 of the Real Property Tax Law encourage rehabilitation through tax incentives. Under New York's 421 program, 100 percent of the first 2 years of increased assessed valuation is exempt. Under the J-51 program, the tax exemption can last up to 32 years. The maximum annual abatement is $8\frac{1}{3}$ percent of the Certified Reasonable Cost of an eligible improvement and a maximum total abatement of up to 100 percent of the CRC. Most of the eligible improvements are major capital improvements.

The Section 8 Moderate Rehabilitation Program, funded by the Department of Housing and Urban Development but administered locally, provides tax incentives to rehabilitate substandard rental units for low-income families. Even in towns of under 100,000, investors working in specially targeted areas may get tax incentives.

Why do cities provide these incentives? Taxes on income property are often based on income potential rather than market value. Deteriorating buildings may be producing little revenue. In some cases, owners may have stopped paying taxes altogether. Even if 75 percent of potential taxes are forgiven, the building may generate more revenue to the city than was received. Any redevelopment of property that isn't producing tax revenue increases the potential for future revenue, even if a 100 percent abatement is granted for a few years.

We cannot deny that tax incentives have helped revitalize previously depressed areas. The revitalization of Chicago's Lincoln Park, Philadelphia's Market Street East, and Boston's Faneuil Hall waterfront testify to the power of these incentives to spur private energies in concert with public purpose. But don't forget bureaucracy's Golden Rule: "He who has the gold makes the rules." And, when it comes to providing subsidies via tax incentives, the rules and red-tape abound. These rules often make demands on an investor's pocketbook, patience, and sanity in excess of the value of the tax forgiveness. Rules routinely cover what projects and items of work are eligible and time, site, and expenditure requirements. They may require rent control and city zoning and code compliance. The documentation process can be onerous. Application forms, affidavits, letters of completion, legal opinions, and inspection certificates rain upon the unhappy investor. The Section 8 program, for example, has a 12-stage application process. The owner cannot terminate it and successive owners must honor it. Frankly, I see little in Section 8 that would induce me to apply. You should evaluate such programs in light of your resources and interests.

BASIS

The IRS uses the term "basis" to describe the value of an asset for tax purposes. It's used to figure the profit or loss when that asset is sold. For many taxpayers, your depreciable basis in a purchase is your cost (IRC Section 1012).

But it's more than the purchase price. IRS Document 5447 says, "Items which are charged to you at settlement or closing are added to the cost . . . and are part of your original basis. These items include attorney fees, abstract fees, utility connection charges, surveys, transfer taxes, title insurance, and any amounts that may be owed by the seller but which you agreed to pay, such as back taxes."

As you claim depreciation deductions each year, your basis goes down.

But it can go up, too. Additions to your basis occur when you make improvements to the property and when you pay attorney fees for property-tax appeals.

You can add money you spend for improving the property (but not what you spend for normal repairs and maintenance). Blacktopping a gravel driveway, putting a light in the backyard, landscaping, adding a fence, or putting in tennis courts or a swimming pool add to the permanent value of the property. Therefore, they should be included in your cost basis.

If the city assesses you for street improvements, save the bills and canceled checks. Special assessments also are improvements. If you pay a lawyer to get an assessment reduced, you can add his fee to your cost basis.

DEPRECIATION

Depreciation means that a building theoretically loses some of its value each year because of damage from the weather, wear and tear, and newer features of competing buildings. While your building may actually increase in market value, the tax laws assume that its value is decreasing and that it will be worthless at the end of a specified time. Depreciation rarely reflects the actual decline in the market value. But it provides a deduction that cuts down your cost of buying your property.

Buildings erected on the owner's land are depreciable. Paving, private streets, curbs and gutters, railroad spurs, and other improvements that have a limited useful life are also depreciable.

Land isn't depreciable. It hasn't a useful life. Land-preparation costs are nondepreciable, unless the costs are in connection with a depreciable improvement. Landscaping isn't depreciable, unless the shrubbery and trees will have to be destroyed at the end of the life of other improvements. In such a case, the landscaping is depreciable over the same useful life as the other improvements.

Depreciation can be taken on business assets even when they aren't in use, such as a rental dwelling without a tenant. A vacant building awaiting resale isn't depreciable, because it's neither used in the trade or business nor held for the production of income.

Deductions for depreciation offset ordinary income. They reduce the basis of the property. When you sell the property, your gain is the difference between the amount realized and the adjusted basis. This may be subject to a capital-gains tax.

The Accelerated Cost Recovery System (ACRS) replaces the old class life system for property placed in service after 1980. Other depreciation methods continue to apply to property placed in service before 1981, as well as to any property not covered by ACRS. See IRS Publication 577 for details on ACRS recovery periods and other depreciation methods. Because ACRS usually gets changed everytime Congress passes a tax-reform act, I'll mislead you if I elaborate on ACRS as it presently exists.

EXCHANGES

If you plan to sell one piece of property and invest the proceeds in another, you should consider the tax advantages of an exchange. You can trade property without recognizing any gain or loss on the transaction.

The property you get in the deal assumes the cost basis of the property you traded for it. You calculate the original cost less the depreciation you have taken plus the improvements you have made in the years you held the property. That becomes the adjusted cost basis you will use on the new property. It's called a "substantial basis."

A trade is usually more advantageous if your property is now worth more than its original basis. The exchange gives you an equivalent value, but you escape the immediate tax you would incur on the appreciation of value if you sold the old property to buy the new one. If your property is worth less than its basis, you should sell it outright and take the benefit of any deductible loss on your tax return.

The exchange of property often occurs with both or at least one of the properties having an existing mortgage. When an investor is relieved of debt by an exchange and the new debt is less than the old, the difference is treated as a boot. This difference is often referred to as the net liability or net debt.

An exchange of a personal residence for business property doesn't qualify for either the rollover "residence replacement rules" (IRC 1034) or a tax-deferred exchange (IRC 1031). You cannot mix personal with business property and defer the tax on the disposal of your old property. However, if you move out of your house and rent it to tenants, thereby converting it to business property, it can qualify for the tax-deferred exchange.

ASSESSMENT

How to Calculate

Market value is how much the county assessor says your property is worth. The assessment level is the fraction of the market value that is taxed. Assessed valuation is market value times the assessment level percentage. The multiplier or equalizer is a number set by the state, designed to make assessments uniform statewide at a percentage of market value. Equalized assessed valuation is the assessed valuation times the multiplier.

Exemptions, if granted, can lower your equalized valuation. They are based on the age of the homeowner, homesteading, and property improvements. The adjusted equalized valuation is the equalized valuation reduced by exemptions.

The tax rate is the amount you pay for each $100 of adjusted equalized valuation. The total tax bill reflects the amount of money local governments serving an area expect to raise through property taxes. Those taxing agencies include city or suburban governments, county governments, county hospitals, forest reserves, school and college districts, the sanitary district, and park districts.

How to Protest

You cannot do much about your tax rate. But you can challenge your assessment. You must either show that your property is overvalued or that the assessment is higher than on comparable property in the same area.

Ask for a reduction just before making necessary repairs of damages that have lowered its value, if local tax records err in description by overstating size or income, or if net income drops due to factors beyond your control. If you doubt that your property is worth as much as your assessment notice says it is, or if you learn neighbors with comparable structures have been given lower values, you should complain.

Get initial advice from your township assessor. Fill out the complaint form. Bring your purchase contract and closing statement if you bought the property recently, photographs of your property in relation to others, and a recent appraisal. Depending on local law, sometimes the complaint must be filed within a certain time period, say within 20 days of your reassessment.

You'll be notified by mail of the results of your complaint. If the complaint is rejected, the letter will explain how to appeal.

TAX SHELTERS

To most Americans, their only tax shelter is the one they live in. They can deduct their mortgage interest and property tax. In fact, that's a poor shelter in that you would pay $70 for $30 of tax benefit, if you're in the 30 percent bracket. But to those who can afford the price of getting in, tax shelters can buy anything from Holstein cattle to roadside billboards. Tax shelters divide into two types. Tax credits figure in such deals as alternative energy, leasing, lithographs, motion pictures, and the like. Energy, investment, and job tax credits are used to compound the tax deduction the investor can write off. Deductions are the second type. For a relatively small investment, often much of it borrowed, a large tax deduction is generated. For example, you might put up $20,000 or 20 percent of a $100,000 real-estate deal and borrow the rest. The law then allows claims for depreciation, tax credits, and everything else associated with the $100,000 investment. Also deductible is the interest on the borrowed money. In the end, a $20,000 stake could result in write-offs of possibly $90,000. For a person in the 30 percent tax bracket, that means a tax saving of $30,000.

Although laws affecting shelters are changing, the government will continue to encourage landlording through tax incentives. Tax shelters are designed to be subsidized investments. If you look at a shelter from the viewpoint of tax evasion, you'll risk losing not only your original stake. You'll face the threat that the IRS will disallow your deductions. They'll force you to pay the unpaid taxes plus penalties.

The investor who knows tax law and itemizes carefully can shelter some of his income. You can offset ordinary income with paper losses. Expenses for improvements, taxes, and upkeep can add up to losses that reduce taxable income. But these expenses not only maintain the value of the property; they improve it.

Depreciation is the deduction that really shelters income. When the depreciation benefits are fully realized, you will have recaptured much of your original investment through write-offs. When you sell the property, the profits are taxed at a favorable capital-gains rate. By generating paper losses, you can shield your cash from the full bite of the IRS. The trick is to cover your ledger with more black than red ink. Thus, the main consideration in any tax-sheltered investment must be its economic viability. You cannot go into it with the idea that it can only be a tax loss. Reformers are writing legislation that makes tax-based investments less lucrative. That is the wave of the future.

Middle-income investors are looking at ways of sheltering income against today's oppressive taxes. But shelters aren't for everyone. The lower the tax bracket, the higher the risk. Investors in income-tax brackets below 40 percent shouldn't enter a partnership. Many brokers will sell to you only if you're in the 50 percent bracket and have $100,000 in assets aside from your house and personal possessions. A typical client who goes into a partnership has a net worth of $250,000, exclusive of his home, its furnishings, and his car. Minimum contributions usually range from $10,000 to $150,000.

What has made shelters particularly fetching is that in most instances the investors had to put up only a small amount of their own cash. As a partnership, they often borrowed the rest on a nonrecourse loan, paper for which the partners aren't personally liable. If the notes defaulted, the lender got the property and the investors got their write-offs and had no worry about being sued for left-over debt: Apartment houses and renovating historical buildings are popular, because Congress took no steps to block nonrecourse financing of them. Thus, a shelter participant might raise $1 million from its members and $4 million in nonrecourse loans to convert a run-down building into a federally subsidized apartment at a total cost of $5 million. Although the property could have a useful life of 30 years, the investors may deduct the mostly borrowed cost over 5 years, providing them with $1 million a year in write-offs that they use to cut their taxable income from other sources. When the depreciation benefits are used up, the partners can sell the apartment, often at a profit.

Real estate is the shelter the IRS is most sympathetic to, because it's based on three factors:

1. Leverage is available in real-estate financing, normally greatest in subsidized projects.
2. The investor can deduct construction loan interest and property taxes.
3. The investor can take advantage of accelerated depreciation based on the total cost of the building, not just the limited partner's equity in it.

Nevertheless, the IRS is stepping up audits of partnerships that have generated big losses. You can get a ruling from the IRS on the legality of your proposed investment in a shelter by writing Assistant Commissioner, Internal Revenue Service, 1111 Constitution Avenue, N.W., Washington, D.C. 20224.

AUDITS

Negligence and Fraud

Negligence involves such things as not keeping good records, not paying on time, and so forth. Fraud is the willful evasion of taxes known to be due. When fraud is involved, there's no statute of limitations. The IRS may reexamine any return the taxpayer filed. Their discovery of a single mishandled item can turn a cursory review into a line-by-line examination.

Underpayment of tax must be repaid with interest. A penalty of 0.5 percent of the unpaid tax is added each month, up to a total of 25 percent of the underpayment. The minimum penalty is 50 percent of the underpayment. You can also be assessed fines of $10,000 and prison terms. Some frauds are misdemeanors; others are felonies.

To convict you of fraud, the government must prove that you intentionally tried to "evade or defeat any tax." Except for fraud, the IRS is presumed correct and you must prove they are wrong. Only in fraud cases do the courts return to the familiar "innocent until proven guilty" approach. Conviction of civil fraud requires "clear and convincing evidence." Conviction for criminal fraud requires proof "beyond a reasonable doubt." Less than 20 percent of fraud investigations end in convictions. Other cases are dropped, the Justice Department refuses to prosecute, or they end with acquittal or dismissal. When tax advisors try to talk clients out of aggressive tax positions, they often cite fraud and negligence penalties. But convictions for negligence and fraud are rare. The conviction rate for negligence is one-tenth of 1 percent of all returns, and for fraud one ten-thousandth of 1 percent of all returns.

Audit Process

Out of every 1,000 returns, the IRS will audit about 24. But your chances of getting caught in their dragnet climb with your income. Some in the higher brackets, such as doctors and lawyers, or those with high gross income, such as real-estate investors, are resigned to annual audits. Even for people in the highest income brackets, the risk of facing an IRS auditor is one in ten. Thus, the odds are nine-to-one that your return will get through IRS processing without problem.

Each return filed with the IRS is checked for mathematical accuracy. The IRS checks for over a dozen simple errors. Refunds are mailed out where appropriate. Only then are returns graded for audit potential by IRS computers. Each area of each return is graded. A comparison is made against the norms to see how your return lines up against others in similar circumstances. The closer to the averages, the lower your chances of an audit. The first stage of an IRS return examination generally involves the use of the computerized discriminant function system (DIF), which uses mathematical formulas to determine if there's a high probability a return merits change. The IRS has assigned numerical ratings to the size of income, exemptions, and deductions to try to gauge the possibilities of error or deceit. If your return includes an unusually high deduction for, say, moving expenses, the computer will flag it for possible audit.

In the second stage, returns with a high DIF score are sent to classifiers who use a handbook to determine if they merit further IRS action. The handbook gives specific information concerning what the IRS considers inordinate deduction amounts for a taxpayer's income level. It identifies areas of high priority to the IRS such as depreciation recapture. Reasonable income in relation to investments and reasonable deductions and exemptions according to income will normally be accepted without further questions. But apparently insufficient listing of income, claiming of unallowable exemptions, and unreasonable deductions may bring the auditors swooping to check over your books. The IRS frequently challenges these parts on income tax returns:

1. Expensive cars used in business. The IRS disallows depreciation of the full cost of a Mercedes, Rolls, or Seville.
2. Bank deposits. Agents may ask for the source of all deposits, including foreign deposits.
3. Change of address. This may flag the return for an examination if no capital gain is reported on the sale of a former home.
4. Travel and entertainment. These deductions are being scrutinized more carefully than ever.

Finally, returns are selected for audit based on information from informants and on discrepancies in income discovered by matching forms filed with the IRS.

If you get a notice by mail, you're probably in for something less than a full audit. The IRS may question one or two items. The audit may be carried out entirely by mail. The letter may ask you to send in further information about specific items or evidence supporting certain figures in your return. If your explanations don't satisfy the agent, you will get another letter telling you that the claim in question has been disallowed, your tax recomputed, and your bill for additional tax is enclosed. But if you see that you're facing a special agent, you had better terminate the interview politely, answer no questions, and phone your attorney. Special agents investigate possible criminal tax fraud. Revenue agents are concerned with ordinary civil tax questions.

Whoever prepares your return should be present during an audit. Sometimes your CPA can handle the whole audit without you being on hand. Legal representation may also be advisable. There have been cases where a taxpayer turned over papers the IRS agent wasn't entitled to see or gave incorrect explanations of transactions through fallible memory, with disastrous consequences. If the IRS detects heightened anxiety, they may expand their inquiry. Let a friend or counselor intercede if nervousness impairs your ability to present your case. Never let an agent browse casually through your papers and records. It will lead to more questions and may expand the scope of your audit. Answer all questions but don't volunteer information or give rambling answers. A loose tongue may incline the IRS to believe that you could be hiding wrongdoing. They may not want to leave until they feel they've justified their visit.

If an examiner discontinues an audit suddenly, don't celebrate too soon. According to Section 10.19 of the IRS Audit Technique Handbook, "The Manual requires that a revenue agent immediately suspend his investigation, without disclosing to the taxpayer or his representative the reason for his action, when he discovers what he believes to be an indication of fraud."

Appealing

If you're unsuccessful in convincing the agent your return was accurate as filed, you'll be asked to pay additional tax plus interest. If you think you're right, pursue your case. There are at least three levels of appeal. The IRS is generally amenable to compromise at the higher levels. Settle out of court if you can. It's cheaper.

If you don't agree with the proposed change, you may be able to get the agent's surpervisor to reverse the agent's decision. If that doesn't work, your next step is a meeting with the examiner in the IRS Appeals Office. The meeting is relatively informal. It's not conducted as a court of law, although you may bring a lawyer or an accountant if you wish. Still unsatisfied at this point, your next step is to go to court: U.S. Tax Court, Court of Claims, or the District Court. You may represent yourself in tax court, but you'll need a lawyer to go higher. If your claim is less than $5,000, you should make your appeal in Small Tax Court. However, before taking your case to court, you should consider how much time and energy you are expending and whether your claims are likely to stand up. The tax laws are complicated and you will be facing skilled government lawyers.

SUMMARY

Here are some of the main points from this chapter:

1. Retain a competent tax accountant.
2. Don't make write-offs an end in themselves.
3. Take advantage of all possible credits and deductions.
4. Consider local tax-incentive programs.
5. Exchanges and installment sales can reduce tax liability.

8

TENANT MANAGEMENT

PROFESSIONAL MANAGEMENT

Consider hiring a professional management firm to handle administrative functions for a percentage of the rent. Compensation is usually a percentage of the gross monthly rent. The manager may also take 25 percent of every new tenant's first month of rent. Some firms have flat fees, such as $25 a month per unit. Because this arrangement reduces the firm's incentive to collect the rent and keep the place full, it's not as desirable as a fee based on a percentage of the gross. Most percentage rates fall in the 5 to 8 percent range.

Having someone manage your properties is another expense. Trying to manage the property yourself could be more costly.

As a real estate investor, you should develop the confidence to delegate your headaches to others. What are the advantages? First, professional managers will rigidly enforce collections and security disbursements. They've heard all the excuses, they don't have the tendency you may show toward charity, and they have the weight of a large organization behind them to enforce their rules. Second, they will shelter you from emergency calls. If you have a full-time job, you won't have the time to snake a pipe or evict a tenant.

A premise of this book is that you aren't a professional. You have a family, a job, and perhaps other hobbies and sports. You're not expected to be on call like a doctor or a cop. For peace of mind, your tenants should have no contact with you. Contact should be through the management office during normal business hours. If there is an emergency involving property damage, your insurance agents and contractors should carry the ball. Finally, they will introduce an element of objectivity in making decisions about what rent to charge, what people to accept as tenants, and what contracts to use. By shielding you from making more repairs and improvements than can be justified and by making sure rent is collected and vacancies are filled, you'll be more than compensated for the commission. In fact, if rental income after carrying costs, including the mortgage, isn't at least 6 percent, the property is probably overfinanced.

Where do you find a professional real-estate manager? The Yellow Pages will usually have a listing under "Real Estate Management." Real-estate agents may also have a managing sideline. The property management firm is better than an agent, as it usually has more contacts and experience.

If your property is too far away to visit regularly, you can also turn it over to a resident manager you can trust. Perhaps you can find a couple who will manage your complex in exchange for rent and perhaps a small salary. You should check their references and resume thoroughly. Sometimes you can share the cost of management with the owner of another building close to you.

Another way to invest at a distance is to buy passive real estate, such as a shopping center partnership. A net-leased, high-credit store would pay a fixed but guaranteed minimum rent. The tenant may pay additional rent based on the volume of sales. It's responsible for all operating expenses, including maintenance and repairs.

The property manager is the owner's agent. He is authorized to negotiate leases, collect rents, make repairs, keep the premises in a rentable condition, pay taxes and the mortgage, and perform other services.

A contract defines your relationship with the manager. This contract includes a description of the property to be managed, the length of time for the agreement to run, cancellation provisions, the amount of compensation to be paid the manager, and the duties and powers given to him. Such contracts are drawn up for specific minimum periods (usually 1 year) with provisions for renewal. The owner often reserves the right to cancel the agreement by giving the manager adequate notice. Sometimes contracts are set up with a trial period of 3 or 6 months (see Appendix E).

In selecting a management firm, examine these areas. The firm and its principals should have professional credentials, such as the Accredited Management Organization and Certified Property Manager designations given by the Institute of Real Estate Management. It's a plus if some of the firm's associates are licensed real-estate brokers. They can help you appraise your property from the standpoint of income. The firm should have been in business long enough to have established a creditable track record. You should talk with the manager who will be assigned to your property, with his backup, and to the head of the financial department to determine their experience. Find out who will be in charge of your property when the manager goes on vacation or is sick. Also, ask if there's an emergency answering service and what is done when the manager is needed quickly during other than the normal business hours.

Scrutinize the financial area. Make certain the firm has good internal controls for processing payables. The firm should have a purchase-order system and an internal accounting procedure that decides how all funds are held.

Find out who controls these funds and who will sign checks written on the account. Make sure you understand how profits are disbursed. Sometimes the company sends out a check every month. Sometimes the money is held in escrow until the account reaches a certain level. Determine whether the company has its accounting functions done manually or by computer.

Ask for 5 references. The main office should be relatively close to your property, so visits aren't inconvenient. If the firm has other client properties in the vicinity, the manager will probably be a regular visitor.

Don't abdicate your responsibility. Your goal is to make the property self-financing, self-managing, self-supporting. However, you shouldn't be indifferent to how it's doing. Insist on written reports, at least monthly. Monitor the financial and operating expenses, particular reports of repairs and vacancies. Visit the property at least once a year. There's no substitute for being on the scene. If there's bad news, the sooner you learn about it, the better.

The remaining chapter will tell you how to manage the property yourself, if that's what you want to do.

SELECTING TENANTS

Renters can be grouped into two categories: renters by choice and renters by necessity. Renters by choice are likely to stay longer and will cause fewer problems. They will commit money and energy to making their apartments nice homes. In this category, you will find career people, childless couples, and senior citizens. They probably don't need the space of a purchased home and won't move unless you dissatisfy them. The increasing divorce rate will improve the over-30 rental market. Empty-nesters—parents whose kids no longer live at home—may also turn to renting. The most profitable tenants are a couple with no pets or children, and with both people employed and away from home most of the time. Pets and kids cause management problems and increase maintenance costs. You are on track of a high-profit investment if you find a building with most married couples or elderly folk who have lived there for years. Single people can be desirable tenants, especially if they are well established in business or a profession. Because they have money and like entertaining, you can usually count on young professionals to maintain and even improve their apartments. However, wealthy tenants often make correspondingly expensive demands.

Your work is easier when the building is fully rented. Many owners ignore the cost of turnover. There is a correlation between tenant stability and allowances you need to make for vacancies, collection problems, and repairs. The owner who has a vacancy must paint the apartment, clean the oven, range, tile, cabinets, shelves, glass, and so on, and shampoo and perhaps replace the rug. The wear caused by moving also reduces the apartment's value. The paperwork of preparing a lease, setting up files, making a credit check, buying advertising space, and spending time showing the unit to prospects are some-times heavy costs. There's also the loss of rent payments and the expense of paying for utilities during the time the apartment is vacant.

How do you find tenants? Tenant referrals are often desirable. Large corporations may be looking for units for employees in need of housing. Area shopping guides provide a good advertising source. Most prospective tenants look at the paper first when they begin apartment shopping. Bulletin boards in grocery stores, public laundries, shopping centers, churches, universities, and company dining halls are also sources of free advertising. If the apartment is located on a busy street, an "Apartment for Rent" sign coupled with a one-page description of the unit and lease terms is an effective draw.

Advertising requires care. It's easy to waste funds on poorly directed advertising. Advertising should entice people to enquire about the unit and screen out people who aren't qualified to rent. The wording is important. The ad or sign should tell enough about the unit to appeal to interested tenants, but it shouldn't go into every detail. You may miss the chance to do some selling. The ad should have these components:

Elements	Example
Title	APARTMENT FOR RENT
Location	Apt. 2, 30 Maple Street, Evanston
Size	Two bedroom
Rent	$300/month
Terms	Utilites not included/1 month security
Optional description	Just rehabbed! New carpeting!
Contact	Call 123–4567

Investigate the applicant's character and background carefully. A bad tenant could drive out good tenants and may mean property damage and lit-igation. It's better to keep the unit vacant than fill it with someone unreliable. These factors are of major importance in tenant selection: stability, house-keeping ability, number and ages of children, and life-style. You should check the applicant's previous place of residence. His length of time at that address and reason for moving may suggest a pattern. Is this a person who moves every few months as an alternative to cleaning his closets? Reject any applicant who doesn't have a steady job, bank account, telephone, or references. Reject him if he has stayed less than 1 year at several previous addresses, hasn't paid his bills on time, doesn't have a weekly income at least equal to the monthly rent, or has been troublesome to managers of other apartments.

Tenants who have employers who are willing to attach the tenant's wages are desirable. You will never have trouble collecting the rent.

The tenant's previous landlord is often an unreliable reference. If the tenant was bad, his landlord will canonize the tenant just to get rid of him.

You should require a signed application for a lease, accompanied by a deposit, to allow time for investigation. The lease is signed later. Don't cash the deposit check until the tenant has signed the lease. If you need to make a refund, you don't have to worry about his check bouncing.

Note in a formal statement the current condition of the apartment. List broken windows, torn carpet, damaged furniture. Beside each item, note if and when you will fix it. This protects the tenant from paying for damage done by a previous renter. It also protects the landlord against tenants who claim the damage they have done to the apartment was done before they moved in. A list signed by both the landlord and the tenant when the apartment is rented prevents misunderstandings later. Some landlords charge the new tenant a nonrefundable cleaning fee to prepare his apartment for occupancy.

Contrary to what some applicants may believe, you are not obligated to let him rent your apartment just because he needs the apartment and he can pay the first month's rent. Some refusals to rent are legal. For example, the size of the family may be too large for the apartment. Some states prohibit discrimination against families with children, but children cause damage. Most states will let you put a cap on how many people you can have in your apartment and will let you ask for extra security and rent for more tenants in the unit. A ceiling of two people for a one bedroom or three people for a two bedroom usually assures that your apartment won't be overrun by juvenile vandals. Your apartment will turn into a slum in short order if you let two or three families squeeze into a single unit.

Ability to pay is another legal ground for refusing to rent. You may check references and credit rating and decide that the applicant may be unable to pay the rent. Family size and income are related to each other. You're not running a charity. Sentimental landlords soon go out of business.

It's illegal, however, for you to refuse to rent because of race, color, national origin or ancestry, sex, religion, or physical or mental handicap. Different laws protect the tenant from these forms of discrimination. Some allow him to sue to get an apartment, while others punish the person who discriminates.

In some cases, a landlord will admit he discriminates by saying, "I don't rent to single women" or "I don't rent to families." Usually, however, a landlord advertises an apartment but says it's already rented when the applicant shows up to see it, delays in acting on the tenant's application and then says someone else has been accepted, or imposes conditions on renting to the tenant but not to other persons. This list is only an illustration, and there may be valid reasons for each of these actions in a specific situation.

On economic grounds, arbitrary discrimination is self-defeating because it restricts you from pools of potentially desirable tenants. As long as they pay the rent and keep up the property, I will rent to anyone.

Two federal laws protect tenants against racial discrimination in renting apartments. Under the Civil Rights Act of 1866, if the tenant can prove discrimination, the court can order the landlord to pay him damages and rent to him either the apartment or a similar one. Title VIII of the Civil Rights Act of 1964 prohibits racial discrimination and discrimination on the basis of religion, sex, and national origin. It doesn't apply to owner-occupied buildings of four units or less if discriminatory advertising isn't used. In other words, if you own a duplex and live in one unit, an applicant couldn't sue you under Title VIII. Title VIII also provides that applicants may file a complaint with HUD, as well as filing their own lawsuit. If HUD's investigation establishes you have discriminated against the applicant, you may be required to rent the apartment to him, pay him damages, and agree not to discriminate against anyone else. If the tenant thinks a landlord has discriminated against him on the basis of origin, ancestry, or religion, he can pursue the same remedies pursued under race discrimination. He couldn't bring suit under the Civil Rights Act of 1866 because that law prohibits only racial discrimination. If the tenant believes the landlord has discriminated against him on the basis of sex or physical or mental handicap, he can sue for damages under Title VIII.

Some state laws also prohibit discrimination in rentals on the basis of marital state. They may also make it illegal for an owner to require that a prospective tenant have no children living with the family as a condition for renting the apartment.

THE SECURITY DEPOSIT

A security deposit is advance payment that gives the landlord assurance that the tenant will abide by the rental agreement. The tenant puts up this money as an advance against any damage. It's to ensure that the tenant will leave the apartment in the same condition he found it. You can withold part or all of the deposit if there is damage or if the unit needs cleaning beyond "reasonable wear and tear." You shouldn't charge the tenant for routine maintenance.

The deposit also serves as a financial reference. If he cannot afford to pay you the security, he won't be able to afford your apartment.

Collecting security deposits requires more bookkeeping, but it's well worth any inconvenience. Without a deposit, you're vulnerable to loss. Loss includes material damage and lost rent. The landlord generally isn't responsible for the tenant's bills, such as unpaid utility bills.

Damages charged against security deposits are generally in kitchens and bathrooms. They consist of missing cabinet doors, burned or stained cabinet tops, broken bathroom mirrors, and broken light fixtures. An apartment usually has to be cleaned up. Although vacancy rates are low, tenants still demand extensive maintenance services before they move in. The unit often needs to be repainted or recarpeted. And it has to be advertised and shown before the cash flow becomes positive again. A damaged rental unit often costs the equivalent of 3 month's rent before it can be rented again. The result of this is increased selectivity among landlords as to their tenants. Future tenants will have to post higher deposits, have longer lists of references, and be willing to put up with more red tape before renting.

Most landlords ask for a security deposit equal to 1 month's rent. In many areas, there's no legal limit on the amount that can be asked. In view of the damages some tenants make, a security deposit, the first month's rent, and the last month's rent is desirable. Most tenants don't have this kind of money. Sometimes, you can arrange to collect the full deposit over a period of 2 or 3 months. If you decide to allow pets, you should set a minimum, nonrefundable deposit of $100 to take care of damage to carpets and draperies. Birds, fish, and a neutered cat usually provide no trouble, but you should flatly prohibit dogs in an apartment. They're often noisy, dirty, destructive, and dangerous.

Write out a separate receipt for the deposit and credit it to the person who paid it. If you don't do this, you may find yourself in a fight over who gets the deposit when roommates separate.

Deposit the security in a collective savings account. Don't use it to pay bills, to invest, or to maintain the property. In some states, landlords are required to pay interest on the deposit. For example, Illinois requires landlords of apartment buildings with 25 or more units (other than public housing) to pay 5 percent interest on security deposits held for more than 6 months. The landlord doesn't have to pay this interest if the tenant is in default under a provision of the lease.

The law isn't always clear as to the proper disposition of a deposit upon a sale of the property. To avoid any personal liability in such a case, the landlord should provide in the lease that on the sale of the premises he may turn over the deposit to the buyer. This relieves the landlord of personal liability to the tenant once he has sold the property.

When renewing a lease at a higher rent, most landlords ask the tenants to pay an additional amount on the security deposit to bring it up to the level of 1 month's rent. This practice is legal. If the tenant has paid his rent on time and has caused no trouble, you may decide to waive this increase.

When tenants sign a lease, they should be given written instructions, such as the following on what must be done when they vacate a unit. They should also be told what they will be charged for things left undone.

RELEASE OF SECURITY DEPOSIT IS SUBJECT
TO THE FOLLOWING PROVISIONS

1. Full term of lease has expired and all provisions herein complied with.
2. Entire apartment, including range, oven, refrigerator, bathroom, closets, cabinets, windows, carpet, balcony, and so on, cleaned.
3. No damage to apartment beyond normal wear and tear.
4. No unpaid late charges or delinquent rents.

5. Forwarding address left with management.
6. No indentations or scratches in wood or resilient floor caused by furniture or other means. Floor must be restored to the original condition if tack-down or wall-to-wall carpeting was installed by lessee.
7. No wallcoverings, stickers, scratches, or large holes on walls.
8. All keys, including those from mailboxes, must be returned.
9. All debris, rubbish, and discards to be placed in proper containers in designated areas.
10. All building-owned carpeting must be professionally cleaned. Tenant must provide manager with receipt upon checkout.

If lessee does not comply with prerequisite conditions, lessee will be charged the current rates lessor is paying to have items repaired or cleaned. The cost of labor and materials for cleaning, repairs, removals, and replacements, where applicable, or rent loss due to necessary repair time, and numerous charges based on actual damages will be deducted from the security deposit.

MINIMUM CHARGES

A. Cleaning
  1. Trash removal $10/hour
  2. Kitchen
    a. Stove $25
    b. Refrigerator $15
    c. Cabinets and countertops $15
    d. Floor $15
    e. Walls $15
  3. Bathroom
    a. Toilet $10
    b. Shower and tub $20
    c. Medicine cabinet $10
    d. Vanity $ 5
    e. Floor $ 5
  4. Closets $10
  5. Windows $5 each
  6. Floors
    a. Vacuum $5
    b. Tile cleaning
      (1) 1 Bedroom $40
      (2) 2 Bedrooms $50
    c. Carpet cleaning
      (1) 1 Bedroom $35
      (2) 2 Bedrooms $45
  7. Excessive cleaning $10/hour
B. Decorating
  1. Patching holes: $\frac{1}{2}$ inch or larger $10 each
  2. Painting, double coating $10 each wall
  3. Removal of wall covering $16/hour

C. Maintenance
    1. Materials plus labor $16/hour
    2. Light bulb replacement $ 1 each

Some courts reject minimal charges on the grounds that you must document the actual loss with invoices and receipts. Your claim will be stronger if you include the Release of Security and Minimal Charges forms as part of the lease. According to contract law, contracts consist of offer, acceptance, and consideration, all components being necessary to its validity. If you simply mail the security deposit information sheet to the tenant a month before he leaves and the tenant has not indicated his agreement with those terms, the court could decide that a contract doesn't exist. For the same reason, you should have the tenant acknowledge any other rules that you wish to enforce in the future or include a clause that he will accept all other rules that you want him to obey in the future before he signs the lease, not after.

Under most circumstances, you should require that the tenant forfeit his security deposit. If he's been in the house for at least a few months, he should by all means give up the deposit. After all, you will have to paint the place again and advertise for new tenants.

In many states, the law concerning security deposits has been put into statutes. These vary widely. They generally require the landlord to return the deposit to the tenant within a certain time or to account for a claim of the deposit or face specified penalties.

Landlords who want to retain the deposit must usually provide the tenant with a statement itemizing the reasons for retention. These reasons include nonpayment of rent or other bills, damage to property, moving without notice, or breach of other conditions. In Illinois, in any building with ten or more apartments, the landlord has 30 days to legally claim the use of any security deposit for the repair of a vacated apartment. He must have sent the tenant an itemized statement of any claimed damage and an estimate or paid receipts for all repairs. Then, within the following 30 days, paid receipts not previously supplied must be given to the tenant. If you fail to provide a written statement, you may lose your right to withhold any portion of his deposit. The court may impose other penalties.

You are entitled to inspect the tenant's apartment before refunding the deposit. At that time, a list should be made and signed by both of you showing the condition of the apartment. This will help eliminate any disagreement over damages.

Sometimes, tenants "live out" a security deposit instead of paying the last month's rent. Unless you have agreed to this, this practice is illegal. The landlord has the right to require the tenant to pay rent until he actually moves out, because the purpose of the deposit is to cover damages caused by him while occupying the premises.

Some landlords refund the deposit in person on the day the tenant vacates the unit. It's better to get the tenant to give you a forwarding address and mail him the deposit. By doing this, you will avoid a scene if the tenant disagrees with your judgment. Many tenants have a higher estimate of their housekeeping abilities than is warranted.

How do you charge for damages or collect from a tenant who uses the deposit as the last month's rent? If damages are under $100, it usually doesn't pay to litigate. Most landlords don't collect. In a typical case, the deposit that was illegally used was $300, the cause was settled for $150, and the landlord eventually got $75.

THE LEASE

A lease is both a contract and a conveyance. It's a contract by the tenant to pay rent to the landlord and usually contains many promises by both the tenant and landlord. The landlord conveys to the tenant the right to occupy the property for the term specified in the lease.

If the contract provides for a specific number of months, it's known as a lease. If it's on a month-to-month basis without specifying any length of time, it's a rental agreement. Tenants usually don't like month-to-month agreements because the landlord can raise the rent and evict on short notice. However, a rental agreement doesn't give the owner the assurance of continuous occupancy. This may be important if tenants are scarce. As a practical matter, if someone breaks a lease by moving out, the only way you can collect is by going into small-claims court month by month. The rent is due only as the month runs out.

A month-to-month cannot be terminated except by giving notice. The landlord cannot evict the tenant unless he first gives the tenant the notice required by law. The tenant continues to be liable for rent unless he gives the landlord the required notice. In many states, a month's notice is required, but this period varies.

When a written lease for a fixed term expires the landlord can renew it or not renew it as he pleases. However, the landlord cannot refuse to renew the tenant's lease because of his race, creed, color, national origin, sex, or marital status. The landlord also cannot refuse to renew his lease because the tenant made a good-faith complaint to a government agency concerning a building code or health regulation violation.

Don't permit your agent or manager to sign a lease for more than 1 year unless it includes a rent escalation clause.

The lease should include a provision to cover periods of holdover tenancy at a higher rent. When most leases expire, the tenancy converts to a month-to-month occupancy until a new lease is signed or the tenant moves out. Thus, there's little incentive for the tenant to renew.

If a tenant has a written lease for a fixed term, it automatically expires at the end of the term without the landlord having to serve notice on the tenant. However, most landlords notify the tenant a month or so before the end of the lease to see if they want to renew the lease. A letter is sent, notifying the tenant of a rent increase effective 30 days after his receipt of the letter and suggesting that he sign a new lease. When should leases commence? Some landlords prefer a month-to-month tenancy until a particular time in the year, such as January 1, when it switches to a 1-year lease. For low-income tenants, early summer is a good time to start. Energy costs are low and they will be able to absorb a rent increase. If they are unwilling to pay, it will be easier to evict. However, tenants are less likely to move if they have to renew in the middle of the winter.

As a rule, once the tenant has a signed a lease, he is bound to it. But a court won't necessarily enforce some lease clauses. Some common clauses are discussed next.

Additional Agreements

Most leases have a box labeled "Additional Agreements." If you've promised to make specific repairs to the apartment or want to stipulate rules not mentioned in a standard lease, they should be listed in this box. If there isn't enough room, get another sheet of paper and attach it to the lease. This paper should be entitled "Additional Agreements" or "Additional Conditions" and be initialed by both parties. The reason for this is because the law says that, if the tenant has a written lease, your prior oral requirements are unenforceable unless they are restated in the lease or in a rider attached to the lease, which is signed by both parties. Apartment managers often use this box to indicate a "no pets" rule. Formal leases rarely include that stipulation.

Condition of the Apartment

The lease has provisions relating to the condition of the apartment. Sections that list duties of the tenant are often headed "Tenant's Use of Apartment," "Tenant's Upkeep," on "Rules and Regulations." Sections listing the landlord's duties are usually headed "Lessor to Maintain" or "Condition of Apartment."

Most leases have a provision that says the tenant has "examined the apartment, accepts its present physical condition," and agrees that the landlord has made "no promises concerning the physical condition except those specifically set forth in this lease." This clause means that if the landlord has orally promised to make certain repairs but hasn't written it into the lease the tenant cannot enforce it. This clause doesn't relieve the landlord from complying with housing code requirements.

In the absence of a specific agreement in the lease, a landlord has no general duty to make repairs to a unit. This absence of responsibility exists because most leases in the past conveyed rural property to tenants who were expected to repair the buildings included in the leased property. Because the tenant takes control of the premises, he is subjected to the responsibilities as owner and occupier of the property. This would include the duty to make repairs in the occupied areas. The law is changing, expanding the landlord's duty to repair.

However, the landlord has always had the duty to repair those areas over which he retains control. These areas, such as stairs and hallways, must be kept in safe repair.

The tenant has a duty to fix self-occupied areas, but is limited to repairs due to negligence or fault, not wear and tear. His duty isn't generally to repair, but to refrain from waste. Voluntary waste is injury or damage caused by a failure to reasonably care for the premises.

Subletting

Many leases provide that the tenant cannot "sublet the apartment" without the written consent of the landlord and that the landlord can reject the new subtenant "for any reason."

However, the courts have held that, whether or not a tenant has signed a lease with this clause, the landlord cannot arbitrarily reject a suitable subtenant the tenant finds. If a tenant wants to move out of an apartment in the middle of the lease and finds a subtenant with similar financial qualifications, family size, and references, the landlord cannot reject the subtenant.

Lockout Clause

Some leases provide that upon the tenancy's termination the landlord "shall have the full and free license, with or without process of law, to take possession of the apartment and remove the tenant." This clause tries to let you throw the tenant into the street without going to court when you claim that his tenancy is over. Some state courts have declared this type of clause invalid. As a result, if you want to evict, you must file a lawsuit against him and have him served with a complaint and summons.

Fire and Casualty

Most leases have a fire and casualty provision, such as, "If the apartment becomes untenantable by reason of fire, explosion, or other casualty, owner may at his option terminate this lease or repair the apartment within 120 days." This paragraph means that you can wait 4 months before repairing an apartment damaged by fire. What the tenant does during this period is up to him. Local code or state law may override this clause.

Penalty for Not Moving Out

Most leases provide for a penalty for each day the tenant remains in possession after the end of the lease. State law may enforce such clauses. For example, an Illinois statute provides that if the tenant deliberately remains in his apartment after the end of his lease and after his landlord serves him with a written demand to move out, the landlord can sue him for double the rent for the period he continues to live in the apartment.

Payment of Rent After Eviction

Most leases provide that, even if the landlord evicts the tenant during the middle of the lease term, he still has to pay rent for the rest of the lease term. As long as the eviction is legal, courts will enforce such a provision. As a result, if the tenant is evicted, he should offer the landlord a suitable sub-tenant for the rest of the lease term.

Waiver of Termination Notices

Most leases provide that the tenant "waives all notices from the landlord whether or not provided by statute, except if waiver is specifically prohibited by statute." If the tenant signed a lease with this clause, the landlord wouldn't have to serve him with a 5-day notice for nonpayment of rent or a 10-day notice for violation of a lease provision. The tenant has waived his right to get these notices.

The Exculpatory Clause

Some leases provide a clause like this: "Neither owner nor owner's agents shall be liable to the tenant for damage to or loss of property." This clause tries to relieve the landlord from being responsible to the tenant for damages. If the court finds that the damage was caused by the landlord's negligence, it won't enforce this law.

Confession of Judgment

Some leases have a clause that says the tenant "authorizes any attorney to appear in court and waives the tenant's right to notice and trial by jury and to confess judgment in favor of the landlord for any rent due." This clause lets the landlord go to court without first telling the tenant and admit on his behalf that a judgment for rent should be entered against him.

Most courts won't enforce a confession of judgment clause.

Abandonment

Some leases provide that if the tenant has been absent from the apartment for, say, 10 days without paying rent and if the landlord has reason to believe that the tenant has "vacated the apartment with no intent to gain residence therein," the tenant will be treated as having abandoned the apartment and his property in it. Title to such property will pass to the landlord, and he may enter the apartment "without due process of law" to evict the tenant.

This clause tries to let you evict a tenant and seize his property without proving in court that the tenant has actually abandoned the apartment. It may be unenforceable.

Waiver of Jury Trial

A clause that tries to take away a residential tenant's right to a jury trial in an eviction action is unenforceable in most states.

Rules and Regulations

Most leases include a set of rules and regulations, such as no waterbeds, no space heaters, or no pets. As long as these provisions aren't petty, they are enforceable. However, a court wouldn't evict for putting a tack in the wall.

Use of the Apartment

Most leases provide that the apartment will be occupied solely as a residence for the tenant's family and that the tenant must do nothing to injure the property or to disturb his neighbors. These clauses are enforceable. A prohibition against the tenant doing anything to "damage the reputation of the building" may be unenforceable because the language is vague.

Alterations

Lease provisions prohibiting the tenant from making alterations or installing major appliances without the landlord's permission are generally enforceable, as are clauses that provide that alterations and additions (including locks and carpeting) shall remain as part of the apartment unless the landlord agrees otherwise. The results could be disastrous if the tenant installs a washing machine on the second floor of your duplex without your permission.

Attorney's Fees

In the absence of an agreement, a tenant isn't obligated to pay a landlord's attorney's fees in enforcing the lease. Many leases, however, have a clause that provides that the tenant must pay the landlord's attorney's fees incurred in enforcing the lease. Courts will only allow a landlord to collect reasonable attorney fees under such a clause.

In any court action against a tenant, make sure that your claim includes not only court costs but legal fees. If you don't explicitly ask to be reimbursed for legal expenses, the award for damages and court costs may not cover your legal fees.

Number of Occupants

Most leases provide that the apartment can be occupied on a regular basis by only the persons listed on the lease or on the lease application. Courts will allow the landlord to evict a tenant who has violated such a provision. An occasional overnight guest is generally allowed.

Local codes may make it illegal for the landlord to allow occupancy unless the apartment meets stated space requirements. For example, these are the requirements of the Chicago Municipal Code:

Floor Area (square feet)	Occupants
125	For each of the first two occupants
100	For each of the next two occupants
75	For each additional occupant

Termination Clause

Courts will enforce a provision that a landlord may terminate the lease simply by serving a 30-day notice on the tenant. Some states require 60 days.

Condominium Conversion

Clauses that violate a tenant's right to receive advance notice of a landlord's intent to convert a building to a condominium are unenforceable.

Although some clauses are applicable everywhere, much of what investors can put into their leases is based on local law and custom. Therefore, novice landlords unfamiliar with the rental market should check with other apartment managers in the area.

There is no such thing as a "standard lease." But every lease should include the following:

1. A complete description of the property the tenant is renting.
2. The exact date the lease will expire.
3. The amount of rent due each month.

4. The date the rent is due. If it's not paid within 5 days of that date, a late charge should be imposed. The late charge should be high enough to discourage late payments. An additional charge should be imposed for each day it's late beyond 5 days.

Optional clauses include the following:

1. The amount of advance payment of rent.
2. The amount of security.
3. A nonrefundable pet deposit.
4. Prohibit assignment or subletting without permission.
5. Use an automatic renewal clause, except for timely notice of termination. The lease should spell out under what terms and conditions the tenant can break it. If his employer transfers him, for example, he should understand his responsibilities.
6. Secure permission to show premises to prospective tenants at reasonable times for 60 days prior to termination date.
7. Use an automatic cost-of-living rent increase tied to the CPI.
8. Limit the number of people allowed to use the apartment.
9. Use a percentage lease on commercial property to permit participation in excess profits of the tenant.
10. Require the tenant to maintain and repair the premises.

If the tenant fails to abide by these requirements, he can be evicted. Unless the lease provides otherwise, you must first serve him a notice specifying the nature of the lease violation.

If you accept a tenant's rent with the knowledge that he has broken a lease provision (such as a ban on pets), a court might conclude that you waived the provision. This rule doesn't apply if the lease has a clause that says the landlord cannot be treated as having waived his right to enforce a lease provision by having failed to enforce it in the past or by having accepted rent with knowledge of the breach. This rule might not apply, also, if you give him a written notice that you will enforce the provision in the future.

Many owners rent their apartments with only an oral understanding. They are afraid that written agreements would give tenants more rights or that they will scare away good tenants. The owner himself has fewer legal rights if there is no written proof of any commitment by either party. A good tenant has nothing to fear by signing a lease. When nothing is in writing, there are more misunderstandings and arguments. Successful operators insist on a signed agreement for each rental unit. It gets new residents off on the right foot by giving them a clear understanding of their obligations.

The law requires that any lease for more than 1 year, to be binding and enforceable, must be in writing. Thus, if you orally agree to rent an apartment for 2 years, the agreement isn't valid. If you change your mind and won't let the tenant into the apartment, he can't do anything about it. If he doesn't move in, you have no remedy against him.

A rental agreement for 1 year or less can be entered into orally. Either side may end a month-to-month tenancy with a 30-day written notice.

Another rule of law says that, if an agreement is put into writing, none of the prior oral agreements are valid unless specifically put into the written agreement. This rule applies to leases. If you promise to paint the tenant's apartment after the tenant moves in but that agreement isn't put into the lease, you're not bound by that promise.

Leases are available in office supply stores, real-estate offices, or apartment associations. These leases may not fit your situation perfectly. If you want to draft your own, make sure your attorney checks every word afterward. Your lease will be legal and enforceable if it contains all the provisions necessary to establish it as a valid contract. Unless you have had a lot of experience drafting contracts, it's risky to try to draft a lease yourself without using one of these preprinted forms as a guide. Most of the fine print in printed lease forms is there to protect the landlord in case there is trouble with the tenant. Don't let a tenant write his own lease. Reject a tenant who returns the lease with modifications. He probably is litigious. A written lease protects the tenant by letting him possess the premises for a fixed term as long as he complies with the lease's requirements. However, most leases have clauses that limit or take away rights the tenants would have if he didn't sign the lease. The courts will enforce most of these clauses.

RIGHTS AND RESPONSIBILITIES

Leases contain certain express and implied covenants, as in the case of all real-estate contracts. The landlord or lessor guarantees the tenant's possession and quiet enjoyment. He promises that the property will be suitable for use. The tenant or lessee guarantees to pay rent, to use the property in the stipulated fashion, and to care for the premises. For business property, the tenant may have to carry insurance. He may also help in paying taxes. Such an agreement in a lease is called a tax-participation clause.

The two sources of law relating to the rights and responsibilities of landlords and tenants are the lease and the city's code. Even if there is no written lease, both parties are bound by the provisions of the building or housing code. The landlord must comply with these provisions even though the tenant's lease says the landlord doesn't have to.

The Tenant's Responsibilities

Tenants must pay rent promptly and regularly, keep the unit in decent and clean order, respect the property of the owner, allow the owner or his agent access for making repairs or improvements, respect the privacy and comfort of neighbors, and follow the terms of the lease.

Chapter 78 of the Municipal Code of Chicago is one section of the ordinances that deals with housing conditions. It spells out the obligations of the landlord and tenant in the condition of a dwelling. Although the following ordinances apply to Chicago, other cities and towns have similar codes.

The code requires the tenant to do the following:

1. Keep the apartment in a clean, sanitary, and safe condition.
2. Keep all plumbing fixtures in the apartment in a clean and sanitary condition, and not abuse them.
3. Not place in the building any material that might cause a fire.
4. Keep out of the apartment any furniture or materials that contain insects or rodents.
5. Dispose of garbage in proper containers, and never leave garbage open in hallways or back porches.
6. Hang or remove screens supplied by the owner unless he has agreed to supply such service.
7. Stay within the housing code rules as to the number of people living in the apartment.

The Landlord's Responsibilities

An owner must keep the premises in good condition and must comply with the local housing code. Here's a list of some of the landlord's obligations under Chicago's code:

1. Heat: You must provide the unit with heat from September 15 to June 1, with the following temperatures:

    65 degrees from 7:30 A.M. to 8:30 A.M.

    68 degrees from 8:30 A.M. to 10:30 P.M.

    63 degrees from 10:30 P.M. to 7:30 A.M.

    You must maintain these temperatures as an average throughout the unit. (The code in areas with warm climates may require the owner to provide the unit with air conditioning.)

2. Hot water: You must provide sinks, bath tubs, and showers with hot water (at least 120 degrees) from 6 A.M. to 10:30 P.M.

3. Toilet: There must be a toilet

4. Public areas: Public areas must be maintained

5. Exterminating: You must keep the building free from rats and reasonably free from insects. You must also exterminate insects and rodents from public areas of your building and from your apartments if two or more are infested

6. Garbage and trash disposal: You must supply and maintain refuse facilities, such as containers

7. Smoke detectors: Multiple dwellings shall have at least one smoke detector per unit and at least one smoke detector at the top of interior stairwells

8. Exterior: The exterior must be maintained

9. Screens: You must provide screens from April 15 to November 15, if the apartment is on the ground floor or floors one to four

10. Lighting of halls and stairways: Halls and stairways must have adequate lighting at all times

11. Exits: Every apartment must have a safe, unobstructed means of exit leading to the ground level

12. Roof: No leaks are permitted in the roof. There must be adequate drainage to prevent rain water from causing dampness in the walls

13. Inside floors, walls, ceilings: Every floor, interior wall, and ceiling must be kept in sound condition and good repair. In addition, "every floor shall be free of loose, warped, protruding, or rotting floor boards" and "all interior walls, ceilings, and interior woodwork shall be free of flaking, peeling, chipped, or loose paint, plaster, or structural material"

14. Poisonous paint: No lead-based paint is allowed anywhere on the building

15. Windows: These must be in good condition, fit reasonably well, and be easily opened

Modern plumbing facilities and the common use of the refrigerator since the 1940s have raised living standards. Health knowledge has taken quantum leaps. For example, modern medicine has greatly reduced the incidence of tuberculosis. Household size has dropped, overcrowding has plummeted. In short, social and technical changes, increased income, government supports, and progressive housing codes have improved living conditions in the past five decades. But some people still live in poor conditions. These advances haven't resolved the dilemma of achieving code compliance:

Tenant: When you make the repairs, I will pay the rent.
Landlord: When you pay the rent, I'll make the repairs

Historically, landlords have always had the right to collect rent while tenants have only slowly gained the right to enforce maintenance standards. The traditional lease relationship between landlord and tenant was derived from feudal property law that reflected an agrarian society where land was the main source of wealth, not buildings. In return for rent for use of the property, the landlord's only obligation was to give the tenant the right to "quiet enjoyment" of the land. To adapt the law to urban conditions, the courts have moved away from the idea of a lease as a conveyance of real property toward acceptance of a lease as a contract. During the past two decades, the rules governing landlord–tenant relations have changed, such as the right of a tenant to sue to correct a violation and the warranty of habitability. The Illinois Supreme Court in the 1972 landmark case of *Spring* v. *Little* established that the law imposes on the landlord an "implied warranty of habitability," whether there is a written lease or not. The landlord warrants to keep the premises in good repair and that a tenant won't be subject to conditions that are dangerous, hazardous, or detrimental to his life, health, or safety, as long as the conditions weren't caused by the tenant's misconduct. Under this case, the court established that if the landlord fails to comply with these health and safety codes, the tenant can withhold all or part of the rent until the premises are put into compliance. The case holds that the landlord cannot evict for nonpayment of rent if rent is being withheld for this reason. The law, however, isn't clear on how much rent the tenant can withhold for each defect.

Some leases have clauses that try to do away with the warranty of habitability and the tenant's right to withhold the rent when the warranty is broken. For instance, the lease might say that the tenant "waives and disclaims any and all warranties, including implied warranties." It may also provide that tenants may not withhold rent when the landlord has failed to make repairs. Courts may not enforce these clauses because they violate public policy as expressed in the building code.

If the tenant withholds his rent to get code violations corrected, you should immediately initiate a nonpayment proceeding. These proceedings differ according to location. In New York, the tenant must answer a dispossess by going to the clerk's office within 5 days. The clerk will give him a tenant-repair-response (TRR) form so that he can request an inspection of the specific condition. The clerk will schedule an inspection by the housing court squad prior to the tenant's first court date. The inspector will prepare a report of violations and submit a copy to the judge to review when the tenant first appears in court.

THE RENT

Structuring the Rent

Rents may be of several types:

1. A flat rate for the period covered.
2. A graded or step-up rental.
3. A percentage rental that depends on the tenant's income.
4. A rental adjusted by reappraisal. Reappraisal leases have seldom worked out, since it's hard to get an appraisal acceptable to both landlord and tenant.

Various combinations of these types of leases may be used. For example, a lease on a business property might provide for a minimum flat rent, plus a percentage of the tenant's gross business receipts, if they exceed a certain stipulated amount.

The gross lease is the most common type of lease. Used for most apartment and house rentals and some commercial rentals, it requires the tenant to pay a monthly rent. The landlord then pays most of the property expenses, such as repairs, property taxes, some utilities, and insurance. The gross lease is practical for office or apartment buildings, because it's virtually impossible to allocate the building's expenses equitably among all renters.

The opposite of the gross lease is the net lease. When a net lease is used, the tenant pays a monthly rent plus the costs of operating the building. Net leases are primarily used on commercial buildings, such as warehouses and supermarkets. There are several varieties of net leases. With the triple net lease, the tenant pays virtually all the property expenses, such as maintenance, insurance, and property taxes. The advantage of this is that it turns your investment into a relatively hands-off undertaking. The tenant pays the bills while you get the profit. The disadvantage is that the tenant gets the write-offs. Your only deduction would be interest and accounting. There are also double net leases, where the tenant pays some of the expenses, such as maintenance and insurance, and the landlord pays the property taxes. Before signing a net lease, make sure both parties understand which expenses they are expected to pay.

A hybrid of the net and gross lease is the discount lease. The tenant earns a rent discount for performing certain minor tasks each month. Suppose the fair market rent for a house is $500. If the landlord offers the tenant a $50 per month discount lease, the tenant only pays $450 monthly. However, the conditions the tenant must meet to earn the discount typically include the following: (1) the rent must be received by the landlord by the first of the month, (2) the tenant must maintain the property and pay for minor repairs up to $50 per month, and (3) the tenant loses the discount for phoning the landlord, except for a major emergency, such as fire or water damage. Some landlords have found that discount leases don't work out. Tenants "forget" to do their chores. I think it's better to use a gross lease and let outside contractors mow the lawn or shovel the snow or do anything else that might have been stipulated in the discount lease.

The percentage lease is primarily used in shopping center rentals. The building's owner shares in the tenant's prosperity if the business does well. If it doesn't do well, the landlord gets only the minimum guaranteed rent. For example, suppose a store in a shopping center rents for $1,000 a month. The landlord might specify that the rent shall be 3 percent of the store's gross monthly income or $1,000 per month, whichever is greater. The store would have to take in a gross of more than $33,000 for the landlord to get a rent above the $1,000 minimum. The argument in favor of percentage leases is that the rental should represent the value of the use of the premises, and the volume of business is the best index of the value of the use of the premises. Therefore, a lease calling for a percentage of gross receipts is the fairest to both parties. However, if the tenant is a poor businessman, he will only get a small volume of business, even if the location is a good one. Also, if the tenant is tempted to chisel on the landlord, litigation may be necessary.

Percentage leases are of different types:

1. Regular percentage form with minimum rent guarantee. This is the simplest and most common form.
2. Straight percentage lease, with no guarantee as to the amount of rent. If this form is used, the following clauses are usually added:
   a. To protect the landlord, a recapture clause gives the landlord the right to cancel the lease after a reasonable time if the tenant's business doesn't come up to expectations.
   b. To protect the tenant, a surrender clause gives the tenant the right to have the lease canceled if business is unsatisfactory.
3. Minimum–maximum form. This provides a minimum guaranteed rental and a fixed maximum that the owner may realize.

The escalation lease is popular with owners of commercial properties, especially office buildings. This lease is basically a gross lease for a fixed time period, such as 10 years, but it contains either a fixed annual rent increase or an annual increase based on an independent index. The consumer price index is the most popular index. For example, if the CPI goes up 4 percent this year, the tenant's rent also escalates by 4 percent. A unique escalation index used in a New York office building is the salary paid to building porters. When their wages go up, office rents escalate.

Raising the Rent

To minimize vacancies, aim for a rent somewhat under, rather than over, the market. Rental units will suffer excessive vacancies if rents exceed the average worker's weekly take-home pay. Another rule of thumb is that an apartment building's total monthly rents should equal about 1.19 percent of the building's sale price. Experts arrive at this figure by reversing the common yardstick that a building's value is about seven times its annual gross rents or ten times its annual net. (Net is the figure you get after subtracting all expenses except debt service from the gross rents.) However, these are crude guides and not iron laws. Your building is unique, and most of your units probably differ slightly from each other, even when they're the same size.

The size of a rent increase seldom matters if there has been an adequate interval since the last one. One substantial raise is better and easier to put across than three smaller raises at intervals of a few months.

If you raise the tenant's rent only once a year and then only in small increments of 5 to 7 percent to counter inflation, you will keep good, reliable tenants and not force them to look elsewhere for housing. Their rental increases won't be out of line with their normal salary increases. During years when the economy is sagging, you may decide not to increase rent at all.

When tenant turnover is almost negligible although the market is tight and tenants don't complain about an increase, the rent hikes may be too low. When you raise rents, you expect a bigger gross each month. But you may not get it if too many tenants move out and you don't fill the vacancies. Refurbishing costs may also shrink your gross. To implement a higher-than-average increase, grant tenants a 1-month rent holiday for the first month of the new lease. This softens the blow for the first year and puts into place a more profitable rent structure for subsequent leases.

You cannot raise rents during the term of the lease unless the lease provides for an increase at your discretion. This provision is called an escalator.

To protect yourself, the lease should call for a predetermined percentage increase in the rent when the lease expires. If the tenant decides to stay on after the lease expires but refuses to sign a new one, you will still get the benefit of the higher rent. The lease might call for an above-average rent increase to induce the tenant to sign on again. As the expiration date nears, you can offer a new lease with less of a markup as an enticement.

Time rent increase to coincide with improvements to the building. Explain the need for the increase to tenants. You should discuss in general terms the rising costs of managing the property.

Keep rents up to market levels by monitoring what competitors are asking. Do this by reading rental ads and by calling managers of local apartments.

Adopt the philosophy that made Las Vegas. Keep prices down, give good value, and keep the place full.

PROBLEM TENANTS

Tenants are guilty until proved innocent. Beware of first impressions. Some tenants are superficially attractive, but can cause considerable headaches. A troublesome tenant can wreak havoc in an apartment building. He can destroy your property and your reputation. To reduce turnover costs, you must try to spot these people before renting to them. Here are some types of troublesome tenants.

The Liar

The liar will tell you that the check is in the mail, that the three extra people in the apartment are visiting relatives from Ohio, that the diarrhetic poodle belongs to a friend and will be out tomorrow. He is an expert in weaving tales to stall and divert. If his fables persist, you had best send the eviction notice.

The Complainer

The complainer will whine about other tenants, your employees, the management, the apartment, the weather, the price of tea in China. Sometimes, his observations are on target. But his unrelenting stream of gripes will poison the atmosphere, disenchant other tenants, and lead to the loss of good tenants.

The Pack Rat

Mr. Rat Man cannot bear to part with anything, including old newspapers and clothes. He lets his children run wild, scribbling on the walls and smashing windows. The housekeeping talents of his wife have much to be desired. Mr. Rat Man's accumulation of junk could turn the apartment into a fire trap and garbage dump. Legal action to evict is in order if reform seems unlikely.

The Entertainer

Mr. Hollywood loves an audience. His apartment is filled with friends and high-decibel rock. Neighbors complain about the constant noise, traffic, and boozing, but he dismisses their criticism as jealousy. A reading of the house rules and lease agreement may pour cold water on his activities. But if he finds your regulations too confining, he should look for another stage.

The Organizer

Let him find one maintenance problem and he's got a petition calling for a rent strike. He handles problems with confrontation and agitation. The Organizer has a broad understanding of his rights but a narrow grasp of his responsibilities.

Take a pass if you spot these types of tenants before leasing. It's better to leave your apartment empty than put up with a nuisance who threatens the comfort and security of your good tenants.

In general, courts tolerate problem tenants. They give greater consideration to demonstrable injuries, such as property destruction or nonpayment of rent. The court doesn't regard a tenant with an ugly personality as grounds for eviction. Therefore, in evicting a tenant, you must veer from subjective opinion and focus on concrete damage or breach of contract. The court has no room for feelings and impressions, no matter how deeply felt and true they may be. Stick to the facts.

Let's look at remedies to two activities courts regard with sympathy as grounds for eviction—property destruction and nonpayment of rent.

Property Destruction

If a tenant has damaged the apartment or failed to comply with the requirements of the lease or the building code as to maintaining the premises, you have several remedies. Some of these depend on the specific wording of the lease, so check the lease first.

1. Ask the tenant to make the repairs.   If the tenant has damaged the apartment, you should first request him to repair the damage. If he has violated a requirement of the lease or the building code as to the condition of the apartment (such as throwing garbage out the window), you should first ask the tenant to comply with the requirement. Make your request in writing and keep a copy in case you need to file a lawsuit.

2. Make the repairs and charge the tenant.   If the tenant has damaged the apartment and failed to repair it, you can make the repairs and charge the cost to the tenant. You have this right even if there's no written lease. It doesn't apply to ordinary wear and tear, because it's your obligation to repair these defects.

If the tenant doesn't pay the cost of the repairs, you can deduct the cost from the security deposit. Make an itemized list of the damage caused by the tenant and keep copies of the receipts of work done. Give the tenant a copy of these after he moves out.

If the lease requires the tenant to pay for the repairs and he fails to do so after you've asked him, you can file an eviction action. See a lawyer first.

3. Sue the tenant for damages.   If the tenant has damaged the apartment, you can sue him for the cost of repairs. You should either hire a lawyer or file a small-claims action of your own.

If other parts of the building have been damaged because of the tenant's negligence (such as damages to the downstairs apartment from the tenant's waterbed bursting), you may be able to claim from the tenant the entire cost of making the necessary repairs.

4. File an eviction action against the tenant.   If the tenant has violated a lease provision by damaging the apartment or by failing to pay your costs for repairing the damage, you can sue to evict the tenant. Unless the lease provides otherwise, you will have to first serve a 10-day notice specifying the nature of the lease violation.

5. Call the police and file a criminal complaint.   If the tenant is deliberately damaging the apartment, call the police. If the damage has already been done, you can still file a criminal complaint against your tenant. To find out the procedure for filing a complaint, call the nearest police station.

6. Raise the rent.   If the tenant has a month-to-month agreement, you can simply raise the rent to compensate for the loss.

7. You can use each of the preceding remedies.   For instance, if your tenant has damaged the apartment, you can sue both to evict him and to have him pay you the cost of repairs.

Before initiating any of these actions, do the following:

1. Call your lawyer. Don't write or say anything to the tenant before you get legal counsel. If you aren't careful, the tenant could cross-file for harassment and even extortion.
2. Make a complete record of the damage. Take photographs of the damage. Have the film developed immediately and get a statement from the developer as to when it was developed. On every picture, indicate when it was taken, by whom, and what the picture represents. Get a receipt for all repairs. Make sure you can clearly associate the price of the material and the labor for each specific damage. The court won't accept a one-figure bill. Try to get someone else to testify as to the damages.
3. Make the repairs. If it's clear that the tenant won't make the repairs, make the repairs yourself. This will give you a precise figure of damages under consideration. The court will reject an estimate. Take to court only bills, invoices, and receipts for service actually rendered.

Nonpayment of Rent

The most important obligation of the tenant is to pay rent. In the absence of a legal justification for not paying the rent, such as your breach of the warranty of habitability, the tenant must pay the rent when it's due or face eviction.

Some leases require the tenant to pay a late charge if rent is late. Unless there's such a lease provision, you cannot charge a late fee. If there is, most courts will enforce such a provision unless the charge is exorbitant.

If a tenant doesn't pay rent when it's due, you have these remedies:

1. Evict the tenant.   If the tenant hasn't paid rent, you can file suit to evict him. Unless the lease provides otherwise, you must first serve the tenant with a written notice giving him a certain amount of time to pay the rent, usually 5 days.

2. Sue the tenant for rent.   You can sue the tenant to collect the amount of the unpaid rent. This claim can be added to the eviction lawsuit. You can also file a separate suit for rent. A separate suit won't proceed as quickly as the suit in the eviction court. In filing a rent-claim suit, you should specify in the complaint your name and that of the tenant, the apartment address and number, the amount of the agreed upon rent, and the amount of rent due but not paid.

3. Seize the tenant's property.   Some states let you or your agents seize as compensation for rent claimed to be due the tenant's property. There are specific procedures, limits, and exemptions in doing this. I don't advise you take this step unless you have the counsel of an attorney.

It's illegal to lock out a tenant who is behind in rent, in most states.

Collection Services

Collection services are useful to collect back rent or unpaid bills. As a rule, you have the right to urge payment of a just debt. The conduct of a collector must be extreme before legal liability is incurred. Have him use a friendly approach that impresses on the debtor a desire to make arrangements for payment that are reasonable.

Don't bring suit with a purpose other than collecting. Combining revenge with collecting is an abuse of the legal process.

Don't file criminal charges. Check with your attorney before undertaking criminal statutes to collect.

Don't use hotheads. They may lead to troubles for which you may be held responsible.

Don't invade the debtor's right to privacy by tricks or expose him to public contempt.

Don't say anything but the truth about the debtor.

Don't threaten or harass. Threats may be deemed extortion or blackmail.

Don't file bankruptcy, receivership, or insolvency proceedings against the debtor except as a last resort.

Don't write or say anything about or to the tenant that you wouldn't want repeated in open court.

TERMINATING THE TENANT-LANDLORD RELATIONSHIP

Tenants move on for many reasons. They may find a better job in another area. They may want to move closer or further from kith and kin. They may want a change of scenery or climate. Some tenants may decide to buy their own house. Most tenant–landlord partings are amiable and routine. But how do you get rid of a problem tenant? This section will discuss the ways in which the landlord–tenant relationship can be terminated. It first describes the legal requirements when a tenant wants to move out of the apartment either at the end of the lease's term or in the middle of it. Next it talks about evictions: grounds, procedures, and defenses. After that, it discusses the circumstances under which the tenant can still be liable to pay rent after moving out voluntarily or being evicted in the middle of the lease's term. Finally, it talks about lockouts and tenants' remedies against illegal lockouts.

Tenant Wants to Move Out

If the tenant has a written lease for a fixed term, such as 1 year, and wants to move out at the end of it, he doesn't have to give advance notice unless the lease specifically requires it. If a tenant has an oral lease, he must give the landlord at least 7-day advance notice if he pays rent weekly or at least 30-day notice if he pays rent by the month. The notice doesn't have to be in any particular form, but it should be in writing. If the rent is due monthly on the first of the month, the tenant can only terminate the tenancy at the end of the month. The notice must be delivered in the previous month. For example, the tenant could deliver a notice dated October 31, saying he will move out on November 30.

You can subject the tenant to one of the following claims or suits if he doesn't move out at the end of the lease:

1. You or the new tenant can file an eviction action against the tenant.
2. You can treat him as a holdover tenant, in effect renewing his lease.

3. You can claim double rent if he has willfully stayed in the apartment after the lease has expired and after you've demanded possession in writing.
4. If the lease has a liquidated damages clause, you might be able to claim damages from him pursuant to the terms of that provision.

Most leases provide that if the tenant moves out before the end of the lease he still has to pay rent for the remainder of the lease term. For instance, if his lease ends on September 30 but he moves out on July 31, he has to pay the August and September rent. You don't have to find a new tenant for the remainder of the lease. The apartment can stay empty, but the tenant must still pay the rent, unless you decide to rerent it for that period for the same or higher rent.

There are several exceptions to this rule:

1. The tenant can find a subtenant.
2. You can cancel the lease.
3. If you interfere with his right to occupy the apartment or fail to make major repairs that you're obligated to make, he might be able to move out and not be liable for the rent thereafter.

1. Subletting.   If the tenant wants to move out before the end of the lease, he must find a suitable subtenant willing to rent the apartment. You have no obligation to find a new tenant, but you cannot refuse a reasonable subtenant. What is "suitable" depends on the circumstances, but it at least means a person who will comply with the lease provisions. If the subtenant doesn't pay the rent, you can claim it from the original tenant. If you refuse to accept the suitable subtenant, the tenant cannot be held liable for rent after the date the subtenant was willing to begin renting. If you accept the subtenant, you can hold the tenant's security deposit until the end of his lease. If the tenant pays the rent, he has the right to collect it from the subtenant.

2. Lease cancellation.   If you cancel the lease, the tenant isn't liable for the remaining rent. It may be in your interest to cancel the lease because it will allow you to rerent the apartment for a new lease term at a higher rent. Tenants don't have the right to compel you to cancel the lease in the middle of the lease term. If you cancel the lease, you may want to charge a fee to cover the costs of finding a new tenant. Some managers simply forfeit their security.

3. Constructive eviction.   Constructive eviction is an old legal doctrine that means that the tenant may move out within a reasonable time and not be liable for subsequent rent if you have deprived him of the use or benefit of the apartment, perhaps because of building code violations. If they do claim this reason upon moving out, don't hesitate to sue for rent due. If they didn't inform you about the problem and give you reasonable time to remedy it, a court might say that they waived their right to move. Make sure that the lease or agreement the tenant signs protects your interests on this point. Tenants sometimes ask if they can move out because you didn't evict a noisy or undesirable tenant. If his neighbor throws a noisy party now and then, you probably have no duty to evict him. On the other hand, if his neighbor is selling hard drugs or assaulting his children, he probably does have the right to break the lease without penalty. However, the tenant should ask you to remedy the situation, and you should act in concert with the police.

Landlord Wants the Tenant to Move Out

Landlords usually evict for one of two reasons. The tenant is a troublemaker or the landlord wants the tenant's premises for personal use. Personal-use evictions are usually easier to accomplish than problem tenant evictions. Most personal-use evictions involve single-room occupancy (SRO) stock. Someone will rent out an extra bedroom. But SROs have a bad reputation, because they attract mental patients, drug addicts, and prostitutes. In major cities, the trend is to put its low life into public housing ghettos. In New York City in the last 10 years, for example, over 85 percent of the SROs have been converted into luxury housing or destroyed. This represents a considerable trauma for the dispossessed. You can feel sorry for low-income displaced people, but you must put your interests first; otherwise you won't have any interests. Your overriding obligation is to make sure that your property stays viable. You cannot solve the problems of the city, but you can manage your quarter-acre.

Subsidized housing evictions are complicated. If you own Section 8 housing, consult the relevant HUD regulations. These apply to all public housing throughout the country. Your local housing authority may spell out additional rules.

Evicting people living in a rent-controlled apartment can also be hard. Perhaps the most straightforward way to get rid of a tenant is to raise the rent. In rent-controlled Manhattan, administrative agencies have let landlords replace a boiler and then pass along the cost to tenants in the form of a major capital improvement charge (MCI). For someone living on a fixed income, a MCI is as good as an eviction notice. But, when rents jump, tenants may double up. This congestion will put additional strain on your property.

Even if you have grounds for asking a tenant to move out, you cannot forcefully evict him without filing an eviction lawsuit and complying with the required procedures. Impatient landlords sometimes resort to illegal ways to get rid of tenants. I don't endorse these methods, but I can understand how landlords can be driven to take these steps. Rising expenses, juvenile vandalism, unfair judges, and an inefficient legal system conspire against the honest landlord:

1. Let the building deteriorate. While the tenants gradually tear it down, milk it for all its cash flow.
2. Reduce services. Cut down on heat, water, and repairs.
3. Money under the table. In a rent-controlled environment, this can be an effective way to get rid of tenants so that you can erect a new uncontrolled building or convert it to condominiums. However, some people can't be bought.

There are two main grounds for you to ask a tenant to vacate the apartment. The first is if the term of the lease has ended. The second is if the tenant has failed to comply with a provision of the lease, such as paying rent.

If the lease is for a fixed term, the tenant must move out at the end of the lease unless it has been renewed. You don't have to give the tenant notice that you want him to move. To avoid problems, however, you should tell the tenant that you don't plan to renew the lease. In all other situations, you must first give the tenant a termination notice advising him that you want him to move. In many states, the most common termination notices are as follows:

1. Five-day notice.   If you claim the tenant owes rent, you can give him a 5-day notice, specifying the amount of rent claimed and give him 5 days to pay it. If the tenant offers the rent due in those 5 days, you must accept it or the court won't allow you to evict him for not paying rent. The nuisance tenant can also be served with a 5-day notice. If he hasn't lived up to a condition of the lease, has broken house rules, or has misbehaved in various other ways, you can serve him. However, the notice should specifically state the reason for dispossessing him. It should be a substantial one, not just some trivial breach of promise. A court won't uphold an eviction and forfeiture of a lease because of a minor infraction. Don't be afraid to go to court if necessary. It's simpler than you think. But the legal phrasing of a 5-day notice, posted on the door or sent by registered mail, almost always frightens people into moving. In some areas, a 3-day notice is used instead of a 5-day notice.

2. Ten-day notice.   If you claim the tenant violated a condition of the lease, you can give him a 10-day notice. This notice must specify the violation. It asks him to move at the end of 10 days. The 10-day notice is usually used in the case of a severe violation of the lease, such as massive, willful property damage.

3. Seven-day or thirty-day notice.   If the tenant pays rent monthly, you must give him a 30-day notice. If he pays rent by the week, you must give him a 7-day notice. If he doesn't have a written lease, you can ask him to move without giving him a reason. You don't have to give a reason with a 30-day notice if the tenant is on a month-to-month rental. You're entitled to your property whenever you see fit. Don't be drawn into discussing why. Just say, "The law provides this procedure for securing possession of the apartment."

In some states, the termination notice is called "Notice to Quit for Violation of Covenant." If the tenant sues you, you will have to prove that he violated the lease.

You're supposed to fill out the termination notice and serve the tenant on the date indicated by the clerk. It should be notarized. Sometimes, if your lawyer drafts a hellfire and brimstone letter to accompany the notice, the tenant will be sufficiently intimidated to leave without any trouble.

Never evict without due process. Some owners think that by serving the 5-day notice and getting no response they can put the tenant out the door. You may be sued if you enter his premises without permission, remove a door, change the locks, cut off his utilities, seize his possessions, or lay hands on him. If the lease says differently, the lease is void.

You can raise an undesirable's rent to pressure a troublemaker (but not a deadbeat) to leave. This avoids unpleasant exchanges. The tenant can save face, telling everyone that he preferred to move rather than pay the higher rent.

If the tenant skips out without paying rent or paying for damage he did, you can get a court judgment against him. After 30 days, you can sell certain of his belongings at a public sale. The newspapers must publish a notice of the sale 2 weeks in advance. The best way to find a missing occupant is through the rental application. It should give the name of his nearest relative or friend, his place of employment, an emergency contact, and so on. You may be able to get his forwarding address from the post office.

You can serve a termination notice in one of four ways:

1. Delivering a copy to the tenant personally.
2. Leaving a copy with a person above the age of 10 who lives in the apartment.
3. Mailing a copy of the notice to the tenant by certified or registered mail, with a return receipt from the tenant.
4. If no one is home, you can post the notice on the premises.

You're not supposed to slip the notice under the door. Only the sheriff can serve the complaint and summons. He must either deliver them to the tenant personally or leave them at his apartment with a member of his family who is 13 years or older and also mail him a copy. If the tenant hasn't moved out at the end of the period provided in the termination notice, you must file an eviction lawsuit to get the tenant to move. This involves filling out a complaint for possession and a complaint for rent and a court summons. After paying a filing fee and a service of summons fee, the sheriff will serve the complaint and summons to the tenant. If you sue just for possession, the sheriff can mail the tenant a copy of the summons or post a notice in a public place. The posted notice is usually in the court building. When the tenant gets the summons, he is ordered to come to court by a certain date (known as the "return" date) to file an appearance and a jury demand, if that's what he wants. Go to the courtroom on the day of the trial. Get to court about 10 minutes early. Check in with the clerk to make sure you're in the right place. Ask him what number your case is on the list. Be prepared to present your case, because continuances are rarely given.

When you hear your case called, step up to the front and show the judge the notarized termination notice served on the tenant, or a copy of the tenant's lease if it provides that a termination notice doesn't need to be served. If the grounds for eviction is nonpayment of rent, bring your records of the tenant's payments. If you have any witnesses, have them join you when your case is called. Eviction courts are crowded and busy. Sometimes the judge will dispose of a case in only a few minutes. You must first present evidence in support of your case. This is called presenting a "prima facie" case. If you claim that the tenant hasn't paid rent, you will have to show that he hasn't paid the full rent due and that you served him with a proper 5-day notice or his lease, provided that you didn't need to serve the notice. The judge will ask the tenant if he owes the rent or if he has a defense.

Tenants can present these defenses:

1. The tenant has paid the rent or has offered to pay the rent within the period of the 5-day notice.
2. The tenant received a termination notice but you filed the lawsuit before the period ran out. For example, if he got a 5-day notice dated November 2 asking him to pay rent by November 7, and you filed the lawsuit on or before November 7, he has a defense.
3. The tenant received too short a termination notice. For example, if you gave the tenant a 25-day notice when you should have given a 30-day notice, he has a defense. The number of days is based on when he last paid his rent. For example, if his lease requires him to pay his rent on the first, but during the previous month he paid the rent on the twentieth, the date of eviction can be the twentieth, not the first.
4. Rent abatement. The tenant may claim that you failed to maintain the property and this has reduced the value of his apartment in at least the amount of rent that he has withheld. The law isn't clear as to how much rent can be withheld for each code violation.
5. Retaliatory eviction. In some states, the law says that you cannot evict a tenant in retaliation for complaining to the city about building code violations or otherwise exercising his rights as a tenant.

6. Discrimination. The tenant has a defense if you seek to evict because of race, creed, color, national origin, or sex. Local ordinances may also prohibit discrimination based on marital status.

7. The tenant may claim that you said he could move out. Generally, this claim won't stand up in court unless the tenant can produce a written statement that you've signed that says the lease will be canceled as of the date he moves out and he won't be liable for rent thereafter. Some landlords agree to sign such a waiver if the tenant forfeits his entire security.

It has been said that a person who tries to represent himself has a fool for a client. Never go to court without a lawyer. Make sure you bring the lease and other supporting documents. If you cannot make it to court, the tenant may challenge your attorney's testimony on grounds that it's hearsay. The judge will usually let him testify after first swearing to tell the truth. Don't give the other side any breaks. Object to all requests for continuances, object to every word the other side utters, and cross-examine to the point of tears. But treat the judge with deference.

If the tenant wins the lawsuit, the judge will dismiss it, in which case he won't have to move. If he loses the suit, the judge will order him to move. The judge must give him at least 5 days to move and will normally give him 14 days.

Here's an example of how fast you can evict someone:

August 1	Rent is due but not paid.
August 2	You serve 5-day notice.
August 7	Last day you must accept rent.
August 8	You file suit. Summons issued.
August 9	Sheriff serves summons.
August 22	Trial date (at least 14 days after summons is issued).
September 5	Eviction date (usually 15 days after trial date).
September 10	The sheriff might not actually evict the tenant until several days after the eviction date.

It will take more time if the tenant asks for a jury trial. Jury trial continuances may last several months. If it's winter, the court may postpone eviction until spring, particularly if the tenant has small children. During this time, you must foot the utility bills as well as the lost rent. Consider the lament of these New York City landlords:

It takes over two weeks for a dispossess. After waiting five to seven days before sending the dispossess, the tenant may owe two to three months rent. It again takes over three weeks, sometimes over a month, before a warrant comes through to evict a tenant and then a show cause will be served. Again, the kangaroo court starts. Sometimes, it takes months by postponement. It's too much suffering. We're all suffering. In the winter, I pay $3,000 per month for fuel no matter who pays or doesn't pay. I have to give heat or I'll be put in jail. The tenants are running away with the rent, but they aren't being put in jail. Only those who are responsible are punished. We're the backbone of the city, yet we're treated as last-class citizens. We pay plenty of taxes whether we collect rent or not. We have to pay water, sewer, real estate taxes, insurance, fuel, lights—I can go on.

Tenants know all the tricks and make use of all the privileges that they have over the owner. We have no rights. This is very wrong. We work hard to keep our buildings, so that we won't lose them. Tenants use minor repairs as an excuse not to pay rent. They tell lots of lies. Judges believe the tenants. It's very discouraging.[1]

A landlord's lot is not a happy one.

If the judge orders the tenant to move, he might say, "Enter the writ and stay it for 15 days." The writ is the name of the court order instructing the sheriff to evict him. When the judge says "stay 15 days," he means that the sheriff can't evict him until 15 days later. Only the sheriff can evict. You cannot. You must pay the sheriff a fee for the eviction. If you don't pay, the sheriff won't evict him, even though the court has authorized it.

If you want to discuss settling the case prior to the trial with the tenant, you may do so. However, neither side is required to discuss settlement because both are entitled to a trial. It may be in your interest to discuss settlement if you think you may not win. If both sides want to discuss settlement, make sure you understand each other's position. Put the settlement in writing and present it to the judge for approval.

If a settlement is reached in which the tenant agrees to move in a certain number of days, the number of days should be specified. If the settlement requires the tenant to pay a certain amount of rent by a certain time, the settlement should say whether the tenant will be allowed to stay if the amount is paid. If the settlement provides for a judgment for you but also allows the tenant to stay if he pays the rent within a certain time, the settlement should provide that you won't vacate the judgment if the rent is paid in time. If the settlement requires either side to pay court costs or attorney fees, the dollar amount should be specified. The court will normally award court costs to the winning side (the cost of filing the lawsuit and issuing summons or the cost of appearing), but will only award attorney fees if there is a lease clause that specifically authorizes them. Legal fees are usually many times more expensive

[1]*Code Inspections and the Housing Court: A Study of the Impact of Pre-Trial Inspections in Non-Payment Proceedings When Tenants Claim Needed Repairs,* Office of Program and Management Analysis, Department of Housing Preservation and Development, New York, 1982, pp. 134–5.

than court costs. Make sure your leases contain that clause. Don't sign settlement agreements drafted by the tenant's lawyer. Instead, wait for the case
to be called and ask the judge to explain it to you. If you like it, you can sign
it. If you don't, you can go to trial. If you settle the case, keep a copy of the
settlement agreement.

If the judge orders the tenant out of the apartment, you can sue him for
the remaining rent for the period after the eviction and before the end of the
lease term. The tenant may need some time to find another apartment. Ask
him to pay all rent that is due plus rent for that extra time. Most judges won't
extend the stay beyond 15 days. Instead, they will hold him to his agreement.
To ask for more time, the tenant must present before the judge a "Motion to
Extend the Stay of the Writ of Restitution." A motion is a request to the court
to take some action. The writ of restitution is the court's order to the sheriff
to evict him. The tenant can also file a notice of appeal. If he wants to stay
in the apartment during the course of the appeal, he must post a bond. Normally, the bond is the full amount of the rent for the next year. When an
appeal is filed, another court (the appellate court) reviews the transcript or
other record of the trial to decide if the trial judge made an error that would
require a reversal of the judgment. The appellate court cannot hear more testimony or examine more evidence. It can take at least 6 months for the appellate court to reach a decision after the appeal has been filed.

You cannot evict a tenant by locking him out. You must file and win the
lawsuit. Only the sheriff can physically evict the tenant. Some states permit
hotel or motel owners to seize all the belongings on the premises of a guest
who has failed to pay his bill. The owner can also lock out the guest. His
action, however, may be subject to legal challenge if the occupant had signed
a lease with the owner (so that he is a tenant and not merely a guest). If you
illegally lock out a tenant or try to evict by cutting off utilities, he has several
remedies. The tenant can file a lawsuit to enjoin you to stop the illegal conduct
and let him back into the apartment. The tenant can also ask the court to
order you to pay him for the loss of the use of the apartment and for any
resulting inconvenience. Finally, the court can order you to pay punitive damages if it decides that you acted maliciously. If you've caused a breach of peace
or damaged the tenant's property in the course of the lock out, the tenant can
call the police or file a criminal complaint against you.

BUILDING GOODWILL

You've seen that a landlord must know something about law, taxes, accounting, finance, and contracting. Your knowledge doesn't have to be as sophisticated as those who devote their lives to specializing in these trades. But you
should have a feeling for what they do and how they can help you. You should
also have some understanding for another area critical to your success as a

landlord. This area is human relations. Personal clashes can mean loss of income and maybe even loss of property. Three kinds of landlords often fail. They are dumbbells, doormats, and dictators. An excessive amount of trust in the goodwill of your tenants and neighbors can lead to bitter disappointment. Submitting to every tenant's demand can lead to bankruptcy. Overreacting to tenant's desires can alienate your tenants.

Owning and managing an apartment is the closest thing our democracy allows that approaches feudalism. The best way to run your property is by being a benevolent monarch. If you try to turn your complex into a commune or a democracy, you'll be plagued by indecision and chaos. It's your responsibility. To paraphrase President Harry S Truman, the buck stops with you. "I've always defined politics to mean the science of government, perhaps the most important science," he said, "for it involves the ability of people to live together." Your complex is a political system. They won't caucus or vote with a ballot, but they can agitate and vote with their feet. There is a balance of power between tenants and landlord. The tenants have the numbers and considerable legal bias in their favor. The landlord has ownership and usually more money. However, the landlord is often outgunned in a class-action suit. Thus, you should never overestimate your own power.

Never look for trouble. Don't be a housemother. Tenants are willing to put up with high rents and poorly maintained units as long as you leave them alone. They bristle if they think you're spying on them. Always give them notice before entering their apartment. Tell them before you turn off their water or electricity. Keep them informed about major repairs. Never get involved in tenant arguments. Never say anything or write anything to them that couldn't stand the scrutiny of a judge. Never lay hands on their children or children in the neighborhood, no matter what damage they're doing. Keep under control. Don't fly off the handle.

Business and personal relationships are driven by self-interest. But they are also formed and sustained by trust and friendship. We do business with people we like. Such goodwill can only be created over time. You must nurture it. Unlike the broker, you don't sell the prospect once. You must keep him sold.

Every manager, by exercising foresight and imagination, can cultivate goodwill. For example, providing safety vaults, parking accommodations, libraries, security, and conference rooms are devices for creating goodwill in managing offices.

Once you've taken over the property, meet with the tenants. But refrain from making commitments. You should be able to contact the tenant by requiring his telephone number and access to his apartment. He should be able to contact your agent. In New York, for example, the law requires the tenant's lease and rental receipt to have your agent's name and address. Also, if your building has more than eight apartments, you must post a sign in the entrance hall with the janitor's name, address, and telephone number. The sign should be on street level and easy to see, such as near the mailbox. New York law also requires the owner to post a certificate of inspection near the mailboxes so that the housing code inspector can sign in on each visit with his name, date, and reason for the inspection. The certificate must have your name, address, and telephone number.

Complaints and requests from desirable tenants require a sympathetic hearing, even when they are unreasonable. Impatient treatment of minor complaints can result in the loss of a good tenant. Establishing rules to which exceptions cannot be made is a device for refusing difficult requests. Rules also help to avoid the charge that the management is playing favorites.

Follow the principle of seeking the greatest good for the greatest number. Some tenants won't recognize the rights of other occupants or won't take care of their apartment. When this happens, remove them as soon as possible, for they can quickly destroy the goodwill you've built up.

SUMMARY

Here are some of the main points from this chapter:

1. Turn your property over to professional management as soon as you can.
2. Require a security deposit and a written lease.
3. You can pursue several remedies against nonpaying or destructive tenants.
4. Screen your tenants carefully.
5. Don't be a housemother.

CONCLUSION:

RISKS AND REWARDS

Of all the dreams and schemes for personal wealth, none fires the imagination like the promise of real-estate investing. But it's not a sure way for getting rich quick. For many, it's a way of getting poor quick. Investing in income real estate is a complex financial and legal process. It demands expertise, patience, and resources. Buying income property is like becoming self-employed. And, as with all types of self-employment, there are risks as well as rewards. If you're in over your head, you can go from sipping the champagne to stomping the grapes in short order. Here are some of the risks.

Market Risk

The value placed on the property may change because of changes in supply and demand. Real estate is basically a local business. Knowledge of the local area is essential for success. You must know what comparable properties are selling and renting for and trends in vacancy, tax rates, and business growth. Decisions of local officials will affect property values, from rent control to busing. Environmental and zoning restrictions could stymie land developers. Investors often fail to reduce market risk by not looking at enough properties. Two properties with the same price can have vastly different profit potential. Investors also often fail to look at the properties closely enough. They trust their own intuition instead of the skills of inspectors, appraisers, lawyers, and contractors.

Buying property is a highly regulated transaction, involving a series of contracts. However, it's also a complex transaction. Because it's complex, you must allow for fraud. Fraud can cost you dearly.

Managerial Risks

Failure to screen tenants, raise rents to market levels, control operating expenses, prevent overcrowding, maintain the property, and put the property to its "highest and best use" are reasons some properties yield low returns. Making money as an investor depends both on making the wise initial investment decision and having the ability to manage properly. A poorly managed and maintained building could decrease in value, driving down rents and attracting a lower grade of tenant. As profits drop, you may fall behind in your mortgage or tax payments and lose the property.

Tax Changes

Shelter is one of life's necessities. The deterioration and destruction of older buildings and population changes and movements contribute to an ever-expanding need for residential buildings. The government, in trying to provide a better life for its citizens, has enacted tax laws creating financial incentives to encourage property ownership. Laws that provide benefits for the real-estate investor are really subsidies for the individual renter. While inflation has increased the costs of housing, the government has failed to adequately increase subsidies for housing. If existing "loopholes" are closed, the incentive to invest in real estate will diminish. Real-estate values will erode while rents will increase to compensate for the lost subsidy. If Congress removes these incentives, tenant interest groups will pressure state legislatures to provide compensatory subsidies, possibly through the use of tax credits.

Congress is under pressure to reduce tax benefits given to real-estate investors for two reasons. First, it has been argued, vast amounts of capital that could have been used to create jobs has been diverted into real estate. Second, property-tax benefits aren't fair, as they largely benefit the rich.

The counterarguments are that housing is a critical component of our society, that supply is well below demand, and that the risks of investing in real property are such that tax incentives are needed.

Energy Costs

Despite the disintegration of OPEC in the early 1980s and the subsequent decline of gasoline prices, the cost of natural gas and electricity has continued to rise at rates well above the rate of inflation. Deregulation and cost overruns in building nuclear power plants are two reasons for these cost increases. Political turmoil in the Middle East could exacerbate these rates. As energy costs increase, property located at great distance from jobs could suffer in value. In buying apartments, you must also take into consideration who pays for the utilities and how well the building is insulated.

Illiquidity

Real estate is among the most illiquid of investments. Raw land and commercial property are particularly difficult to dispose of. Be wary of investing in managerial-intensive property if you have a slender profit margin and there's some chance you will have to move to another part of the country.

Interest Rate Changes

Fluctuations in the cost of money affects your ability to buy and improve income property.

Reduce the Risks

Here are 3 things to do to reduce your risks in owning real estate:

1. Buy adequate insurance.
2. Maintain your property.
3. Screen your tenants thoroughly.

Here are some of the benefits you can expect to enjoy by investing in real estate.

Safety

A *need* is an item people have to have for basic human existence. A *want* is an item people desire after they've taken care of their needs. There's always a high demand for a need, but the demand for a want varies according to incomes, tastes, and the economy. Housing is an example of a need. Real estate is a commodity with a limited supply and an ever-increasing demand. The pressure pushing up rents comes from the high cost of replacing obsolete housing and the population growth. In some areas, prospective renters are literally standing in line. The high interest rates are uncomfortable for many young couples who would rather buy their house. An increasing number of families are forming. The traditional new household, usually a newly married couple, has changed. Today, single men and women are forming new households. They include not only the never-married, but divorced and widowed as well. The trend toward smaller family size means that the need for a home is less urgent. Couples who choose not to have children can participate in leisure activities that they would have to forego if they were tied down to a home. Mobility is on the rise. Younger professionals and executives who expect to be transferred find rentals more logical than homes. We live in a more transient society. People don't put down roots like they did a generation ago. Renting makes it easier for people to pick up and go. Increasing lifespans are another force motivating people to rent. People are living longer and are seeking more convenient housing alternatives to single-family homes.

Any number of catastrophies can damage or destroy your property, but you can insure against most of these risks. "Real estate can't be lost or stolen, nor can it be carried away," President Franklin D. Roosevelt said. "Managed with reasonable care, it's about the safest investment in the world."

Appreciation

Despite fluctuations in real-estate values, the long-term trend for sound, well-located income property has been toward increased values. If you're prepared to hold the property for at least 5 years, you can usually expect to sell it at a profit. Part of the increase in value derives from those forces we mentioned in the last section. As rents increase, the value of your property increases. This lessens the bite of inflation. In a rising housing market, tenants suffer as rents go up, but homeowners profit as their houses increase in value. The value of real estate increases at a rate comparable to the rate of inflation. Real estate also lets you enjoy the inflation rate on money you don't have. It lets you accumulate capital while deferring taxes on the gain until you decide to sell. Property ownership gives the middle-income person a tremendous investment base—his down payment plus the lender's money—on which appreciation is growing.

Leverage

Few investments let you control so much equity for so little money. You may put down 10 percent or even nothing, but still get the benefit of the investment value of the entire property—all income and appreciation. Income property offers you one of the highest ratios of leverage available in legitimate investment. Used wisely, leverage can be a powerful wealth-building tool.

Equity Buildup

Once rent money is spent, it's gone forever. But each monthly mortgage payment reduces the principal amount of the loan while building equity on the property. For rental properties, the property is self-amortizing. It pays for itself out of its own income. As time goes by, interest as a proportion of the mortgage declines as the principal increases. You will be able to see a fair contribution to your net worth halfway through your mortgage term. Equity buildup also provides greater financial security for longtime property owners. You can draw on their equity for personal loans. When it comes time to sell, property equity can generate a steady flow of income during the retirement years, with the proper structuring of the sale.

Government Subsidies

If you invest in certain kinds of property, the government will give you many economic benefits, ranging from low-interest loans to grants.

Income

If the property had a favorable price/profit ratio and it wasn't overleveraged, you will get a steady positive income month after month. Your net may not be much, but, over time, it will accumulate and grow. The French have an appropriate saying: "Light gains make a heavy purse."

Tax Benefits

Because of the tax benefits of real estate, it's possible to have a positive cash flow without having any taxable income. Even repair and maintenance costs, although deductible, nevertheless contribute to preserving and increasing the value of your property. The investor who bought his property with an eye toward cash flow and appreciation instead of tax write-offs has nothing to fear from tax reform.

Stability

The value of stocks and collectibles undulate like an epileptic squirrel. But income property appeals to the conservative investor because it lets him predict, with reasonable accuracy, income, expenses, and profit. Also, the mortgage is stable or at least predictable over the life of the loan. Raw land and new construction are speculative because they don't have tenant track records.

Independence

When you invest in real estate, you see and control what your dollars are doing. Little luck is involved in your gains or losses. You decide when to sell, buy, or refinance. You don't have to worry about corporate politics. You're your own boss.

A visitor attending President Andrew Jackson's funeral asked one of his slaves whether he thought the general would go to heaven. The slave replied, "He will if he wants to." When you own property, you can do what you want to, within the bounds of common law and common sense.

Pleasure

Property is destiny. It's a tangible link with the past and the future. Your identity fuses with the property you own and nourish. You'll not only earn a financial return, but a psychic one. You'll feel satisfaction in working hard and seeing the results of your labor. There's joy in honest sweat, even at the cost of a banged thumb or a scraped shin. Income property is a place of freedom, a greenhouse for personal growth, and a laboratory for experimentation. For here—and perhaps nowhere else—we can indulge our whims.

When you own income real estate, you'll enjoy an improved quality of life, pride of ownership, and greater participation in the democratic process in your community, as well as many economic benefits.

SUMMARY

Here are some of the main points from this section:

1. Buying income property involves inherent risk, such as fraud, poor management, and tax rule changes.
2. Don't overextend yourself.
3. Because income property fulfills a basic need, it's generally a safe investment.
4. Appreciation, equity buildup, income, and tax benefits are some benefits from owning income real estate.
5. Owning and managing income property is fun.

CODA

Throughout this book, I've stressed several points. These include the following:

1. Make the 5-year plan the unit of personal financial planning.
2. Have the property inspected before you buy.
3. Retain legal counsel before you sign anything.
4. Put all verbal understandings in writing.
5. Preventive care is the best insurance.
6. Don't overfinance.
7. Keep accurate records.
8. Screen your tenants carefully.

9. Require a security deposit and a written lease.
10. Turn your property over to professional management as soon as you can.

As you review them, you may be thinking, "That's obvious!" That these assertions are self-evident to you doesn't cancel your need to internalize and apply them. "Knowing is not enough," said Goethe. "We must apply. Willing is not enough. We must do." Not a week goes by without a story in the press disclosing the tale of an expensive, embarrassing debacle because people who knew better violated these rules. Before you buy that time share, partnership, or apartment, read these rules again.

On the other hand, as you read these rules, you may be thinking, "That's nonsense!" Based on your achievements, you may have solid grounds for thinking thusly. I accept that. I don't want to replace one dogma with another. These rules aren't meant to handcuff you into patterns of behavior that go against your interests. Rather, they're meant to provide a framework within which you can make sound decisions. All things being equal, these rules have proved their validity. Not just in my experience, but in the experiences of others from around the country and in the past. As you get more experience as an investor, you'll know when it's right to break the rules to your advantage. Rules are just guideposts, showing you that well-trod path to financial security. But you must walk that path. And the choices that you'll make along the way will require flexibility, common sense, and courage. Keep learning, keep striving, keep buying and "the earth shall be yours and its fullness thereof."

GLOSSARY

Acceleration clause: A clause in a mortgage or trust deed that lets the lender call for payment in full if the borrower defaults.

Acre: A unit of land measurement that is 43,560 square feet or 4,890 square yards.

Adjustable rate mortgage (ARM):   A mortgage on which the interest rate may change according to a predetermined index.

Ad valorem taxes: Counties, cities, and school districts levy real-estate taxes according to the value of each property subject to these taxes. Ad valorem is the Latin term meaning "according to value."

Agent: A person acting on behalf of another, called the principal.

Agreement of sale: A contract in which a seller agrees to sell and a buyer agrees to buy, under specific terms spelled out in writing and signed by both parties. It's also known as a contract of purchase, purchase agreement, sales agreement, or binder depending on location or jurisdiction.

Amortization: The gradual paying off of the loan. Only the payment of principal is amortization.

Annual percentage rate (APR):   The APR incorporates the total finance charge of the loan, including interest, loan fees, and other fees. Federal laws require that it be furnished to the borrower.

Bill of sale: A document that transfers title to personal property. A deed transfers real property.

Blanket mortgage: A single mortgage covering the units and common areas of a multifamily building or complex, held by a cooperative housing corporation.

Building code: The law established by a governmental agency to regulate the construction of buildings within its jurisdiction.

Capital gain: The gain realized from the sale of a capital asset, such as real estate.

Carrying charges: Amount required to continue ownership of a property. Some investors confine this term just to mortgage payments.

Cash flow: The direction money flows between an owner and a piece of investment property, after all expenses except depreciation. Positive cash flow is when the property generates income over outgo. Negative cash flow is when the owner must put in money to keep the property solvent.

Cash on cash: The ratio of cash throw-off to your original investment. This is also known as your equity dividend rate.

Cash throw-off: The net operating income minus the annual debt service.

Certificate of title: A document signed by a title examiner or attorney stating that the seller has an insurable title to the property.

Chattel mortgage: The creation of a loan on personal property as security for payment on a real estate loan.

Closing costs: The various expenses involved in arranging a real-estate transfer that are in addition to the actual sale price of the property.

Closing statement: The computation of financial adjustments between buyer and seller to determine the net amount of money the buyer must pay to the seller to complete the purchase of the real estate and the seller's net proceeds.

Cloud: Any condition that may affect the title to property, usually a minor matter that a quitclaim deed or court judgment can settle.

Commission: The payment of money or other valuable consideration to a real-estate broker for service performed.

Condominium: Units owned by individuals within a multifamily building. The unit's owner gets an interest in the common areas and voting rights in the owner's association.

Contempt: The willful disregard of the authority of the court or disobedience to its lawful orders.

Contingency clause: A clause in a contract that comes into effect upon the occurrence of a specified event.

Convey: To transfer title of property from one person or organization to another.

Cooperative: A housing corporation in which individual households own shares entitling them to live in a particular unit in a multifamily building.

Cooperative mortgage: The long-term loan made to the purchaser of a share in a cooperative housing corporation.

Credit report: A report on the credit history of a potential borrower.

Dealer: One whose occupation is the buying and selling of real estate. Special, usually less favorable, tax rules apply to real-estate dealers.

Debt–service ratio: The ratio of the annual mortgage payments to the gross annual income.

Deed: A formal written document by which title to real property is transferred from one owner to another.

Deed of trust: A security document whereby real property is given as security for a debt.

Default: The failure to perform to the terms of a contract.

Defendant: The person against whom relief is sought in a legal action.

Defense: The response by a defendant which, if accepted by the court, will defeat the action against him.

Deficiency judgment: The obtaining by the lender of a money judgment against the borrower after a foreclosure, when the proceeds from the sale of property don't satisfy the outstanding loan.

Depreciation: The degree to which an asset deteriorates with time.

Dismissed without prejudice: An order or judgment that disposes of a case, usually on a technicality, but gives the petitioner the right to commence a new proceeding on the same claim.

Dismissed with prejudice: An order or judgment that not only dismisses the petitioner's case, but bars him from instituting a new action on the same claim.

Disposition: The final outcome of a court case.

Down payment: The difference between the selling price and the mortgage or trust deed amounts in the purchase of real property.

Earnest money: The money given to the seller by the potential buyer upon the signing of the agreement of sale to show that the buyer is serious about buying the property.

Easement: The right of an individual, company, or agency to trespass on the property of another owner. Easements can be perpetual or finite.

Equity: The difference between the current market value of the property and the value of any claims or liens against the property.

Escalation clause: This clause provides that a tenant's rent increases automatically if the landlord's expenses increase.

Escape clause: This clause allows one party to break the contract, usually with little or no penalty.

Escrow: Funds, property, or other things of value left in trust with a third party. The escrow may be released upon the fulfillment of certain conditions or by agreement of the parties.

Expense ratio: The ratio of total expenses, exclusive of mortgage payments, to the gross annual income.

Fannie Mae: Federal National Mortgage Association (FNMA). Originally created by the federal government in 1938 to help the nation recover from the depression, FNMA is now a privately owned corporation operating in the public interest. FNMA's role in the secondary market is to borrow money from the capital markets when mortgage money is tight and use the funds to buy mortgages, primarily from mortgage banks.

Fee: The basic right to ownership of land. The most basic type of unencumbered ownership is fee simple.

Fiduciary: A person in a position of trust, such as an agent, broker, or manager.

Fixture: Those things that formerly were personal property that now are permanently attached to real property and go with the property when it's sold. Fixtures include towel racks, shower heads, and built-in appliances.

Foreclosure: To sell real property to pay the obligation on a mortgage or trust deed when the borrower is in default.

Freddie Mac: Federal Home Loan Mortgage Corporation (FHLMC). An organization Congress chartered in 1970 to help develop and maintain a secondary mortgage market in conventional home loans. FHLMC buys mortgages, mainly from savings and loans associations, and resells them in the secondary market.

Gain: For tax purposes, the difference between the adjusted sales price and the adjusted basis upon sale of property.

Grace period: A period of time after the regular due date of a loan payment during which a late penalty isn't charged.

Graduated payment mortgage (GPM):   Under this type of mortgage, the mortgagor makes low monthly payments for the first few years of the mortgage term. The payments gradually increase for the next few years until they reach a level where they remain for the balance of the mortgage.

Gross income: The total income from all sources on a piece of investment property.

Gross-income multiplier: A predetermined number multiplied by the gross income, used to determine the value of a piece of investment property.

Gross leasable area: The area upon which a tenant actually pays rent under a lease. It excludes common areas shared by all tenants.

Hazard insurance: The pay for damage losses caused to property by fire, windstorms, and other hazards. Doesn't include losses caused by acts of war or flooding of property in perennial floodplain.

Holdback: A certain portion of a construction loan held back by the lender until completion of the project or until specified actions have been performed.

Homeowner's policy: The home insurance package of coverages, including fire insurance, burglary and theft, and personal liability coverage.

Homestead exemption: A tax relief aimed at reducing the property tax burden to encourage homeownership.

Judgment: The official decision of the court on a case or proceeding before it. A *default* judgment is rendered in favor of the petitioner due to the non-appearance of the respondent. In a *consent* judgment, the provisions and terms are settled and agreed to by the parties to the proceeding. A *conditional* judgment depends on the preformance of certain acts by one or both of the parties in a proceeding.

Junior mortgage: A mortgage that is in an inferior position to another mortgage. A second mortgage is a junior mortgage. A mortgage that has a subordination clause is usually referred to as a junior mortgage.

Late charge: A penalty charged by the lender for late loan payments, as specified in the loan contract.

Leaseback: A situation where the seller of a piece of property agrees to lease it back from the buyer.

Leverage: The ratio of an investor's money to borrowed money in the purchase of property. The greater the borrowed money, the greater the leverage.

Lien: A legal claim by a person or institution against the property or any other asset. The most common lien is a mortgage.

Limited partnership: A form of partnership in which some or most partners have limited liability.

Listing contract: An agreement between a property owner as principal and a real-estate broker as agent for the broker to sell the owner's property within a given time for a commission.

Litigant: Any party in a lawsuit.

Loan closing: The final step in the property-buying process, the closing includes the signing of notes, financial adjustments, and any disbursements of funds in the transaction.

Loan origination fee: A one-time fee usually charged by a lender for making a mortgage or trust deed.

Loan processing: The work done by a lender from the time a home buyer applies for a mortgage to the time the loan is approved. This includes the application, property appraisal, a credit investigation, establishment of the loan terms, and other legal and financial paperwork.

Market study: An analysis of the prevailing or future market for a specific type of real estate in a particular area.

Market value: That amount of money for which a willing seller will sell property, a willing buyer will buy it, neither of them being under compulsion to buy and sell and both being aware of the best and highest use to which the property can be put.

Monthly payment: The payment to be made by the borrower each month based on the stated interest rate, the amount borrowed, the term, and any escrow amount to be paid each month.

Month-to-month tenancy: A real-estate rental for which the rent is paid monthly for an unspecified term.

Mortgage: A security instrument used for borrowing money. The borrower is the mortgagor. The lender is the mortgagee.

Mortgage assignment: The borrower can transfer his debt to someone else, usually someone to whom he sells the property while the mortgage is still on it.

Mortgage commitment: A promissory document in which a lender tells a future borrower that he will, under specified conditions, give him a mortgage loan at some specified future date.

Mortgage note: A written agreement to repay a loan. The agreement is secured by a mortgage, serves as proof of an indebtedness, and states the manner in which the debt shall be paid. Also called deed or trust note.

Motion: An application for relief during a legal proceeding.

Net income: The income from property, usually after all expenses have been deducted, except for mortgage payments.

Net lease: A lease in which the tenant pays a portion of the expenses of the property, such as taxes, maintenance, utilities, and repairs.

Offer: Usually a written contract to purchase property offered by a buyer to a seller and frequently accompanied by earnest money.

Option: The right to buy or rent a piece of property within a certain period of time upon certain conditions.

Ordinary income: For tax purposes, income received from a regular job as opposed to investment income, such as might be received from ownership of real estate.

Paper loss: A loss on the ownership of property, not in the form of cash, but in the form of an accounting entry.

Percentage lease: A lease in which the rent payment is partly based on the sales of the tenant.

Percentage mortgage: A mortgage based on a percentage of the value of the real estate.

PITI: Abbreviation for principal, interest, taxes, and insurance, which many residential mortgages include.

Plaintiff: The person who brings a legal action.

Points: A fee to reimburse the lender for the costs of processing the paperwork involved in creating a mortgage loan. One point is equal to 1 percent of the loan amount.

Prepay: To pay off the loan before the due date.

Prepayment penalty: A money penalty assessed by lenders for early payment of loans.

Principal: Capital sum lent on interest; either party to a contract; one who appoints an agent to act in his stead; the most important.

Property management: The operation of real property, including the leasing of space, collection of rent, selection of tenants, and the repair and renovation of buildings and grounds.

Prorate: To divide certain expenses such as taxes and insurance between buyer and seller at time of sale.

Pro se litigant: Any person in a lawsuit who represents himself without an attorney.

Purchase money mortgage: Money granted directly by a seller to the buyer of the seller's property, in which the seller may take back the property if the buyer doesn't pay off the mortgage as agreed.

Qualify: To meet all lender's requirements, including a sufficient income and good credit, to get a mortgage or trust deed.

Quitclaim deed: A deed that releases any interest a seller or other individual may have in a given piece of land.

Real estate investment trust (REIT):   A mutual fund that borrows funds in private capital markets. The proceeds are used to make construction and development loans, long-term mortgage loans, and loans for buying income-producing real estate.

Realized gain: The gain received upon the sale of property.

Refinance: To replace an existing mortgage with a new, usually higher, mortgage.

Rehab: A revitalization project, usually of a run-down building in a run-down area.

Revitalization: Improving the condition of land and structures in a deteriorated area.

Sales agreement: An offer to purchase property.

Sales leaseback: An arrangement under which the owner of a property sells his land to another but retains the right to continue occupancy as a tenant under a lease.

Second mortgage: A junior or subordinate mortgage, sometimes also referred to as a second trust deed.

Self-amortizing mortgage: The constant payments in the liquidation of the mortgage's principal at maturity.

Setback: A zoning provision specifying the distances a new house must be set back from a road or from the lot boundaries.

Sheriff's deed: A deed granted by a court as part of the forced sale of property to satisfy a judgment.

Subordination clause: A clause in a mortgage keeping it in a secondary or subordinate position to another mortgage.

Summons: A notice of the commencement of an action against a person, requiring him to appear in court to answer the complaint.

Survey: A map or plat of the land and its improvements.

Syndicate: A group of investors organized for the purpose of buying property.

Tax bracket: In income taxes, a particular percentage of taxes owed for a particular income range.

Tax lien: A claim made against the property when the property's owner is delinquent in paying his taxes.

Tax shelter: Offsetting regular income with a (paper) loss on an investment such as real estate.

Time share: The exclusive right to occupy a unit in a development for a specified period of time each year.

Title: A document that indicates rights of ownership and possession of a particular property.

Title closing: The meeting at which title to a property is conveyed from one owner to another.

Title insurance: Protects lenders and home owners against loss of their interest in property due to legal defects in the title.

Title search: A check of the title records, generally at the local courthouse, to make sure that the buyer is buying the house from the legal owner and that there are no liens, overdue assessments, or other claims.

Torrens system: The system maintained by some cities that keep a municipal record with title records of all properties current.

Transfer tax: The state tax, local tax, or tax stamps required when the title passes from one owner to another.

VA: The Veterans Administration, a federal agency that guarantees special loans to qualified veterans.

Vacancy factor: A percentage subtracted from calculations of gross rental income for vacancy, even if the property is fully rented.

Valuation: The estimated worth or price.

Warranty of habitability: An implied covenant between landlord and tenant that the premises are free of any condition dangerous to life, health, or safety.

Zoning: The legal restrictions that help shape a community's character and development.

A
AMORTIZATION CHART

To determine your monthly payments, find the value for the term (number of years) and the interest rate and multiply by the number of thousands of dollars loaned. For example, a 30-year mortgage with an interest rate of 12 percent for $50,000 requires monthly payments of 10.29 × 50 = $514.50.

AMORTIZATION CHART
Monthly Payment Per $1,000

# Yrs.	10%	10¼%	10½%	10¾%	11%	11¼%	11½%	11¾%	12%	12¼%	12½%
5	$21.25	21.38	21.50	21.62	21.75	21.87	22.00	22.12	22.25	22.38	22.50
10	13.22	13.36	13.50	13.64	13.78	13.92	14.06	14.21	14.35	14.50	14.64
12	11.95	12.10	12.25	12.39	12.54	12.69	12.84	12.99	13.14	13.29	13.44
15	10.75	10.90	11.06	11.21	11.37	11.53	11.69	11.85	12.01	12.17	12.33
16	10.46	10.62	10.78	10.94	11.10	11.26	11.42	11.58	11.74	11.91	12.07
17	10.21	10.38	10.54	10.71	10.86	11.02	11.19	11.35	11.52	11.68	11.85
18	10.00	10.16	10.33	10.49	10.66	10.82	10.99	11.16	11.32	11.49	11.67
19	9.81	9.98	10.15	10.31	10.48	10.65	10.82	10.99	11.16	11.33	11.50
20	9.65	9.82	9.99	10.16	10.33	10.50	10.67	10.84	11.02	11.19	11.37
21	9.51	9.68	9.85	10.02	10.19	10.37	10.54	10.72	10.89	11.07	11.25
22	9.38	9.56	9.73	9.90	10.08	10.25	10.43	10.61	10.78	10.96	11.14
23	9.27	9.45	9.62	9.80	9.98	10.15	10.33	10.51	10.69	10.87	11.05
24	9.17	9.35	9.53	9.71	9.89	10.06	10.25	10.43	10.61	10.79	10.98
25	9.09	9.27	9.45	9.63	9.81	9.99	10.17	10.35	10.54	10.72	10.91
26	9.01	9.19	9.37	9.55	9.74	9.92	10.10	10.29	10.47	10.66	10.85
27	8.94	9.13	9.31	9.49	9.67	9.86	10.05	10.23	10.42	10.61	10.80
28	8.88	9.07	9.25	9.43	9.62	9.81	9.99	10.18	10.37	10.56	10.75
29	8.83	9.01	9.20	9.38	9.57	9.76	9.95	10.14	10.33	10.52	10.71
30	8.78	8.97	9.15	9.34	9.53	9.72	9.91	10.10	10.29	10.48	10.68
35	8.60	8.79	8.99	9.18	9.37	9.57	9.77	9.96	10.16	10.36	10.56
40	8.49	8.69	8.89	9.09	9.29	9.49	9.69	9.89	10.09	10.29	10.49

# Yrs.	12¾%	13%	13¼%	13½%	13¾%	14%	14¼%	14½%	14¾%	15%	15¼%
5	22.63	22.76	22.89	23.01	23.14	23.27	23.40	23.53	23.66	23.79	23.93
10	14.79	14.94	15.08	15.23	15.38	15.53	15.68	15.83	15.99	16.14	16.29
12	13.60	13.75	13.91	14.06	14.22	14.38	14.53	14.69	14.85	15.01	15.18
15	12.49	12.66	12.82	12.99	13.15	13.32	13.49	13.66	13.83	14.00	14.17
16	12.24	12.40	12.57	12.74	12.91	13.08	13.25	13.43	13.60	13.77	13.95
17	12.02	12.19	12.36	12.53	12.71	12.88	13.05	13.23	13.41	13.58	13.76
18	11.84	12.01	12.18	12.36	12.53	12.71	12.89	13.06	13.24	13.42	13.60
19	11.68	11.85	12.03	12.21	12.39	12.56	12.74	12.92	13.10	13.29	13.47
20	11.54	11.72	11.90	12.08	12.26	12.44	12.62	12.80	12.99	13.17	13.36
21	11.43	11.61	11.79	11.97	12.15	12.33	12.52	12.70	12.89	13.08	13.26
22	11.33	11.51	11.69	11.87	12.06	12.24	12.43	12.62	12.81	12.99	13.18
23	11.24	11.42	11.61	11.79	11.98	12.17	12.35	12.54	12.73	12.92	13.12
24	11.16	11.35	11.53	11.72	11.91	12.10	12.29	12.48	12.67	12.86	13.06
25	11.10	11.28	11.47	11.66	11.85	12.04	12.23	12.43	12.62	12.81	13.01
26	11.04	11.23	11.42	11.61	11.80	11.99	12.19	12.38	12.57	12.77	12.97
27	10.99	11.18	11.37	11.56	11.76	11.95	12.14	12.34	12.54	12.73	12.93
28	10.94	11.14	11.33	11.52	11.72	11.91	12.11	12.31	12.50	12.70	12.90
29	10.91	11.10	11.29	11.49	11.68	11.88	12.08	12.28	12.47	12.67	12.87
30	10.87	11.07	11.26	11.46	11.66	11.85	12.05	12.25	12.45	12.65	12.85
35	10.76	10.96	11.16	11.36	11.56	11.76	11.96	12.17	12.37	12.57	12.78
40	10.70	10.90	11.10	11.31	11.51	11.72	11.92	12.13	12.33	12.54	12.74

# Yrs.	15½%	15¾%	16%	16¼%	16½%	16¾%	17%	17½%	18%
5	24.06	24.19	24.32	24.46	24.59	24.72	24.86	25.13	25.40
10	16.45	16.60	16.76	16.91	17.07	17.23	17.38	17.70	18.02
12	15.34	15.50	15.66	15.83	15.99	16.16	16.32	16.66	17.00
15	14.34	14.52	14.69	14.87	15.04	15.22	15.40	15.75	16.11
16	14.12	14.30	14.48	14.65	14.83	15.01	15.19	15.55	15.92
17	13.94	14.12	14.30	14.48	14.66	14.84	15.02	15.39	15.76
18	13.78	13.96	14.15	14.33	14.51	14.70	14.88	15.26	15.63
19	13.65	13.84	14.02	14.21	14.39	14.58	14.77	15.15	15.53
20	13.54	13.73	13.92	14.11	14.29	14.48	14.67	15.05	15.44
21	13.45	13.64	13.83	14.02	14.21	14.40	14.59	14.98	15.37
22	13.37	13.56	13.75	13.95	14.14	14.33	14.53	14.91	15.31
23	13.31	13.50	13.69	13.89	14.08	14.27	14.47	14.86	15.26
24	13.25	13.44	13.64	13.83	14.03	14.23	14.42	14.82	15.21
25	13.20	13.40	13.59	13.79	13.99	14.18	14.38	14.78	15.18
26	13.16	13.36	13.56	13.75	13.95	14.15	14.35	14.75	15.15
27	13.13	13.32	13.52	13.72	13.92	14.12	14.32	14.72	15.13
28	13.10	13.30	13.50	13.70	13.90	14.10	14.30	14.70	15.11
29	13.07	13.27	13.47	13.67	13.87	14.08	14.28	14.68	15.09
30	13.05	13.25	13.45	13.65	13.86	14.06	14.26	14.67	15.08
35	12.98	13.19	13.39	13.59	13.80	14.00	14.21	14.62	15.03
40	12.95	13.16	13.36	13.57	13.77	13.98	14.19	14.60	15.02

B

SETTLEMENT COSTS

The law requires the lender to give you a copy of this booklet when you apply for a loan. But, when you apply for a loan, you've committed yourself to buy the property. Since this booklet contains much that you should know before you make an offer, I've included it in this appendix.

Settlement Costs

A HUD Guide

Revised Edition

The content of this booklet has been prepared, prescribed and approved by the U.S. Department of Housing and Urban Development, as required by Section 5 of the Real Estate Settlement Procedures Act of 1974 (Public Law 93-533), effective on June 30, 1976.

This publication may be reprinted. However, in no case may any change, deletion, or addition be made in its content.

For sale by the Superintendent of Documents, U.S. Government Printing Office
Washington, D.C. 20402

Settlement Costs

Introduction

For many people, buying a home is the single most significant financial step of a lifetime. The Real Estate Settlement Procedures Act (RESPA), a Federal statute, helps to protect you at this step.

Settlement is the formal process by which ownership of real property passes from seller to buyer. It is the end of the home buying process, the time when title to the property is transferred from the seller to the buyer.

RESPA covers most residential mortgage loans used to finance the purchase of one- to four-family properties, such as a house, a condominium or cooperative apartment unit, a lot with a mobile home, or a lot on which you will build a house or place a mobile home using the proceeds of the loan.

RESPA was not designed to set the prices of settlement services. Instead, it provides you with information to take the mystery out of the settlement process, so that you can shop for settlement services and make informed decisions.

This information booklet was prepared as provided in RESPA by the Assistant Secretary for Housing – Federal Housing Commissioner of the U.S. Department of Housing and Urban Development.

Part One of this booklet describes the settlement process and nature of charges and suggests questions you might ask of lenders, attorneys and others to clarify what services they will provide you for the charges quoted. It also contains information on your rights and remedies available under RESPA, and alerts you to unfair or illegal practices.

Part Two of this booklet is an item-by-item explanation of settlement services and costs, with sample forms and worksheets that will help you in making cost comparisons. Remember that terminology varies by locality so that terminology used here may not exactly match that used in your area. For example, settlement is sometimes called closing and settlement charges are frequently referred to as closing costs.

Part I

What Happens and When

Suppose you have just found a home you would like to buy. In a typical situation, when you reach an agreement with the seller on the price, you then sign a sales contract. The terms of the sales contract can be negotiated to your benefit, as the booklet explains below.

Next you will probably seek a mortgage to finance the purchase. This booklet suggests questions you should raise as you shop for a lender.

When you file your application for a loan, the lender is required by RESPA to provide a good faith estimate of the costs of settlement services and a copy of this booklet. The lender has three business days, after written loan application, to mail these materials to you.

Between loan application time and settlement, you usually have a chance to shop for settlement services, to ensure that you will obtain good value for your money.

Finally, one business day before settlement, if you so request, the person conducting the settlement must allow you an opportunity to see a Uniform Settlement Statement that shows whatever figures are available at that time for settlement charges you will be required to pay. At settlement, the completed Uniform Settlement Statement will be given to you.

Note: In some parts of the country where there is no actual settlement meeting, or in cases where neither you nor your authorized agent attends the closing meeting, the person conducting settlement has the obligation to deliver the Uniform Settlement Statement to you by mail.

There is no standard settlement process followed in all localities; therefore, what you experience, involving many of the same services, will probably vary from the description in this booklet.

Shopping for Services

When settlement arrives, you are committed to the purchase of the property and may have made a partial payment, sometimes called earnest money, to the seller or his agent. Services may have been performed for which you are obligated to pay. Unless a seller fails to perform a legally binding promise or has acted in a fraudulent fashion, you are normally obligated to complete your part of the contract and pay settlement costs. Thus the time to decide the terms of sale, raise questions, and establish fair fees is not at time of settlement, but earlier, when you negotiate with the seller and providers of settlement services. By the time of settlement, any changes in settlement costs and purchase terms may be difficult to negotiate.

You can also negotiate with the seller of the house about who pays various settlement fees and other charges. There are generally no fixed rules about which party pays which fees, although in many cases this is largely controlled by local custom.

Among the many factors that determine the amount you will pay for settlement costs are the location of your new home, the type of sales contract you negotiate, the arrangements made with the real estate broker, the lender you select, and your decisions in selecting the various firms that provide required settlement services. If the chosen house is located in a "special flood hazard area," identified as such by HUD on a flood insurance map, the lender may require you to purchase flood insurance pursuant to Federal law (See page 26). Information on flood insurance availability, limits of coverage and copies of maps can be obtained through the National Flood Insurers Association servicing company for your State or by calling HUD toll free numbers 800-638-6620.

Role of the Broker
Although real estate brokers provide helpful advice on many aspects of home buying, and may in some areas supervise the settlement, they normally serve the interests of the seller, not the buyer. The broker's basic objective is to obtain a signed contract of sale which properly expresses the agreement of the parties, and to complete the sale. However, as State licensing laws require that the broker be fair in his dealings with all parties to the transaction, you should feel free to point this out to the broker if you feel you are being treated unfairly.

A broker may recommend that you deal with a particular lender, title company, attorney, or other provider of settlement services. Ask brokers why they recommend a particular company or firm in preference to others. Advise them that while you welcome their suggestions (and, indeed, they probably have good contacts), you reserve the right to pick your own providers of services.

Negotiating a Sales Contract

If you have obtained this booklet before you have signed a sales contract with the seller of the property, here are some important points to consider regarding that contract.

The sales agreement you and the seller sign can expressly state which settlement costs you will pay and which will be paid by the seller although some may be negotiable up to time of settlement. Buyers can and do negotiate with sellers as to which party is to pay for specific settlement costs. The success of such negotiations depends upon factors such as how eager the seller is to sell and you are to buy, the quality of the house itself, how long the house has been on the market, whether other potential buyers are interested, and how willing you are to negotiate for lower costs. If the contract is silent on these costs, they are still open to negotiation.

There is no standard sales contract which you are required to sign. You are entitled to make any modifications or additions in any standard form contract to which the seller will agree. You should consider including the following clauses:

• The seller provides title, free and clear of all liens and encumbrances except those which you specifically agree to in the contract or approve when the results of the title search are reported to you. You may negotiate as to who will pay for the title search service to determine whether the title is "clear."

• A refund of your deposit (earnest money) be made by the seller or escrow agent, and cancellation of the sale if you are unable to secure from a lending institution a first mortgage or deed-of-trust loan with an amount, interest rate, and length of term, as set forth in the contract, within a stated time period.

• A certificate be provided at time of settlement, stating that the house is free from termites or termite damage.

• A certificate that the plumbing, heating, electrical systems and appliances are in working order, and that the house is structurally sound. Negotiate who pays for any necessary inspections. There is no uniform custom in most areas. Many buyers prefer to pay for these inspections because they want to know that the inspector is conducting the service for them, not for the seller.

(You can also purchase a warranty to back up the inspection, if you wish).

• An agreement be reached on how taxes, water and sewer charges, premiums on existing transferable insurance policies, utility bills, interest on mortgages, and rent (if there are tenants) are to be divided between buyer and seller as of the date of the settlement.

Before you sign the sales contract, make sure that it correctly expresses your agreement with the seller on such important details as the sales price of the home, method of payment, the time set for your taking possession, what fixtures, appliances, and personal property are to be sold with the home, and the other items described above.

The above list is not complete, but does illustrate the importance of the sales agreement and its terms. Before you sign a sales contract you may want to ask an attorney to review the proposed agreement and determine if it protects your interests, for once signed, the contract is binding on you and the seller. If you do not know of an attorney you may wish to consult the local bar association referral service or neighborhood legal service office.

Selecting an Attorney

If you seek the aid of an attorney, first ask what services will be performed for what fee. If the fee seems too high, shop for another lawyer. Does the attorney have substantial experience in real estate? The U.S. Supreme Court has said that it is illegal for bar associations to fix minimum fee schedules for attorneys, so do not be bashful about discussing and shopping for legal fees you can afford. Your attorney will understand.

Questions you may wish to ask the attorney include: What is the charge for reading documents and giving advice concerning them? For being present at settlement? Will the attorney represent any other party in the transaction in addition to you? In some areas attorneys act as closing agents handling the mechanical aspects of the settlement. A lawyer who does this may not fully represent your interests since, as closing agent, he would be representing the seller and other interests as well.

Selecting a Lender

Your choice of lender will influence not only your settlement costs, but also the monthly cost of your mortgage loan.

Lending institutions require certain settlement services, such as a new survey or title insurance, or they may charge you for other settlement-related services, such as the appraisal or credit report. You may find, in shopping for a lender, that other institutions may not have such requirements. Part Two of this booklet provides a description of the various kinds of services that may be required and fees that may be charged to you. You will also find a worksheet in Part Two, which you can use to compare requirements and cost estimates from different lenders.

Many lending institutions deal regularly with certain title companies, attorneys, appraisers, surveyors, and others in whom they have confidence. They may want to arrange for settlement services to be provided through these parties. This booklet discusses your rights in such a situation under the section below on Home Buyer's Rights.

If you choose a lending institution which allows you a choice of settlement service providers, you should shop and compare among the providers in your area, to find the best service for the best price. Where the lender designates the use of particular firms, check with other firms to see if the lender's stated charges are competitive.

Questions you may want to ask the lender should include these:

● Are you required to carry life or disability insurance? Must you obtain it from a particular company? (You may prefer no insurance or may wish to obtain it at a better premium rate elsewhere.)

● Is there a late payment charge? How much? How late may your payment be before the charge is imposed? You should be aware that late payments may harm your credit rating.

● If you wish to pay off the loan in advance of maturity (for example, if you move and sell the house), must you pay a prepayment penalty? How much? If so, for how long a period will it apply?

● Will the lender release you from personal liability if

your loan is assumed by someone else when you sell your house?

• If you sell the house and the buyer assumes your loan, will the lender have the right to charge an assumption fee, raise the rate of interest, or require payment in full of the mortgage?

• If you have a financial emergency, will the terms of the loan include a future advances clause, permitting you to borrow additional money on the mortgage after you have paid off part of the original loan?

• Will you be required to pay monies into a special reserve (escrow or impound) account to cover taxes or insurance? If so, how large a deposit will be required at the closing of the sale? The amount of reserve deposits required is limited under RESPA. Some recent State laws have required that these accounts bear interest for the benefit of the borrower (buyer). If reserve requirements can be waived, you will be responsible for paying the particular charges for taxes or insurance directly to the tax collector or insurance company. Further information is in "Reserve Accounts" in Part Two of this booklet.

• In looking for the best mortgage to fit your particular financial needs, you may wish to check the terms and requirements of a private conventional loan versus a loan insured through the Federal Housing Administration or Farmers Home Administration or guaranteed by the Veterans Administration. The FHA, VA, and Farmers Home Administration loans involve Federal ceilings on permissible charges for some settlement services, which may be of interest to you. Ask lenders about these programs. Another source of information about the federally insured or guaranteed programs is from public documents, some of which are listed in the bibliography of this booklet.

• If you are dealing with the lender who holds the existing mortgage, you might be able to take over the prior loan, in a transaction called "assumption." Assumption usually saves money in settlement costs if the interest rate on the prior loan is lower than that being asked in the market. In times of inflation in the housing market, a higher downpayment might be required than if you had obtained a new loan. You may want to ask the seller whether he would be willing to "take back" a second mortgage to finance part of the difference between the assumed loan and the sales price.

Selecting a Settlement Agent

Settlement practices vary from locality to locality, and even within the same county or city. In various areas settlements are conducted by lending institutions, title insurance companies, escrow companies, real estate brokers, and attorneys for the buyer or seller. By investigating and comparing practices and rates, you may find that the first suggested settlement agent may not be the least expensive. You might save money by taking the initiative in arranging for settlement and selecting the firm and location which meets your needs.

Securing Title Services

A title search may take the form of an abstract, a compilation of pertinent legal documents which provides a condensed history of the property ownership and related matters. In many areas title searches are performed by extracting information from the public record without assembling abstracts. In either situation, an expert examination is necessary to determine the status of title and this is normally made by attorneys or title company employees. In areas where both title insurance companies and attorneys perform these and other settlement services, compare fees for services (such as title certification, document preparation, notary fee, closing fee, etc.), provided by each to determine the better source for these services.

In many jurisdictions a few days or weeks prior to settlement the title insurance company will issue a binder (sometimes called a Commitment to Insure) or preliminary report, a summary of findings based on the search or abstract. It is usually sent to the lender for use until the title insurance policy is issued after the settlement. The binder lists all the defects in and liens against the title identified by the search. You should arrange to have a copy sent to you (or to an attorney who represents you) so that you can raise an objection if there are matters affecting the title which you did not agree to accept when you signed the contract of sale.

Title insurance is often required to protect the lender against loss if a flaw in title is not found by the title search made when the house is purchased. You may also get an owner's title policy to protect yourself. In some States, attorneys provide bar-related title insurance as part of their services in examining title and providing a title opinion. In these States the attorney's fee may include the title insurance premium, although the total title-related charges in the transaction should be taken into account in determining whether you will realize any savings.

Bear in mind that a title insurance policy issued only to the lender does not protect you. Similarly, the policy issued to a prior owner, such as the person from whom you are buying the house, does not protect you. To protect yourself from loss because of a mistake made by the title searcher, or because of a legal defect of a type which does not appear on the public records, you will need an owner's policy. Such a mistake rarely occurs but, when it does, it can be financially devastating to the uninsured. If you buy an owner's policy it is usually much less expensive if purchased simultaneously with a lender's policy.

To reduce title insurance costs, be sure to compare rates among various title insurance companies, and ask what services and limitations on coverage are provided by each policy so that you can decide whether a higher rate is consistent with your needs.

Depending upon practice in your jurisdiction, there may be no need for a full historical title search each time title to a home is transferred. If you are buying a home which has changed hands within the last several years, inquire at the title company that issued the previous title insurance policy about a "reissue rate," which would be a lower charge than for a new policy. If the title insurance policy of the previous owner is available, take it to the title insurer or lawyer whom you have selected to do your search.

To mark the boundaries of the property as set out in the title, lenders may require a survey. A home buyer may be able to avoid the cost of a repetitive complete survey of the property if he can locate the surveyor who previously surveyed the project which he can update. However, the requirements of investors who buy loans originated by your lender may limit the lender's discretion to negotiate this point. Check with the lender or title company on this.

Home Buyer's Rights

Information Booklet
When you submit or the lender prepares your written application for a loan, the lender is legally required, under RESPA to give you a copy of this booklet. If the lender does not give it to you in person on the day of your loan application, he must put it in the mail to you no later than three business days after your application is filed.

Good Faith Estimates
When you file your application for a loan, the lender must also, under the terms of RESPA, provide you with good faith estimates of settlement services charges you will likely incur. If he does not give it to you, he has three business days in which to put it in the mail.

See Part Two of this booklet for a full item-by-item discussion of settlement services. On the form entitled "Settlement Statement," you will find Section L, which lists possible settlement services and charges you will encounter.

The lender is required to give you his good faith estimate, based upon his experience in the locality in which the property is located, for each settlement charge in Section L that he anticipates you will pay, except for paid-in-advance hazard insurance premium (line 903) and reserves deposited with the lender (all Section 1000 items). The estimate may be stated as either a dollar amount or range for each charge. Where the lender designates the use of a particular firm, the lender must make its good faith estimate based upon the lender's knowledge of the amounts charged by the firm. The form used for this good faith estimate must be concise and clear, and the estimates must bear a reasonable relationship to the costs you will likely incur. If the lender provides you good faith estimates in the form of ranges, ask the lender what the total settlement costs will most likely be. While the lender is not obligated to provide this information under RESPA, it is important for you to know as you evaluate the different mortgage packages being offered you.

Lenders were not required to give good faith estimates for reserves deposited with them or for the prepaid hazard insurance premium because these charges require information not normally known to the lender at time of loan application. It is important for you to make these calculations because they can represent a sizeable cash payment you may have to make at settlement. Calculation of the reserve items is presented later in this booklet under "Reserve Accounts." Ask the lender what his policies are in terms of reserve accounts, for what items the lender requires reserves and for what period of time. You may want to ask the lender to run through a hypothetical calculation for you based upon the date you will most likely close on the house. Other assumptions may be necessary, for example, the assessed value of the property for determining property taxes. The lender can probably be more specific on hazard insurance premiums, particularly for those coverages which a lender requires.

Once you have obtained these estimates from the lender be aware that they are only estimates. The final costs may not be the same. Estimates are subject to changing market conditions, and fees may change. Changes in the date of settlement may result in changes in escrow and proration requirements. In certain cases, it may not be possible for the lender to anticipate exactly the pricing policies of settlement firms. Moreover, your own careful choice of settlement firms might result in lower costs, just as hasty decisions might result in higher costs. Remember that the lender's estimate is not a guarantee.

Lender Designation of Settlement Service Providers
Some lending institutions follow the practice of designating specific settlement service providers to be used for legal services, title examination services, title insurance, or the conduct of settlement.

Where this occurs the lender, under RESPA, is required to provide you as part of the good faith estimates a statement in which the lender sets forth:

1. The name, address and telephone number of each provider he has designated. This must include a statement of the specific services each designated firm is to provide for you, as well as an estimate of the amount the lender anticipates you will have to pay for the service, based on the lender's experience as to what the designated provider usually charges. If the services or charges are not clear to you, ask further questions.

2. Whether each designated firm has a business relationship with the lender.

While designated firms often provide the services needed, a conflict of interest may exist. Take, for example, the situation where the provider must choose between your interests and those of the lender. Where legal services are involved, it is wise to employ your own attorney to ensure that your interests are properly protected. It is wise for you to contact other firms to determine whether their costs are competitive and their services are comparable.

Disclosure of Settlement Costs One Day Before Closing and Delivery

One business day before settlement, you have the right to inspect the form, called the Uniform Settlement Statement, on which are itemized the services provided to you and fees charged to you. This form (developed by the U.S. Department of Housing and Urban Development) is filled out by the person who will conduct the settlement meeting. Be sure you have the name, address, and telephone number of the settlement agent if you wish to inspect this form or if you have any questions.

The settlement agent may not have all costs available the day before closing, but is obligated to show you, upon request, what is available.

The Uniform Settlement Statement must be delivered or mailed to you (while another statement goes to the seller) at or before settlement. If, however, you waive your right to delivery of the completed statement at settlement, it will then be mailed at the earliest practicable date.

In parts of the country where the settlement agent does not require a meeting, or in cases where you or your agent do not attend the settlement, the statement will be mailed as soon as practicable after settlement and no advance inspection is required.

The Uniform Settlement Statement is not used in situations where:

1. there are no settlement fees charged to the buyer (because the seller has assumed all settlement-related expenses), or

2. the total amount the borrower is required to pay for all charges imposed at settlement is determined by a fixed amount and the borrower is informed of this fixed amount at the time of loan application. In the latter case,

the lender is required to provide the borrower, within three business days of application, an itemized list of services rendered.

Escrow Closing

Settlement practices differ from State to State. In some parts of the country, settlement may be conducted by an escrow agent, which may be a lender, real estate agent, title company representative, attorney, or an escrow company. After entering into a contract of sale, the parties sign an escrow agreement which requires them to deposit specified documents and funds with the agent. Unlike other types of closing, the parties do not meet around a table to sign and exchange documents. The agent may request a title report and policy; draft a deed or other documents; obtain rent statements; pay off existing loans; adjust taxes, rents, and insurance between the buyer and seller; compute interest on loans; and acquire hazard insurance. All this may be authorized in the escrow agreement. If all the papers and monies are deposited with the agent within the agreed time, the escrow is "closed."

The escrow agent then records the appropriate documents and gives each party the documents and money each is entitled to receive, including the completed Uniform Settlement Statement. If one party has failed to fulfill his agreement, the escrow is not closed and legal complications may follow.

Truth-in-Lending

The lender is required, usually within three days of receiving your application, to give you or place in the mail to you a Truth in Lending statement that will disclose the "annual percentage rate" (APR). The APR reflects the cost of your mortgage loan as a yearly rate. This rate may be higher than the rate stated in your mortgage or deed of trust note because the APR includes, in addition to interest, loan discount (points), fees, and other credit costs. The Truth in Lending statement also discloses other useful information, such as the finance charge, schedule of payments, late payment charges, and whether or not additional charges will be assessed if you pay off the balance of your loan before it is due (prepayment penalty).

Some of the information that the lender is required to disclose may not be certain at the time the lender is required to give you the Truth in Lending statement. If so, the lender will indicate that the uncertain disclosures are estimates. Should the actual APR differ by more than a small amount from the lender's estimate, the lender must give you a corrected Truth in Lending statement no later than at settlement. However, if the estimated APR proves to be correct, the lender *need not* give you a new Truth in Lending statement, even if other disclosures have changed. For this reason, you may want to ask the lender shortly before settlement if all the Truth in Lending disclosures are still accurate.

Protection Against Unfair Practices
A principal finding of Congress in the Real Estate Settlement Procedures Act of 1974 is that consumers need protection from ". . . unnecessarily high settlement charges caused by certain abusive practices that have developed in some areas of the country." The potential problems discussed below may not be applicable to most loan settlements, and the discussion is not intended to deter you from buying a home. Most professionals in the settlement business will give you good service. Nevertheless, you may save yourself money and worry by keeping the following considerations in mind:

Kickbacks. Kickbacks and referrals of business for gain are often tied together. The law prohibits anyone from giving or taking a fee, kickback, or anything of value under an agreement that business will be referred to a specific person or organization. It is also illegal to charge or accept a fee or part of a fee where no service has actually been performed. This requirement does not prevent agents for lenders and title companies, attorneys, or others actually performing a service in connection with the mortgage loan or settlement transaction, from receiving compensation for their work. It also does not prohibit payments pursuant to cooperative brokerage, such as a multiple listing service, and referral arrangements or arrangements between real estate agents and brokers.

The prohibition is aimed primarily at eliminating the kind of arrangement in which one party agrees to return part of his fee in order to obtain business from the referring party. The danger is that some settlement fees can be inflated to cover payments to this additional party, resulting in a higher total cost to you. There are criminal penalties of both fine and imprisonment for any violation of these provisions of law. There are also provisions for you to recover three times the amount of the kickback, rebate, or referral fee involved, through a private lawsuit. In any successful action to enforce your right, the court may award you court costs together with a fee for your attorney.

Title Companies. Under the law, the seller may not require, as a condition of sale, that title insurance be purchased by the buyer from any particular title company. A violation of this will make the seller liable to you in an amount equal to three times all charges made for the title insurance.

Fair Credit Reporting. There are credit reporting agencies around the Nation which are in the business of compiling credit reports on citizens, covering data such as how you pay your bills, if you have been sued, arrested, filed for bankruptcy, etc.. In addition, this file may include your neighbors' and friends' views of your character, general reputation, or manner of living. This latter information is referred to as an "investigative consumer report."

The Fair Credit Reporting Act does not give you the right to inspect or physically handle your actual report at the credit reporting agency, nor to receive an exact copy of the report. But you are entitled to a summary of the report, showing the nature, substance, and sources of the information it contains.

If the terms of your financing have been adversely affected by a credit report, you have the right to inspect the summary of that report free of charge (there may otherwise be a small fee). The accuracy of the report can also be challenged, and corrections required to be made. For more detailed information on your credit report rights, contact the Federal Trade Commission (FTC) in Washington, D.C. or the nearest FTC regional office. *The FTC Buyer's Guide No. 7: Fair Credit Reporting Act* is a good summary of this Act.

Equal Credit Opportunity

The Equal Credit Opportunity Act prohibits lenders from discriminating against credit applicants on the basis of race, color, religion, national origin, sex, marital status, age (provided that the applicant has the capacity to enter into a binding contract), because all or part of the applicant's income derives from any public assistance program, or because the applicant has in good faith exercised any right under the Consumer Credit Protection Act. If you feel you have been discriminated against by any lender, you may have a private right of legal action against that lender and you may wish to consult an attorney; or you may wish to consult the Federal agency that administers compliance with this law concerning the lender you suspect has violated your rights thereunder. Inquire of the lender regarding the identity of that agency. You may also contact your regional Federal Reserve Bank about your rights under this Act.

The Right to File Complaints

As with any consumer problems, the place to start if you have a complaint is back at the source of the problem (the lender, settlement agent, broker, etc.). If that initial effort brings no satisfaction and you think you have suffered damages through violations of the Real Estate Settlement Procedures Act of 1974, as amended, you may be entitled to bring a civil action in the U.S. District Court for the District in which the property involved is located, or in any other court of competent jurisdiction. This a matter best determined by your lawyer. Any suit you file under RESPA must be brought within one year from the date of the occurrence of the alleged violation. You may have legal remedies under other State or Federal laws in addition to RESPA.

You should note that RESPA provides for specific legal sanctions only under the provisions which prohibit kickbacks and unearned fees, and which prohibit the seller from requiring the buyer to use a particular title insurer. If you feel you should recover damages for violations of any provision of RESPA, you should consult your lawyer.

Most settlement service providers, particularly lenders, are supervised by some governmental agency at the local, State and/or Federal level. Others are subject to the control of self-policing associations. If you feel a provider of settlement services has violated RESPA, you can address your complaint to the agency or association which has supervisory responsibility over the provider. For the names of such agencies or associations, you will have to check with local and State Governments or consumer agencies operating in your area. You are also encouraged to forward a copy of complaints regarding RESPA violations to the HUD Office of Single Family Housing and Mortgagee Activities, which has the primary responsibility for administering the RESPA program. Your complaints can lay the foundation for future legislative or administrative actions.

Send copies of complaints, and inquiries, to:

U.S. Department of Housing and Urban Development
Office of Single Family Housing and
Mortgagee Activities
451 7th Street S.W.
Washington, D.C. 20410

The Home Buyer's Obligations (Repayment of Loan and Maintenance of Home)

At settlement you will sign papers legally obligating you to pay the mortgage loan financing the purchase of your home. You must pay according to the terms of the loan – interest rate, amount and due date of each monthly payment, repayment period – specified in the documents signed by you. You will probably sign at settlement a note or bond which is your promise to repay the loan for the unpaid balance of the purchase price. You will also sign a mortgage or deed of trust which pledges your home as security for repayment of the loan.

Failure to make monthly mortgage payments on time may lead to a late payment charge, if provided for in the documents. If you default on the loan by missing payments altogether and do not make them up within a period of time usually set by State law, the documents also specify certain actions which the lender may take to recover the amount owed. Ultimately, after required notice to you, a default could lead to foreclosure and sale of the home which secures your loan.

You should also be careful to maintain your home in a proper State of repair, both for your own satisfaction and comfort as the occupant and because the home is security for your loan. The mortgage or deed of trust may in fact specifically obligate you to keep the property in good repair and not allow deterioration.

Read the documents carefully at or before settlement, and be aware of your obligations as a homeowner.

Part II

This part of the booklet provides an item-by-item discussion of possible settlement services that may be required and for which you may be charged. It also provides a sample of the Uniform Settlement Statement form, and worksheets which you may find handy for comparing costs from different service providers.

Sections A through I of the Uniform Settlement Statement contain information concerning the loan and parties to the settlement. Sections J and K contain a summary of all funds transferred between the buyer, seller, lender, and providers of settlement services. The bottom line in the left-hand column shows the net cash to be paid by the borrower, while the bottom line in the right-hand column shows the cash due the seller.

Section L is a list of settlement services that may be required and for which you may be charged. Blank lines are provided for any additional settlement services.

You would add up the costs entered on the lines of Section L, and carry them forward to Sections J and K, in order to arrive at the net cash figures on the bottom lines of the left and right columns.

Uses of This Form

1. **Settlement services comparisons.** As you shop for settlement services, you can use the Settlement Costs Worksheet as a handy guide, noting on it the different services required by different lenders and the different fees quoted by different service providers.

2. **Disclosure of actual settlement costs.** A copy of this form, or one with similar terminology, sequence and

numbering of line items, must be filled out by the person conducting the settlement meeting. Your right to inspect the form one business day before settlement was discussed earlier in this booklet. The form will be completely filled in at the settlement meeting.

Specific Settlement Services

The following defines and discusses each specific settlement service. The numbers correspond to the items listed in Section L of the Uniform Settlement Statement form.

700. Sales/Broker's Commission

This is the total dollar amount of sales commission, usually paid by the seller. Fees are usually a percentage of the selling price of the house, and are intended to compensate brokers or salesmen for their services. Custom and/or the negotiated agreement between the seller and the broker determine the amount of the commission.

701-702. Division of Commission

If several brokers or salesmen work together to sell the house, the commission may be split among them. If they are paid from funds collected for settlement, this is shown on lines 701-702.

703. Commission Paid at Settlement

Sometimes the broker will retain the earnest money deposit to apply towards his commission. In this case, line 703 will show only the remainder of the commission which will be paid at settlement.

800. Items Payable in Connection with Loan

These are the fees which lenders charge to process, approve and make the mortgage loan.

801. Loan Origination

This fee covers the lender's administrative costs in processing the loan. Often expressed as a percentage of the loan, the fee will vary among lenders and from locality to locality. Generally the buyer pays the fee unless another arrangement has been made with the seller and written into the sales contract.

802. Loan Discount

Often called "points," a loan discount is a one-time charge used to adjust the yield on the loan to what market conditions demand. It is used to offset constraints

A.

U. S. DEPARTMENT OF HOUSING AND URBAN DEVELOPMENT

SETTLEMENT STATEMENT

B. TYPE OF LOAN

1. ☐ FHA 2. ☐ FmHA 3. ☐ CONV. UNINS.
4. ☐ VA 5. ☐ CONV. INS.

6. File Number: 7. Loan Number:

8. Mortgage Insurance Case Number:

C. NOTE: *This form is furnished to give you a statement of actual settlement costs. Amounts paid to and by the settlement agent are shown. Items marked "(p.o.c.)" were paid outside the closing; they are shown here for informational purposes and are not included in the totals.*

D. NAME OF BORROWER:	E. NAME OF SELLER:	F. NAME OF LENDER:

G. PROPERTY LOCATION:	H. SETTLEMENT AGENT:	
	PLACE OF SETTLEMENT:	I. SETTLEMENT DATE:

J. SUMMARY OF BORROWER'S TRANSACTION	
100. GROSS AMOUNT DUE FROM BORROWER:	
101. Contract sales price	
102. Personal property	
103. Settlement charges to borrower *(line 1400)*	
104.	
105.	
Adjustments for items paid by seller in advance	
106. City/town taxes to	
107. County taxes to	
108. Assessments to	

K. SUMMARY OF SELLER'S TRANSACTION	
400. GROSS AMOUNT DUE TO SELLER:	
401. Contract sales price	
402. Personal property	
403.	
404.	
405.	
Adjustments for items paid by seller in advance	
406. City/town taxes to	
407. County taxes to	
408. Assessments to	

(Form Continues on Next Page)

109.			409.	
110.			410.	
111.			411.	
112.			412.	
120.	GROSS AMOUNT DUE FROM BORROWER		420.	GROSS AMOUNT DUE TO SELLER

200. AMOUNTS PAID BY OR IN BEHALF OF BORROWER:		500. REDUCTIONS IN AMOUNT DUE TO SELLER:	
201. Deposit or earnest money		501. Excess deposit *(see instructions)*	
202. Principal amount of new loan(s)		502. Settlement charges to seller *(line 1400)*	
203. Existing loan(s) taken subject to		503. Existing loan(s) taken subject to	
204.		504. Payoff of first mortgage loan	
205.		505. Payoff of second mortgage loan	
206.		506.	
207.		507.	
208.		508.	
209.		509.	

Adjustments for items unpaid by seller (borrower) / *Adjustments for items unpaid by seller*

210. City/town taxes	to		510. City/town taxes	to	
211. County taxes	to		511. County taxes	to	
212. Assessments	to		512. Assessments	to	
213.			513.		
214.			514.		
215.			515.		
216.			516.		
217.			517.		
218.			518.		
219.			519.		
220.	TOTAL PAID BY/FOR BORROWER		520.	TOTAL REDUCTION AMOUNT DUE SELLER	

300. CASH AT SETTLEMENT FROM/TO BORROWER		600. CASH AT SETTLEMENT TO/FROM SELLER	
301. Gross amount due from borrower *(line 120)*		601. Gross amount due to seller *(line 420)*	
302. Less amounts paid by/for borrower *(line 220)*	( )	602. Less reductions in amount due seller *(line 520)*	( )
303. CASH (□ FROM) (□ TO) BORROWER		603. CASH (□ TO) (□ FROM) SELLER	

Previous Edition is Obsolete

(Back of Form Continued on Next Page)

HUD-1 (5-76)

L. SETTLEMENT CHARGES

	PAID FROM BORROWER'S FUNDS AT SETTLEMENT	PAID FROM SELLER'S FUNDS AT SETTLEMENT
700. TOTAL SALES/BROKER'S COMMISSION *based on price* $ @ % =		
Division of Commission (line 700) as follows:		
701. $ to		
702. $ to		
703. Commission paid at Settlement		
704.		
800. ITEMS PAYABLE IN CONNECTION WITH LOAN		
801. Loan Origination Fee %		
802. Loan Discount %		
803. Appraisal Fee to		
804. Credit Report to		
805. Lender's Inspection Fee		
806. Mortgage Insurance Application Fee to		
807. Assumption Fee		
808.		
809.		
810.		
811.		
900. ITEMS REQUIRED BY LENDER TO BE PAID IN ADVANCE		
901. Interest from to @ $ /day		
902. Mortgage Insurance Premium for months to		
903. Hazard Insurance Premium for years to		
904. years to		
905.		
1000. RESERVES DEPOSITED WITH LENDER		
1001. Hazard insurance months @ $ per month		
1002. Mortgage insurance months @ $ per month		
1003. City property taxes months @ $ per month		
1004. County property taxes months @ $ per month		
1005. Annual assessments months @ $ per month		
1006. months @ $ per month		
1007. months @ $ per month		

(Form Continues on Next Page)

249

1008. months @ $ per month

1100. TITLE CHARGES

1101.	Settlement or closing fee	
1102.	Abstract or title search	to
1103.	Title examination	to
1104.	Title insurance binder	to
1105.	Document preparation	to
1106.	Notary fees	to
1107.	Attorney's fees	to
	(includes above items numbers;	)
1108.	Title insurance	to
	(includes above items numbers;	)
1109.	Lender's coverage	$
1110.	Owner's coverage	$
1111.		
1112.		
1113.		

1200. GOVERNMENT RECORDING AND TRANSFER CHARGES

1201.	Recording fees: Deed $	; Mortgage $; Releases $
1202.	City/county tax/stamps: Deed $	; Mortgage $
1203.	State tax/stamps: Deed $	; Mortgage $
1204.		
1205.		

1300. ADDITIONAL SETTLEMENT CHARGES

1301.	Survey	to
1302.	Pest inspection	to
1303.		
1304.		
1305.		

1400. TOTAL SETTLEMENT CHARGES *(enter on lines 103, Section J and 502, Section K)*

HUD—1 (5—76)

250

SETTLEMENT COSTS WORK SHEET

(Use this worksheet to compare the charges of various lenders and providers of settlement services.)

	PROVIDER 1	PROVIDER 2	PROVIDER 3
800. ITEMS PAYABLE IN CONNECTION WITH LOAN			
801. Loan Origination Fee %			
802. Loan Discount %			
803. Appraisal Fee to			
804. Credit Report to			
805. Lender's Inspection Fee			
806. Mortgage Insurance Application Fee to			
807. Assumption Fee			
808.			
809.			
810.			
811.			
900. ITEMS REQUIRED BY LENDER TO BE PAID IN ADVANCE			
901. Interest from to @ $ /day			
902. Mortgage Insurance Premium for months to			
903. Hazard Insurance Premium for years to			
904. years to			
905.			
1000. RESERVES DEPOSITED WITH LENDER			
1001. Hazard insurance months @ $ per month			
1002. Mortgage insurance months @ $ per month			
1003. City property taxes months @ $ per month			
1004. County property taxes months @ $ per month			
1005. Annual assessments months @ $ per month			
1006. months @ $ per month			
1007. months @ $ per month			
1008. months @ $ per month			

(Form Continues on Next Page)

1100. TITLE CHARGES

1101.	Settlement or closing fee	to
1102.	Abstract or title search	to
1103.	Title examination	to
1104.	Title insurance binder	to
1105.	Document preparation	to
1106.	Notary fees	to
1107.	Attorney's fees	to
	(includes above items numbers;	
1108.	Title insurance	to
	(includes above items numbers;	
1109.	Lender's coverage	$
1110.	Owner's coverage	$
1111.		
1112.		
1113.		

1200. GOVERNMENT RECORDING AND TRANSFER CHARGES

1201.	Recording fees: Deed $	; Mortgage $	; Releases $
1202.	City/county tax/stamps: Deed $	; Mortgage $	
1203.	State tax/stamps:	Deed $	; Mortgage $
1204.			
1205.			

1300. ADDITIONAL SETTLEMENT CHARGES

1301.	Survey	to
1302.	Pest inspection	to
1303.		
1304.		
1305.		

1400. TOTAL SETTLEMENT CHARGES (enter on lines 103, Section J and 502, Section K)

placed on the yield by State or Federal regulations. Each "point" is equal to one percent of the mortgage amount. For example, if a lender charges four points on a $30,000 loan this amounts to a charge of $1,200.

803. Appraisal Fee

This charge, which may vary significantly from transaction to transaction, pays for a statement of property value for the lender, made by an independent appraiser or by a member of the lender's staff. The lender needs to know if the value of the property is sufficient to secure the loan if you fail to repay the loan according to the provision of your mortgage contract, and the lender must foreclose and take title to the house. The appraiser inspects the house and the neighborhood, and considers sales prices of comparable houses and other factors in determining the value. The appraisal report may contain photos and other information of value to you. It will provide the factual data upon which the appraiser based the appraised value. Ask the lender for a copy of the appraisal report or review the original.

The appraisal fee may be paid by either the buyer or the seller, as agreed in the sales contract. In some cases this fee is included in the Mortgage Insurance Application Fee. See line 806.

804. Credit Report Fee

This fee covers the cost of the credit report, which shows how you have handled other credit transactions. The lender uses this report in conjunction with information you submitted with the application regarding your income, outstanding bills, and employment, to determine whether you are an acceptable credit risk and to help determine how much money to lend you.

Where you encounter credit reporting problems you have protections under the Fair Credit laws as summarized under "Home Buyer's Rights" in this booklet.

805. Lender's Inspection Fee

This charge covers inspections, often of newly constructed housing, made by personnel of the lending institution or an outside inspector. (Pest or other inspections made by companies other than the lender are discussed in connection with line 1302).

This fee covers processing the application for private mortgage insurance which may be required on certain loans. It may cover both the appraisal and application fee.

806. Mortgage Insurance Application Fee

This fee is charged for processing papers for cases in which the buyer takes over the payments on the prior loan of the seller.

807. Assumption Fee

You may be required to prepay certain items, such as interest, mortgage insurance premium and hazard insurance premium, at the time of settlement.

900. Items Required by Lender to Be Paid in Advance

Lenders usually require that borrowers pay at settlement the interest that accrues on the mortgage from the date of settlement to the beginning of the period covered by the first monthly payment. For example, suppose your settlement takes place on April 16, and your first regular monthly payment will be due June 1, to cover interest charges for the month of May. On the settlement date, the lender will collect interest for the period from April 16 to May 1. If you borrowed $30,000 at 9 percent interest, the interest item would be $112.50. This amount will be entered on line 901.

901. Interest

Mortgage insurance protects the lender from loss due to payment default by the homeowner. The lender may require you to pay your first premium in advance, on the day of settlement. The premium may cover a specific number of months or a year in advance. With this insurance protection, the lender is willing to make a larger loan, thus reducing your downpayment requirements. This type of insurance should not be confused with mortgage life, credit life, or disability insurance designed to pay off a mortgage in the event of physical disability or death of the borrower.

902. Mortgage Insurance Premium

This premium prepayment is for insurance protection for you and the lender against loss due to fire, windstorm, and natural hazards. This coverage may be included in a Homeowners Policy which insures against additional risks which may include personal liability and theft. Lenders often require payment of the first year's premium at settlement.

903. Hazard Insurance Premium

A hazard insurance or homeowner's policy may not protect you against loss caused by flooding. In special flood-prone areas identified by HUD, you may be required by Federal law to carry flood insurance on your home. Such insurance may be purchased at low federally subsidized rates in participating communities under the National Flood Insurance Act.

1000. Reserves Deposited With Lenders

Reserves (sometimes called "escrow" or "impound" accounts) are funds held in an account by the lender to assure future payment for such recurring items as real estate taxes and hazard insurance.

You will probably have to pay an initial amount for each of these items to start the reserve account at the time of settlement. A portion of your regular monthly payments will be added to the reserve account. RESPA places limitations on the amount of reserve funds which may be required by the lender. Read "Reserve Accounts" in this booklet for reserve calculation procedures. Do not hesitate to ask the lender to explain any variance between your own calculations and the figure presented to you.

1001. Hazard Insurance

The lender determines the amount of money that must be placed in the reserve in order to pay the next insurance premium when due.

1002. Mortgage Insurance

The lender may require that part of the total annual premium be placed in the reserve account at settlement. The portion to be placed in reserve may be negotiable.

1003-1004. City/County Property Taxes

The lender may require a regular monthly payment to the reserve account for property taxes.

1005. Annual Assessments

This reserve item covers assessments that may be imposed by subdivisions or municipalities for special improvements (such as sidewalks, sewers or paving) or fees (such as homeowners association fees).

1100. Title Charges

Title charges may cover a variety of services performed by the lender or others for handling and supervising the settlement transaction and services related thereto. The specific charges discussed in connection with lines 1101 through 1109 are those most frequently incurred at settlement. Due to the great diversity in practice from area to area, your particular settlement may not include all these items or may include others not listed. Ask your settlement agent to explain how these fees relate to services performed on your behalf. An extended discussion is presented in "Securing Title Services" earlier in this booklet.

1101. Settlement or Closing Fee

This fee is paid to the settlement agent. Responsibility for payment of this fee should be negotiated between the seller and buyer, at the time the sales contract is signed.

1102 – 1104. Abstract or Title Search, Title Examination, Title Insurance Binder

These charges cover the costs of the search and examination of records of previous ownership, transfers, etc., to determine whether the seller can convey clear title to the property, and to disclose any matters on record that could adversely affect the buyer or the lender. Examples of title problems are unpaid mortgages, judgment or tax liens, conveyances of mineral rights, leases, and power line easements or road right-of-ways that could limit use and enjoyment of the real estate. In some areas, a title insurance binder is called a commitment to insure.

1105. Document Preparation

There may be a separate document fee that covers preparation of final legal papers, such as a mortgage, deed of trust, note, or deed. You should check to see that these services, if charged for, are not also covered under some other service fees. Ask the settlement agent.

1106. Notary Fee

This fee is charged for the cost of having a licensed person affix his or her name and seal to various documents authenticating the execution of these documents by the parties.

1107. Attorney's Fees

You may be required to pay for legal services provided to the lender in connection with the settlement, such as examination of the title binder or sales contract. Occasionally this fee can be shared with the seller, if so stipulated in the sales contract. If a lawyer's involvement is required by the lender, the fee will appear on this part of the form. The buyer and seller may each retain an attorney to check the various documents and to represent them at all stages of the transaction including settlement. Where this service is not required and is paid for outside of closing, the person conducting settlement is not obligated to record the fee on the settlement form.

1108. Title Insurance

The total cost of owner's and lender's title insurance is shown here. The borrower may pay all, a part or none of this cost depending on the terms of the sales contract or local custom.

1109. Lender's Title Insurance

A one-time premium may be charged at settlement for a lender's title policy which protects the lender against loss due to problems or defects in connection with the title. The insurance is usually written for the amount of the mortgage loan and covers losses due to defects or problems not identified by title search and examination. In most areas this is customarily paid by the borrower unless the seller agrees in the sales contract to pay part or all of it.

1110. Owner's Title Insurance

This charge is for owner's title insurance protection and protects you against losses due to title defects. In some areas it is customary for the seller to provide the buyer with an owner's policy and for the seller to pay for this policy. In other areas, if the buyer desires an owner's policy he must pay for it.

1200. Government Recording and Transfer Charges

These fees may be paid either by borrower or seller, depending upon your contract when you buy the house or accept the loan commitment. The borrower usually pays the fees for legally recording the new deed and mortgage (item 1201). These fees, collected when property changes hands or when a mortgage loan is made, may be quite large and are set by State and/or local governments. City, county and/or State tax stamps may have to be purchased as well (item 1201 and 1203).

1300. Additional Settlement Charges

The lender or the title insurance company may require that a surveyor conduct a property survey to determine the exact location of the house and the lot line, as well

as easements and rights of way. This is a protection to
the buyer as well. Usually the buyer pays the surveyor's fees, but sometimes this may be handled by the
seller.

1301 Survey

This fee is to cover inspections for termite or other pest
infestation of the house. This may be important if the
sales contract included a promise by the seller to
transfer the property free from pests or pest-caused
damage. Be sure that the inspection shows that the
property complies with the sales contract before you
complete the settlement. If it does not you may wish to
require a bond or other financial assurance that the
work will be completed. This fee can be paid either by
the borrower or seller depending upon the terms of the
sales contract. Lenders vary in their requirements as
to such an inspection.

   Fees for other inspections, such as for structural
soundness, are entered on line 1303.

**1302. Pest and Other
Inspections**

All the fees in the borrower's column entitled "Paid
from Borrower's Funds at Settlement" are totaled here
and transferred to line 103 of Section J, "Settlement
charges to borrower" in the **Summary of Borrower's
Transaction** on page 1 of the Uniform Settlement
Statement. All the settlement fees paid by the seller are
transferred to line 502 of Section K, **Summary of
Seller's Transaction** on page 1 of the Uniform Settlement Statement.

**1400. Total Settlement
Charges**

Comparing Lender Costs

If a lender is willing to reduce his fees for such items as
loan origination, discount points and other one-time
settlement charges, he may gain it back if he charges a
higher mortgage interest rate.

   Here is one rule of thumb which you can use to
calculate the combined effect of the interest rate on
your loan and the one-time settlement charges (paid
by you) such as "points." While not perfectly accurate,
it is usually close enough for meaningful comparisons
between lenders. The rule is, that one-time settlement
charges equaling one percent of the loan amount
increase the interest charge by one-eight (1/8) of one
percent. The 1/8 factor corresponds to a pay back

period of approximately 15 years. If you intend instead to hold the property for only five years and pay off the loan at that time, the factor increases to 1/4.

Here is an example of the rule. Consider only those charges that differ between lenders. Suppose you wish to borrow $30,000. Lender A will make the loan at 8.5 percent interest, but charges a two percent origination fee, a $150.00 application fee, and requires that you use a lawyer, for title work, selected by the lender at a fee of $300.

Lender B will make the loan at 9 percent interest, but has no additional requirements or charges. As part of that nine percent interest, though, Lender B will not charge an application fee and will absorb the lawyer's fee. What are the actual charges for each case?

Begin by relating all of Lender A's one-time charges to percentages of the $30,000 loan amount:

2 percent origination fee=	2 percent of loan amount
$150 application fee	= 0.5 percent of loan amount
$300 lawyer's fee	= 1 percent of loan amount
Total	3.5 percent of loan amount

Since each 1 percent of the loan amount in charges is the equivalent of 1/8 percent increase in interest, the effective interest rate from Lender A is the quoted or "contract" interest rate, 8.5 percent plus .44 percent (3.5 times 1/8), or a total of 8.94 percent interest. Since Lender B has offered a nine percent interest rate, Lender A has made a more attractive offer. Of course, it is more attractive only if you have sufficient cash to pay Lender A's one-time charges and still cover your downpayment, moving expenses, and other settlement costs. This is simply a method to compare diverse costs on an equal basis. In the above illustration, Lender A does not receive the $300 lawyer fee.

The calculation is sensitive to your assumption about the period of time you plan to own the house before paying off the mortgage. As indicated above, the factor increases to 1/4 if you expect to pay off the mortgage in five years. Applying this new factor to the above illustration, the effective interest rate for Lender A would be 8.5 percent plus .87 (3.5 x 1/4) for a total of 9.37 percent interest. Lender A's offer is no longer more attractive than Lender B's which was 9.0 percent.

In doing these calculations you should also be careful as to which one-time fees you place into the calculation. For example, if Lender B in the above illustration did not include in his charge a legal fee but told you that you had to secure legal services in order to obtain the loan from him, you would have to add to Lender B's interest rate the legal fee that you had to incur.

You can use this method to compare the effective interest rates of any number of lenders as you shop for a loan. If the lenders have provided Truth-in-Lending disclosures, these are an even better comparative tool. You should question lenders carefully to make sure you have learned of all the charges they intend to make. The good faith estimate you receive when you make a loan application is a good checklist for this information, but it is not precise. Thus, you should ask the lender how the charges and fees are computed.

CALCULATING THE BORROWER'S TRANSACTIONS

A Sample Worksheet

This page is a sample worksheet for a family purchasing a $35,000 house and getting a new $30,000 loan. Line 103 assumes that their total settlement charges are $1,000. (This figure is the sum of all the individual settlement charges, which will be listed in detail in Section L, of their Uniform Settlement Statement.) The $1,000 figure is merely illustrative. The amount may be higher in some areas and for some types of transactions, and lower for others.

J. SUMMARY OF BORROWER'S TRANSACTION	
100. GROSS AMOUNT DUE FROM BORROWER:	
101. Contract sales price	35,000.00
102. Personal property	200.00
103. Settlement charges to borrower *(line 1400)*	1,000.00
104.	
105.	
Adjustments for items paid by seller in advance	
106. City/town taxes to	
107. County taxes to	
108. Assessments 6/30 to 7/31 (owners assn)	20.00
109. Fuel oil 25 to gal. @.50/gal	12.50
110.	
111.	
112.	
120. GROSS AMOUNT DUE FROM BORROWER	36,232.50
200. AMOUNTS PAID BY OR IN BEHALF OF BORROWER:	
201. Deposit or earnest money	1,000.00
202. Principal amount of new loan(s)	30,000.00
203. Existing loan(s) taken subject to	
204.	
205.	
206.	
207.	
208.	
209.	
Adjustments for items unpaid by seller	
210. City/town taxes to	
211. County taxes 1-1 to 6-30 @$600/yr	300.00
212. Assessments 1-1 to 6-30 @100/yr	50.00
213.	
214.	
215.	
216.	
217.	
218.	
219.	
220. TOTAL PAID BY/FOR BORROWER	31,350.00
300. CASH AT SETTLEMENT FROM/TO BORROWER	
301. Gross amount due from borrower *(line 120)*	36,232.50
302. Less amounts paid by/for borrower *(line 220)*	(31,350.00)
303. CASH (☒ FROM) (☐ TO) BORROWER	4,882.50

Your Financial Worksheet

Once you have decided which providers you wish to use for your settlement services and have selected the lender who will make your loan, you can calculate the total estimated cash you will need to complete the purchase. The form below, which is a part of the Uniform Settlement Statement, can be used as a worksheet for this purpose.

J. SUMMARY OF BORROWER'S TRANSACTION	
100. GROSS AMOUNT DUE FROM BORROWER:	
101. Contract sales price	
102. Personal property	
103. Settlement charges to borrower *(line 1400)*	
104.	
105.	
Adjustments for items paid by seller in advance	
106. City/town taxes to	
107. County taxes to	
108. Assessments to	
109.	
110.	
111.	
112.	
120. GROSS AMOUNT DUE FROM BORROWER	
200. AMOUNTS PAID BY OR IN BEHALF OF BORROWER:	
201. Deposit or earnest money	
202. Principal amount of new loan(s)	
203. Existing loan(s) taken subject to	
204.	
205.	
206.	
207.	
208.	
209.	
Adjustments for items unpaid by seller	
210. City/town taxes to	
211. County taxes to	
212. Assessments to	
213.	
214.	
215.	
216.	
217.	
218.	
219.	
220. TOTAL PAID BY/FOR BORROWER	
300. CASH AT SETTLEMENT FROM/TO BORROWER	
301. Gross amount due from borrower *(line 120)*	
302. Less amounts paid by/for borrower *(line 220)*	( )
303. CASH (☐ FROM) (☐ TO) BORROWER	

100. Gross Amount Due From Borrower

Page 1 of the Uniform Settlement Statement summarizes all actual costs and adjustments for the borrower and seller, including total settlement fees and charges found on line 1400 of Section L.

101. Contract Sales Price

This is the price of the home agreed to in the sales contract between the buyer and seller.

102. Personal Property

If, at the time the sales contract was made, you and the seller agreed that some items were to be transferred with the house, the price of those items is entered here. If it was agreed to include these items in the price of the home, their cost will be part of the sales price recorded on line 101. Personal property could include items such as carpets, drapes, stove, refrigerator, etc.

103. Settlement Charges to Borrower

The total charges detailed in Section L and totaled on line 1400, are recorded here. This figure includes all of the items payable in connection with the loan, items required by the lender to be paid in advance, reserves deposited with the lender, title charges, government recording and transfer charges, and any additional related charges.

104-105. Additional Costs

This space is for listing any additional amounts owed the seller, such as reserve funds if the buyer is assuming the seller's loan. This may not be applicable to your settlement.

106-112. Adjustments

These include taxes, front footage charges, insurance, rent, fuel and other items that the seller has previously paid for covering a period which runs beyond the settlement date. The costs are usually divided on a proportional basis with the seller being reimbursed for charges accruing after the date of transfer of title.

120. Gross Amount Due

This is the total of lines 101 through 112.

200. Amounts Paid By Or On Behalf Of Borrower

(See items 201-220)

201. Deposit or Earnest Money

This is the amount which you paid against the sales price when the sales contract was signed. It is credited to the purchase.

This is the amount of the new mortgage which you will repay to the lender in the future.

202. Principal Amount of New Loan

If you are taking over the seller's mortgage(s) instead of obtaining a new loan or paying all cash, the amount still owed on those prior loans will be shown here.

203. Existing Loan(s)

This includes taxes or assessments which become due after settlement, but which the seller pays because they cover a period of time prior to settlement. See "Reserve Accounts" for a further discussion of these matters.

210-219. Adjustments

This is the sum of lines 201 through 219.

220. Total Amounts Paid By/For Borrower

Remaining are the summary lines which are 301-303 for the borrower (and 601-603 for the seller). Subtracting line 302 (gross amount paid by or for the borrower) from line 301 (gross amount due from the borrower) results in the net cash the borrower must pay at settlement.

300. Cash At Settlement From/To Buyer

RESERVE ACCOUNTS

In most instances, a monthly mortgage payment is made up of a payment on the principal amount of the mortgage debt which reduces the balance due on the loan, an interest payment which is the charge for use of the borrowed funds, and a reserve payment (also known as an escrow or impound payment) which represents approximately one-twelfth of the estimated annual insurance premiums, property taxes, assessments and other recurring charges.

When settlement occurs you may need to make an initial deposit into the reserve account; otherwise, your regular monthly deposits to it will not accumulate enough to pay the taxes, insurance or other charges when they fall due. Under RESPA, the maximum amount that the lender can require borrowers or prospective borrowers to deposit into a reserve account at settlement is a total gross amount not to exceed the sum of: (a) an amount that would have been sufficient to pay taxes, insurance premiums, or other charges which would have been paid under normal lending practices, and **ending** on the **due date** of the first full monthly mortgage installment payment; plus (b) an additional amount not in excess of one-sixth (2 months) of the estimated total amount of taxes, insurance premiums and other charges to be paid on the dates indicated above during any twelve month period to follow

An illustration will help clarify this calculation. Assume the following set of facts on a loan, and that taxes are paid at the end of the period against which taxes are assessed.

Example:

Settlement date	April 30, 1977
Due Date of first mortgage loan repayment	June 1, 1977
Taxes due yearly	$360.00
Monthly tax accrual	$30.00
Due date for taxes	December 1st for the calendar year

The reserve amount for category (a) is $180.00. This represents the amount of taxes accruing between December 1, 1976 (the last tax due date) and May 30, 1977 ($30.00 x 6 months). Reserve amounts chargeable under category (b) could be up to two months advance payment times $30.00 or a total of $60.00. Therefore, total reserve deposits for taxes at settlement would be a maximum of $240.00. Changing the due date for taxes and/or the first mortgage payment results in a different reserve amount for the same illustration.

The same procedure is used to determine the maximum amounts that can be collected by the lender for insurance premiums or other charges. You need to know the charges and due dates in order to compute the amounts.

Once you begin your monthly mortgage payments, you cannot be required to pay more than one-twelfth of the annual taxes and other charges each month, unless a larger payment is necessary to make up for a deficit in your account or to maintain the cushion of the one-sixth of annual charges mentioned in (b) above. A deficit may be caused, for example, if your taxes or insurance premiums are raised.

You should note that the above monthly mortgage payments reserve limitations apply to all RESPA covered mortgage loans whether they were originated before or after the implementation of RESPA.

Adjustments Between Buyer and Seller

The previous section dealt with setting up and maintaining your reserve account with the lender. At settlement it is also usually necessary to make an adjustment between buyer and seller for property taxes and other charges. This is an entirely separate matter from the initial deposit which the borrower makes into the new reserve account.

The adjustments between buyer and seller are shown in Sections J and K of the Uniform Settlement Statement. In the example given in the foregoing section, the taxes, which are payable annually, had not yet been paid when the settlement occurs on April 30. The home buyer will have to pay a whole year's taxes on the following December 1. However, the seller lived in the house for the first four months of the year. Thus, one-third of the year's taxes are to be paid by the seller. Accordingly, lines 208 and 508 on the Uniform Settlement Statement would read as follows:

County taxes
1/1/77 to 4/30/77 $120.00

The buyer would be given credit for this amount in the settlement and the seller would have to pay this amount or count it as a deduction from sums payable to the seller.

In some areas taxes are paid at the beginning of the taxable year. If, in our example, the taxes were paid by the seller on January 1, 1977 for the following tax year ending December 31, 1977, the buyer will have to compensate the seller for the taxes paid by the seller for those months that the buyer will be in possession of the property (April 30–December 31). This adjustment will be shown on lines 107 and 407 of the Uniform

Settlement Statement. With settlement occurring on April 30, those lines will read as follows:

County taxes

4/30/77 to 12/31/77

$240.00

This amount would be credited to the seller in the settlement.

Similar adjustments are made for insurance (if the policy is being kept in effect), special assessments, fuel and other utilities, although the billing periods for these may not always be on an annual basis. Be sure you work out these prorations with the seller prior to settlement. It is wise for you to notify utility companies of the change in ownership and ask for a special reading on the day of settlement, with the bill for pre-settlement charges to be mailed to the seller at his new address. This will eliminate much confusion that can result if you are billed for utilities which cover the time when the seller owned the unit.

C

TOOLS AND SUPPLIES

If you plan to rehab or repair rental property, you should have these tools and supplies on hand.

Plumbing Tools
- Open-end wrench set
- Vise grips
- Channel-lock pliers
- 14-inch pipe wrench
- Basin wrench
- Tubing cutter
- Propane torch
- Hacksaw

Electrical Tools
- Wire strippers
- Insulated pliers
- Screwdrivers
- Half-inch electric drill and auger bits
- Keyhole saw
- Test light

Mason's Tools
- Trowel
- Wire brush
- Brick hammer
- Chisel
- Mortar hoe
- Wheelbarrow

Carpentry Tools
- Crosscut saw
- Framing square
- Phillips and straight-blade screwdrivers
- Claw hammer
- Jack plane
- Miter box
- Chalk string
- Measuring tape

Garden Tools
- Leaf rake
- Metal rake
- Hoe
- Dirt shovel
- Snow shovel
- Pickax
- Hedge clipper
- Lawn mower
- Extension ladder

House-wrecking Tools
    Crowbar   Rope
    Pry bar   Four-pound hammer
    Come-along   Extension cord and spotlight
Power Tools
    Safety goggles   Chain saw
    Circular saw   Bench saw
    Sabre saw   Radial arm saw
    Power sander   Electric drill
Supplies
    Lightbulbs   Fuses
    Salt   Paint supplies
    Ducting tape   Sandpaper
    Drywall patching Glazier's points
    Calk   Nails
    Weatherstripping Screws
    Washers   Bolts
    Wire   Furnace filters and belts
    Epoxy

D

FEDERAL TAXES

Before starting your taxes, write to the IRS asking for its most recent version of Publication 527, "Rental Property." This publication reviews tax regulations that concern the small-income property investor. You should also get the following forms, as necessary:

1. Schedule E, Supplemental Income Schedule
2. Form 3468, Computation of Investment Credit
3. Form 4562, Depreciation and Amortization
4. Form 4592, Investment Interest Expense Deductions
5. Form 4797, Supplemental Schedule of Gains and Losses

If you want a more exhaustive examination of different tax issues, you should write to the following: The Superintendent of Documents, U.S. Government Printing Office, Washington, D.C. 20402. Ask for their *Subject Bibliography Index*. The *Subject Bibliography Index* contains a listing of about 240 catalogs organized according to topic. The "Taxes and Taxation" catalog (SB-195) should appeal to the tax specialist.

E

PROPERTY MANAGEMENT CONTRACT

This appendix contains a standard property management contract. Stetson Management operates about 15,000 units from three offices in suburban Chicago. It takes 6 percent of the monthly gross of all rent. It also charges 25 percent of the first month's rent on any new lease.

B E T W E E N

OWNER   Philip G. Wik
_____

AGENT   Stetson Management, Inc.
_____

For Property Located At_____

Beginning   April 1st   85
_____ 19___

Ending   March 31st   87
_____ 19___

MANAGEMENT AGREEMENT

In consideration of the covenants herein contained _____
_____ Philip G. Wik _____(hereinafter called
"OWNER") and ___ Stetson Management, Inc. ___(hereinafter called
"AGENT"), agree as follows:

1. The OWNER hereby employs the AGENT exlusively to rent
and manage the property (hereinafter called the "Premises")
known as _____

_____
upon the terms hereinafter set forth, for a period of $\frac{2}{}$ years
beginning on the ___1st___ day of ___April___, 19$\frac{85}{}$ and ending
on the ___31st___ day of ___March___, 19$\frac{87}{}$, and thereafter
for yearly periods from time to time, unless on or before __days

Individualized Service for the Property Owner
217 West Main Street   West Dundee, IL 60118   312.428.5080

prior to the date last above mentioned on or before_____
days prior to the expiration of any such renewal period, either
party hereto shall notify the other in writing that it elects
to terminate this Agreement, in which case this Agreement shall
be thereby terminated on said last mentioned date. (See
also Paragraph 6 (c) below).

    2. THE AGENT AGREES:

    (a) To accept the management of the Premises, to the extent,
for the period, and upon the terms herein provided and agrees
to furnish the services of its organization for the rental operation and management of the Premises.

    (b) To render a monthly statement of receipts, disbursements
and charges to the following person at the address shown:

      NAME   ADDRESS

  Philip G. Wik [*]
_____

_____

_____

and to remit each month the net proceeds (provided AGENT is not
required to make any mortgage, escrow or tax payments on the first
day of the following month). AGENT will remit the net proceeds
or the balance thereof after making allowance for such payments
to the following persons, in the percentages specified and at
the addresses shown:

      NAME   PERCENTAGE   ADDRESS

  Philip G. Wik   100%
_____

_____

_____

In case the disbursements and charges shall be in excess of the
receipts, the OWNER agrees to pay such excess promptly, but
nothing herein contained shall obligate the AGENT to advance its
own funds on behalf of the OWNER.

(c) To cause all employees of the AGENT who handle or are
responsibile for the safekeeping of any monies of the OWNER to
be covered by a fidelity bond in an amount and with a company
determined by the AGENT at no cost to the OWNER.

3. THE OWNER AGREES: To give the AGENT the following
authority and powers (all or any of which may be exercised in
the name of the OWNER) and agrees to assume all expenses in
connection therewith:

(a) To advertise the Premises or any part therof, to dis-
play signs thereon and to rent the same; to cause references
of prospective tenants to be investigated; to sign leases for
terms not in excess of one years and to renew and/or cancel
the existing leases and prepare and execute the new lease without additional charge to the OWNER; provided, however, that the
AGENT may collect from tenants all or any of the following: a
late rent administrative charge, a non-negotiable check charge,
credit report fee, a subleasing administrative charge and/or
broker's commission and need not account for such charges and/
or commission to the OWNER; to terminate tenancies and to sign
and serve such notices as are deemed needful by the AGENT; to
institute and prosecute actions to oust tenants and to recover
possession of the Premises; to sue for and recover rent; and,
when expedient, to settle, compromise and release such actions
or suits, or reinstate such tenancies.

(b) To hire, discharge and pay all engineers, janitors and
other employees; to make or cause to be made all ordinary repairs
and replacements necessary to preserve the Premises in its present condition and for the operating efficiency thereof and all
alterations required to comply with lease requirements, and to

do decorating on the Premises; to negotiate contracts for non-
recurring items not exceeding $ _400.00_____ and to enter into
agreements for all necessary repairs, maintenance, minor alterations
and utility services; and to purchase supplies and pay all bills.

(c) To collect rents and/or assessments and other items due
or to become due and give receipts therefore and to deposit all
funds collected hereunder in the AGENT'S custodial account.

(d) To refund tenants' security deposits at the expiration
of leases and, only if required to do so by law, to pay interest
upon such security deposits.

(e) To execute and file all returns and other instruments
and do and perform all acts required of the OWNER as an employer with respect to the Premises under the Federal Insurance
Contributions Acts, the Federal Unemployment Tax Act and Sub-
title C of the Internal Revenue Code of 1954 with respect to
wages paid by the AGENT on behalf of the OWNER and under any
similar Federal or State law now or hereafter in force (and
in connection therewith the OWNER agrees upon request to
promptly execute and deliver to the AGENT all necessary powers
of attorney, notices of appointment and the like).

4. THE OWNER FURTHER AGREES:

(a) To indemnify, defend and save the AGENT harmless from
all suits in connection with the Premises and from liability
for damage to the property and injuries to or death of any
employee or other person whomsoever, and to carry at his (its)
own expense public liability, elevator liability (if elevators
are part of the equipment of the Premises), and workmen's compensation insurance naming the OWNER and the AGENT and adequate
to protect their interests and in form, substance and amounts
reasonably satisfactory to the AGENT, and to furnish to the
AGENT certificates evidencing the existence of such insurance.
Unless the OWNER shall provide such insurance and furnish such
certificate within ___ days from the date of this Agreement, the
AGENT may, but shall not be obligated to, place said insurance
and charge the cost thereof to the account of the OWNER.

(b) To pay all expenses incurred by the AGENT, including,
without limitation, attorney's fees for counsel employed to
represent the AGENT or the OWNER in any proceeding or suit involving an alleged violation by the AGENT or the OWNER, or both,
of any constitutional provision, statute, ordinance, law or regulation of any governmental body pertaining to fair employment,
Federal Fair Credit Reporting Act, environmental protection, or
fair housing, including, without limitation, those prohibiting
or making illegal discrimination on the basis or race, creed,
color, religion or national origin in the sale, rental or other
disposition of housing or any services rendered in connection
therewith (unless the AGENT if finally adjudicated to have
personally and not in a representative capacity violated such
constitutional provision, statute, ordinance, law or regulation),
but nothing herein contained shall require the AGENT to employ
counsel to represent the OWNER in any such proceeding or suit.

(c) To indemnify, defend and save the AGENT harmless from
all claims, investigations and suits with respect to any alleged
or actual violation of state or federal labor laws, it being
expressly agreed and understood that as between the OWNER and
the AGENT, all persons employed in connection with the Premises
are employees of the OWNER not the AGENT. The OWNER'S obligation
under this paragraph 4 (c) shall include the payment of all
settlements, judgments, damages, liquidated damages, penalties,
forfeitures, back pay awards, court costs, litigation expense
and attorneys' fees.

(d) To give adequate advance written notice to the AGENT if
payment of mortgate indeptedness, general taxes or special assessments or the placing of fire, steam boiler or any other insurance
is desired.

5. TO PAY THE AGENT EACH MONTH:

(a) FOR MANAGEMENT: XXXXXXXXXXXXXXXXXXXX per month or 6%
percent _____ of the monthly gross receipts from the operation of the
Premises during the period this Agreement remains in full force and
effect, whichever is the greater amount. A _25_ % fee will be
charged on any new tenant lease.

6. IT IS MUTUALLY AGREED THAT:

(a) The OWNER expressly withholds from the AGENT any power
or authority to make any structural changes in any building or
to make any other major alterations or additions in or to any
such building or equipment therein, or to incur any expense
chargeable to the OWNER other than expenses related to
exercising the express powers above vested in the AGENT without the prior written direction of the following person:

         NAME   ADDRESS

     Philip Wik
_____

_____

_____

except such emergency repairs as may be required because of danger
to life or property or which are immediately necessary for the
preservation and safety of the Premises or the safety of the
tenants and occupants thereof or are required to avoid the
suspension of any necessary service to the Premises.

(b) The AGENT does not assume and is given no responsibility
for compliance of any building on the Premises or any equipment
therein with the requirements of any statute, ordinance, law or
regulation of any governmental body or of any public authority
or official thereof having jurisdiction, except to notify the
OWNER promptly or forward to the OWNER promptly any complaints,
warnings, notices or summonses received by it relating to such
matters. The OWNER represents that to the best of his (its)
knowledge the Premises and such equipment comply with all such
requirements and authorizes the AGENT to disclose the ownership
of the Premises to any such officials and agrees to indemnify
and hold harmless the AGENT, its representatives, servants and
employees, of and from all loss, cost, expense and liability
whatsoever which may be imposed on them or any of them by reason
of any present or future violation or alleged violation of such
laws, ordinances, statutes or regulations.

(c) In the event it is alleged or charged that any building on the Premises or any equipment therein or any act or
failure to act by the OWNER with respect to the Premises or

the sale, rental or other disposition thereof fails to comply with or is in violation of, any of the requirements of any constitutional provision, statute, ordinance, law or regulation or any governmental body or any order or ruling of any public authority or official thereof having or claiming to have jurisdiction thereover, and the AGENT, in its sole and absolute discretion, considers that the action or position of the OWNER or registered managing agent with respect thereto may result in damage or liability to the AGENT, the AGENT shall have the right to cancel this Agreement at any time by written notice to the OWNER of its election so to do, which cancellation shall be effective upon the service of such notice. Such notice may be served personally or by registered mail, or to the person named to receive the AGENT'S monthly statement at the address designated for such person as provided in Paragraph 2 (b) above, and if served by mail shall be deemed to have been served when deposited in the mail. Such cancellation shall not release the indemnities of the OWNER set forth in Paragraph 4 and 6 (b) above and shall not terminate any liability or obligation of the OWNER to the AGENT for any payment, reimbursement or other sum of money then due and payable to the AGENT hereunder.

7. This Agreement may be cancelled by OWNER before the termination date specified in Paragraph 1 on not less than _____ days prior written notice to the AGENT, provided that such notice is accompanied by payment to the AGENT of a cancellation fee in an amount equal to _____% of the management fee that would accrue over the remainder of the stated term of the Agreement. For this purpose, the monthly management fee for the remainder of the stated term shall be presumed to be the same as that of the last month prior to service of the notice of cancellation.

This Agreement shall be binding upon the successors and assigns of the AGENT and their heirs, administrators, executors, successors and assigns of the OWNER.

This Agreement executed at _____, Illinois,
this _____day of _____, 19__ .

_____
"Manager"

_____
"Owner"

F

TENANT MANAGEMENT

1. Tenant Information Sheet
2. Tenant Rejection Letter
3. Apartment Inspection Sheet
4. Rent Not Paid Letter
5. Landlord's Five Days' Notice
6. Thirty-day Eviction Notice
7. Small-claims Complaint Form
8. Court Summons
9. Rent Increase Notification
10. Entry Notification

TENANT INFORMATION SHEET

Dear Applicant:

Please fill out this form to the best of your ability.

Address of the apartment you want to rent   _____

Date apartment will be rented   _____

Your name   _____

Names and ages of people who will be living in apartment

_____

_____

_____

Previous address   _____

Length of time at that address   _____

Reason for leaving   _____

Place of employment   _____

Length of time at that job   _____
Gross weekly income   _____
Social Security number   _____
Car model   _____
Car license number   _____
Business phone number   _____
Home phone number   _____
Emergency contact name and phone   _____
Credit references   _____

TENANT REJECTION LETTER

Dear Applicant:

I'm sorry to inform you that your application for residency at _____ has been declined. Therefore, we are returning your deposit, which was made by check number __ , dated _____ , in the amount of $ _____ . Thank you for your interest in _____ Apartments.

Cordially:

Manager

APARTMENT INSPECTION

Dear New Resident:

Please use this list to check your apartment for damages or needed repairs according to your rental agreement. Return this sheet to the office within one week of your arrival at the building. Our maintenance staff will attend to all the repairs as soon as possible.

Bedrooms
  Closets
  Floors
  Walls
Bathroom
  Tub
  Shower
  Sink
  Toilet
Kitchen
  Stove
  Refrigerator
  Counters
Other
Unit # __ Date _____ Name _____

RENT NOT PAID

Address:
Date:

Dear Occupant:

Our records indicate that your rent is not yet paid. To avoid unnecessary legal action, please remit your past due rent immediately.

Please be reminded that, as we are members of the credit bureau, continual late payments on your behalf could possibly affect your credit standing.

Should you fail to pay the amount due or make satisfactory payment arrangements within ten days of the date of this letter, we will proceed with preparations for filing a complaint against you for the amount due, plus court costs and attorney's fees as allowed by law, without further notice.

Guide yourself accordingly.

Cordially:

Manager

THIRTY-DAY NOTICE OF TERMINATION OF TENANCY

To _____ or any persons in possession of the property located at _____

Notice is hereby given that your tenancy of the above described premises is terminated as of _____ , and you are hereby required to quit and deliver up possession to the undersigned on or before said date.

This is intended as thirty days' notice to terminate said tenancy.

Dated _____ 19 ____.

Manager _____   Apartments _____

LANDLORD'S FIVE DAYS' NOTICE

To_____(Tenant)_____

You are hereby notified that there is now due the undersigned landlord the

sum of _____(rent)_____ Dollars and _____ Cents, being rent for the

premises situated in the City of _____Chicago_____ , County of _____Cook_____

and State of Illinois, described as follows, to wit:_____

_____
(address)

_____

together with all buildings, sheds, closets, out-buildings, garages and barns used in connection with said premises.

And you are further notified that payment of said sum so due has been and is hereby demanded of you, and that unless payment thereof is made on or before the expiration of five days after service of this notice your lease of said premises

will be terminated_____November 8, 1977_____

_____(Name)_____ is hereby authorized to receive and

rent so due, for the undersigned.

Dated this _____2nd_____ **day of** _____November_____ , 19__77__

_____(Name)_____

                                                              Landlord
By _____(signature)_____

                                          Agent or Attorney

STATE OF ILLINOIS ⎫
                  ⎬ S.S.   AFFIDAVIT OF SERVICE-When served by a person
COUNTY OF_____ ⎭   not an officer

(Name)_____ , being duly sworn, on oath deposes and says that on

the _____2nd_____ day of _____November_____ , 19__77__ he served the within notice on the
tenant named therein, as follows:*

(1) by delivering a copy thereof to the within named tenant. _____(name)_____

(2) by delivering a copy thereof to _____ , a person above the
age of ten years, residing on or in charge of the within described premises.

(3) by sending a copy thereof to said tenant by ** ⎰ certified ⎱ mail, with request for return of
⎱ registered ⎰
receipt from the addressee.

(4) by posting a copy thereof on the main door of the within described premises, no one being in actual possession thereof.

Subscribed and sworn to before me this

__2nd__ day of _____November_____ 19 __77__ ⎫   _____(signature)_____
                                             ⎬
_____(signature)_____   ⎬   *Strike out all paragraphs not applicable.
                                             ⎬   **Strike out word not applicable.
              Notary Public   ⎭

SMALL CLAIMS COMPLAINT

CIRCUIT COURT FOR THE 16TH JUDICIAL CIRCUIT
KANE COUNTY, ILLINOIS

Case Number_____

Amount Claimed $_____ Plus Costs

VS.

PLAINTIFF(S)   DEFENDANT(S)

I, the undersigned, claim that the defendant is indebted to the plaintiff in the sum of $ _____

for (The Nature of the Plaintiff's Claim, Giving Dates and other relevant information): _____

_____

_____

_____

_____

_____

_____

_____

_____

and that the plaintiff has demanded payment of said sum; that the defendant refused to pay the same and no part thereof has been paid.

Plaintiff Resides At:	Defendant Resides At:
	(Give residence address — not service instructions)
Name_____	Name_____
Address _____	Address _____
City _____	City _____
State _____ Zip____	State _____ Zip____
Phone _____	Phone _____

Date _____
       (Month - Day - Year)   _____
                                                (Signature of Plaintiff)

WHITE — Court Copy   PINK — Defendant's Copy   CANARY — Plaintiff's Copy

P2-SC-002

SUMMONS

IN THE CIRCUIT COURT OF COOK COUNTY, ILLINOIS
MUNICIPAL DEPARTMENT FIRST DISTRICT

LANDLORD

Plaintiff . . .

No. . . 82 MI-234592 . . . .

Action for: .Possession . . . .

v.

Rent Amount Claimed $. 0 . . . .

TENANT

Trial Date . May 28, 1982 . . . .

Defendant . . .

Trial Time .9:30 a.m. . . . .

SUMMONS FOR TRIAL

You are hereby summoned and required to appear in person on *
. . May 28, 1982 . . . at . . . .9:30 a.m. . . . . , in Courtroom . . . . . .1502 . . . . . of the Richard J. Daley Center for TRIAL of this case.

You are further required to file your written appearance by yourself or your attorney at the same time and place. A statutory fee of $14.00 is due and payable when you file your appearance.

If you fail to appear for TRIAL, a Judgment by default may be taken against you for the relief asked in the complaint, a copy of which is hereto attached. After the Judgment is entered, the Sheriff may evict you.

This summons may not be served later than seven (7) days before the trial date.

WITNESS . . . . May 14 . . . . , 19 82.

. . . .
Clerk of Court

Name: John Shirk
Attorney For: Landlord
Address: etc.
City:
Telephone:

DATE OF SERVICE . . . . , 198 . . .
(To be inserted by officer on copy
left with defendant or other person)

NOTICE TO PLAINTIFF

*Not less than 14 days nor more than 40 days after issuance of summons.

RENT INCREASE NOTIFICATION

Date: _____

Dear Occupant:

Due to increased operating costs, we are forced to increase your rent. Effective _____ , your rent will be $_____.

Thank you for being a good tenant.

Cordially:

Manager

_____ Apartments

ENTRY NOTIFICATION

Dear Occupant:

On the following date and time, we will be entering your apartment for the purpose of

_____

_____ .

Date: _____   Approximate Time: _____

We apologize for any inconvenience this may cause you.

Thank you for your cooperation.

Cordially:

Manager

_____ Apartments

SELECTED BIBLIOGRAPHY

BOOKS

ALLEN, ROBERT J. *Nothing Down*. New York: Simon & Schuster, 1980.

COHEN, HERB. *You Can Negotiate Anything*. New York: Bantam Books, 1980.

DAVIS, JOSEPH C. *Buying Your House: A Complete Guide to Inspection and Evaluation*. New York: Berkley Publishing, 1978.

FRANKEL, WILLIAM, ed. *Home Repair and Improvement Series*. Chicago: Time-Life Books, 1978.

FREEDMAN, ANN. *The 20 Biggest Mistakes Real Estate Salespeople Make and How to Correct Them*. Englewood Cliffs, N.J.: Prentice-Hall, 1980.

FRIEDMAN, MILTON. *Capitalism and Freedom*. Chicago: University of Chicago Press, 1963.

GAINES, KENNETH S. *How to Sell (and Buy) Your Home without a Broker*. New York: Coward, McCann & Geoghegan, 1975.

HASSE, PAUL, and others. *Small Claims Courts*. Washington, D.C.: HALT, 1983.

HOFFMAN, GEORGE C. *Don't Go by Appearances: A Manual for House Inspection*. Corte Madera, Calif.: Woodward Books, 1975.

IRWIN, ROBERT. *How to Buy a Home at a Reasonable Price*. New York: McGraw-Hill, 1979.

McNEIL, JOSEPH G. *Homeowner's Guide to Buying, Evaluating, and Maintaining Your Home*. New York: Van Nostrand Reinhold, 1979.

NUNN, RICHARD V. *The Big Apple Fix-Up Book*. Upper Saddle River, N.J.: Creative Homeowner Press, 1980.

REED, JOHN T. *Aggressive Tax Avoidance for Real Estate Investors*. Danville, Calif.: Reed Publishing, 1981.

RIFENBACK, RICHARD K. *How to Beat the Salary Trap*. New York: McGraw-Hill, 1978.

RUFF, HOWARD J. *How to Prosper During the Coming Bad Years.* New York: Warner Books, 1979.

SAMUELSON, PAUL A. *Economics.* New York: McGraw-Hill, 1973.

WALDRON, GORDON, and ROBERT UNGERLEIDER, eds. *Tenant–Landlord Handbook.* Chicago: Legal Assistance Foundation of Chicago, Chicago Council of Lawyers, 1982.

WEIMER, ARTHUR, and others. *Real Estate.* New York: Ronald Press, 1972.

WIEDEMER, JOHN P. *Real Estate Finance.* Reston, Va.: Reston Publishing, 1977.

ZUCCHERO, VINCENT W. *Rental Homes: The Tax Shelter That Works and Grows for You.* Reston, Va.: Reston Publishing, 1983.

GOVERNMENT PUBLICATIONS

DEPARTMENT OF AGRICULTURE. *Farm Real Estate Market Developments.* Washington, D.C.: Government Printing Office, 1984.

———. *Renovate an Old House?* Washington, D.C.: Government Printing Office, 1978.

DEPARTMENT OF HOUSING AND URBAN DEVELOPMENT. *Buying Lots from Developers.* Washington, D.C.: Government Printing Office, 1982.

———. *The Conversion of Rental Housing to Condominiums and Cooperatives.* Washington, D.C.: Government Printing Office, 1980.

DEPARTMENT OF HOUSING PRESERVATION AND DEVELOPMENT. *Be Prepared for Housing Problems: How to Complain Effectively.* New York: Citybooks, 1983.

———. *Code Inspections and the Housing Court.* New York: Citybooks, 1982.

———. *Housing Maintenance Code.* New York: Citybooks, 1984.

DEPARTMENT OF INTERIOR. *The Economics of Revitalization.* Washington, D.C.: Government Printing Office, 1981.

LAW ENFORCEMENT ASSISTANCE ADMINISTRATION. *How to Crimeproof Your Home.* Washington, D.C.: Government Printing Office, 1979.

U.S. FIRE ADMINISTRATION. *After the Fire: Returning to Normal.* Washington, D.C.: Government Printing Office, 1980.

MISCELLANEOUS

Local and state real-estate boards
Chamber of Commerce
Loan associations and banks
Newspaper real-estate supplements
Better Business Bureau and other consumer-advocate groups

Accounting associations, such as the American Institute of Accountants
Internal Revenue Service
Bar associations
Contractors and managers of hardware supply stores
Other apartment owners and managers

INDEX

INDEX

A

Accelerated Cost Recovery System (ACRS), 161–62
Acceleration clause, 61, 215
Acres, 37, 215
Adjustable Rate Mortgage (ARM), 75–78, 215
Advertising, 172
Alarm systems, 149
Alterations, 182
Amortization, 4, 215, 223–24
Apartments, 49–50, 108–10
Appearance, 43–44
Appraiser, 96–100, 253
Assumption, 79–80
Attorney. *See* Lawyer
Auctions, 85–87

B

Balance sheet, 132–33
Balloons, 61, 81
Banker, 102–4
Basis, 160–61

Bookkeeping, 127–34
Broker, 9, 52–53, 55, 93–96, 230
Budget, 4, 6

C

Capitalism, 1, 3, 20
Capitalization rate, 33–34
Cash flow, 30–32, 216
Cash throw-off, 31, 216
Civil Rights Act (1866), 173–74
Civil Rights Act (1964), 174
Clause(s):
    adjustable rate mortgage, 75–78
    contingency, 55–58
    contracting, 105
    financing, 57
    kickout, 65
    lease, 178–85
    mortgage, 60–61
    record, 57
    tax, 57
    termination, 183
    time is of the essence, 58, 65
Closing, 61–63, 216

Code, 186–88, 215
Collection services, 195–96
Commercial banks, 72
Commercial property, 50–51, 110–11
Condominium, 48–49, 115–21, 183, 216
Confession of judgment, 181
Constructive eviction, 197–98
Contempt, 216
Contract, property management, 170, 271–79
Contract sales, 78–79
Contract of sale, 53–58, 231–32
Contractor, 45, 104–6
Co-operative, 115
Correlation, 99
Creative financing, 74–75, 93
Credit report, 216, 253
Credits, 155–57
Credit union, 73
Crime, 148–52

D

Debt, 8, 68, 216
Deductions, 157–59
Deed, 59, 217
Default, 58, 66
Defense, 201–2, 217
Depreciation, 4, 19, 33, 98–99, 109, 133–34, 161–62, 217
Diary, 127
Discounted cash flow, 36
Discrimination, 26, 173–74, 202
Disinvestment, 28
Dispossess, 188, 202 (*See also* Eviction)
Documentation, 37–39
Double-entry, 128–29

Down payment, 68–70, 217
Due on encumbrance, 61
Due on sale, 79–80
Duplex, 109

E

Earnest money, 54, 217
Electrical, 42, 100
Equity, 81–82
Equity loan. *See* Refinancing
Escrow, 217, 240
Eviction, 181, 197–204
Exchanges, 162
Exculpatory clause, 181
Exemptions, 162–63

F

Fannie Mae, 217–18
Farms, 69, 112
Federal Housing Administration (FHA), 15, 73–74
Financial control, 134–35
Fire, 144–47, 180
Five-year plan, 5–6
Foreclosure, 38, 88, 218
Fraud, 112–13, 165–66

G

Gain, 19, 218
Gangs, 150–51
Ginnie Mae, 15–16
Greater fool theory, 124

H

Hard money, 14, 17
Heating, 41–42, 100
House, single-family, 48–49,
    107–8

I

Incentives, 159–60
Income, 29–36, 99, 155, 211
Index, ARM, 77
Inflation, 16–17
Inspection, 48, 56, 100–101,
    253–54
Insulation, 40–41
Insurance:
  companies, 72
  federal, 151–52
  homeowner's, 140–43, 218
  liability, 143–44
  title, 138–39, 257
Interest, 17–19, 157, 209, 254
Interstate Land Sales Act,
    112–13

J

Junior mortgage. See Second
    mortgage

K

Kiting, 70

L

Land, 51–52, 111–15
Land-lease, 84–85
Lawyer, 57, 101–2, 182–83, 202,
    232
Lease, 9, 178–85
Leverage, 67–68, 137, 210, 219
Lighting, 148–49
Loan:
  acceptance form, 26
  processing, 71, 219
  sources, 71–75, 233–34
Location. See Neighborhood
Lock-out, 180, 204
Loss adjustment, 146–47
Lots. See Land

M

Major Capital Improvement
    (MCI), 198
Management. See Property
Market risk, 207
Market value, 97
Misrepresentation, 58
Money market, 18
Mortgage, 37, 72
Motivated seller, 52
Multiple Listing Service (MLS),
    25, 66

N

Negative amortization, 76–77
Negative cash flow, 11, 69
Negligence, 165–66
Negotiating, 53, 231–32

Neighborhood, 26–29, 118
Net losses, 159
Net worth, 8–10
No money down, 11, 69–70
Non-payment of rent, 188, 195
Number of occupants, 183

O

Offer, 53–59, 65–66, 220
Office of Interstate Land Sales
    Registration, 113
Operating statement, 32–33,
    129–32
Options, 84, 108, 220
Ordinary income, 19, 220
Other People's Money (OPM),
    69
Owner, 37

P

Partnerships, 123–25, 163–65,
    170, 222
Payback, 35
Pension funds, 73
Percentage lease, 190, 220
Percentage mortgage, 103,220
Personal property, 57–58,
    139–40
Planning, 3–6
Plumbing, 41, 101
Points, 70–71, 220
Prepayment, 61, 78
Profit and loss statement. *See*
    Operating statement
Property:
    analysis, 36–52
    destruction, 193–94

management, 169–71, 221,
    271–86
Purchase money mortgage, 83,
    221

Q

Qualitative analysis, 28, 45–48
Quantitative analysis, 28, 48–52

R

Ratios:
    debt-service, 104, 217
    financial analysis, 136–37
    income analysis, 29–30
    purchase analysis, 34–36
Real Estate Investment Trust
    (REIT), 73, 221
Real Estate Limited Partnership
    (RELP). *See* Partnership
Real Estate Settlement Proce-
    dures Act (RESPA), 59–60,
    93
Recordkeeping, 126–27, 154–55
Refinancing, 12, 69, 81–83, 221
Renovation, 45, 89–92, 117–19
Rent, 134–35, 189–91
Rent control, 28–29
Return on investment, 26, 36
Risks, 207–10

S

Sales-leaseback, 221
Savings, 10–12
Savings and loans, 71–72

Second mortgage, 80–81, 219, 221
Section 8, 159–60, 198
Security deposit, 174–78
Selling, 63–66, 95–96
Seminars, 19–20
Settlement, 59–60, 225–67
Shared appreciation mortgage, 85
Single room occupancy (SRO), 198
Smoke detectors, 144–46
Special service districts, 27
Speculation, 4, 13–14
Spring v. Little (1972), 188
Stocks, 15–16
Subletting, 180, 197
Sweat equity. *See* Renovation

T

Tax(es):
  ad valorem, 215
  assessment, 162–63
  auctions, 87
  audits, 165–68
  benefits, 18–19, 211
  calculation, 31
  credits, 155–57
  deductions, 157–59
  federal, 153, 270
  incentives, 159–60
  increment financing, 27
  lien, 222
  records, 154–55
  reform, 153, 208

  shelters. *See* Partnerships
  stamps, 37
  unpaid, 37
Tenant:
  eviction, 193–204
  management forms, 280–86
  problem tenants, 192–96
  selection, 171–74
Termites, 42–43, 100
Time share, 121–23, 222
Title:
  closing, 240
  insurance, 138–39
  search, 235–38
Tools, 89–92, 268–69

V

Veteran's Administration (VA), 15, 73–74, 222

W

Waiver of jury, 182
Waiver of termination, 181
Warranty of habitability, 188, 222
Wraparound mortgage, 83–84

Z

Zoning, 90, 114–15, 222